Especially for

....

From

....

Date

....

DAILY WISDOM
FOR MEN

The Power of
Godly Transformation

2020 DEVOTIONAL COLLECTION

BARBOUR BOOKS
An Imprint of Barbour Publishing, Inc.

Scripture quotations marked KJV are taken from the King James Version of the Bible.

Scripture quotations marked NKJV are taken from the New King James Version®. Copyright © 1982 by Thomas Nelson, Inc. Used by permission. All rights reserved.

Scripture quotations marked NIV are taken from the HOLY BIBLE, NEW INTERNATIONAL VERSION®. NIV®. Copyright © 1973, 1978, 1984, 2011 by Biblica, Inc.™ Used by permission. All rights reserved worldwide.

Scripture quotations marked MSG are from *THE MESSAGE*. Copyright © by Eugene H. Peterson 1993, 1994, 1995, 1996, 2000, 2001, 2002. Used by permission of NavPress Publishing Group.

Scripture quotations marked ESV are from The Holy Bible, English Standard Version®, copyright © 2001 by Crossway Bibles, a publishing ministry of Good News Publishers. Used by permission. All rights reserved.

Scripture quotations marked NLT are taken from the *Holy Bible*. New Living Translation copyright© 1996, 2004, 2015 by Tyndale House Foundation. Used by permission of Tyndale House Publishers, Inc. Carol Stream, Illinois 60188. All rights reserved.

Scripture quotations marked AMPC are taken from the Amplified® Bible, Classic Edition © 1954, 1958, 1962, 1964, 1965, 1987 by The Lockman Foundation. Used by permission.

Scripture quotations marked NASB are taken from the New American Standard Bible, © 1960, 1962, 1963, 1968, 1971, 1972, 1973, 1975, 1977, 1995 by The Lockman Foundation. Used by permission.

Cover photograph: AlexZhilkin / Creative Market

Published by Barbour Books, an imprint of Barbour Publishing, Inc., 1810 Barbour Drive, Uhrichsville, Ohio 44683, www.barbourbooks.com

Our mission is to inspire the world with the life-changing message of the Bible.

Member of the
Evangelical Christian
Publishers Association

Printed in China.

INTRODUCTION

As you begin 2020, it's a great time to "see" God's bigger picture for you and your life. The key word this year is *transformation.* You will have the privilege of "seeing" this vital, overarching biblical theme explored from cover to cover. That's the first purpose for this book.

The second purpose of this book is to encourage you to use our popular "Read Thru the Bible in a Year Plan," which each of the devotions follows. The full "Plan" appears near the back of this book. Do this daily reading and you'll enjoy more of God's blessings in more areas of your life than you ever thought possible. Miss fifteen minutes of sleep if necessary, but don't miss feasting on three portions of God's Word daily.

It's an understatement to say the Bible is filled with the theme of *transformation.* Important aspects of biblical transformation include how we can be courageous as the Holy Spirit continues to mold and shape us and our paths, how God the Father loves to hear and answer our heartfelt prayers, and how Jesus Christ is changing us to be more like Him—humble, gentle, confident, noble, loving, and grace-filled.

Yes, 2020 is a great time to embrace God's transformational power. Each day will be a gift from God. Enjoy the adventure!

The Editors

ARE YOU LIKE ADAM?

*Then God said, "Let us make human
beings in our image, to be like us."*
GENESIS 1:26 NLT

Who doesn't enjoy wandering through the woods, looking out over the desert, walking along an ocean shore, or standing on a prominent hill just before sunset?

God's handiwork shines everywhere you see the beauty of nature. What you see now, however, is dulled and damaged by the ravages of thousands of years of sin.

Imagine what Adam must have experienced when he first viewed creation fresh from the Creator's hand. Every tree Adam climbed, every lion cub he stroked, every rock he skipped on the Tigris River must have radiated something of God's glory. But no plant, animal, or jewel compared with the wonder of Adam caring for the Garden, conversing with the Lord, and listening to his wife's first songs.

The wonders of nature have immense worth because God created them. But the human race holds an incredible place of honor within the universe (Psalm 8). Why? Because you are made in the image of God.

Of course, sin has ravaged more than nature. The entire human race has been infected with this fatal disease.

Thankfully, through Jesus Christ you can receive forgiveness of sins and the sure hope of new, eternal life.

Lord, transform me. Like Adam, I am created by You and endowed with dignity and worth. This year, I want to become a nobler man.

ARE YOU LIKE EVE?

And the LORD God made clothing from
animal skins for Adam and his wife.

GENESIS 3:21 NLT

Meet the woman who gets blamed for everything. "If only Eve hadn't eaten the forbidden fruit." Not that Adam helped matters any! Who knows what life would have been like without the original sin? But Bible readers do know what life is like afterward. And, like Eve, you know that God will not forsake you when you sin.

As soon as Adam and Eve ate the fruit, they experienced the bitter aftertaste of sin—exposure, shame, and physically painful consequences. Quickly, God also gave them the taste of forgiveness. Later, after a sobering discussion, God would give them coverings for their physical nakedness.

First, though, God gave them hope for their souls. His forgiveness did not undo the damage, but He promised that one day the serpent and sin would be defeated by the Lord Jesus. In the meantime, despite the presence of sin and death, humanity would continue—with Eve becoming the mother of all people.

Your sin brings pain to you and others. Like Eve, you can be confident that God will do more than just forgive you. In fact, the Lord promises one day to remove the curse from the ground (Romans 8:20–23) and live with His people once again in the garden of eternity (Revelation 22:1–2).

Lord, transform me. Like Eve, I know for
certain that You forgive even the worst of sins.

ARE YOU LIKE DAVID?

A psalm of David. When he fled from his son Absalom.
TITLE OF PSALM 3 NIV

Why was David a man after God's own heart? Perhaps because David's every heartbeat pulsed in rhythm with God's own. Few thoughts crossed his mind that did not find their way to David's Lord. His conversation with God was rarely put on hold and never abandoned with disinterest. No matter what happened to David, God was the first to hear about it.

David called out to the Lord for mercy when his reputation was attacked (Psalm 4:1–2).

He pleaded with God for compassion when he was weak in body and sick of heart (Psalm 6:1–3, 6).

He expressed marvel and wonder as he spent the night under the sky—and told God how he wondered at the exaltation of humanity (Psalm 8:3–4).

He questioned the Lord when he felt like God was far away and wicked people were getting away with murder (Psalm 10:1–6).

David's heart lay open before God in anguish, grief, joy, and exaltation—every emotion expressed to God in prayer. David spoke his heartfelt prayers to God, and later God gave his prayers back to humanity as part of scripture.

Whether you echo David's words, or express your own thoughts and feelings, you can share your whole heart and life with the Lord.

Lord, transform me. Like David, I want to share my heart with You in any and every circumstance.

ARE YOU LIKE NOAH?

But God remembered Noah and all the wild animals
and livestock with him in the boat. He sent a wind to blow
across the earth, and the floodwaters began to recede.

GENESIS 8:1 NLT

I f Noah had been interviewed by Gallup on issues of morality and godliness, he would have found himself completely outnumbered. To his credit, that did not stop Noah from living a blameless life. For the first five hundred years of his life, Noah kept on doing right in a world that was going very wrong.

Even after God called him to make a boat that would be his means of rescue from the coming judgment, Noah endured another hundred years of standing against the tide of growing violence and hatred. But now he was a public spectacle, building a ship that no one but his family and the animals would choose to enter, no matter how diligently Noah warned his fellow citizens. No one listened and no one cared—and Noah and his family alone were left when the Flood swept the inhabited world away.

In the end, Noah received the approval that really mattered. He found favor with God and salvation from otherwise certain destruction.

Like Noah, you are never so outnumbered that it is impossible to live by faith, pleasing God.

Lord, transform me. Like Noah, I want to live a
blameless life, even if I am the only one who does so.

HEARING THE BEATITUDES
AS A COMMONER

*Arriving at a quiet place, he sat down and taught his
climbing companions. This is what he said: "You're blessed
when you're at the end of your rope. With less of you
there is more of God and his rule."*

MATTHEW 5:2–3 MSG

What if you heard Jesus Christ's Beatitudes as a common person of the time? If you did, what Jesus says almost sounds like a fairy tale. After all, Jesus offers you entry into the realm of God's kingdom. Jesus urges you to happily wait to talk with God, for He will grant your wish. Indeed, you can inherit the earth and enjoy its fruitful bounty. Don't worry that God will tell His angels to toss you out of His kingdom. No, God will show you mercy, invite you into His throne room, and adopt you as one of His children. After that, still greater rewards are yours given your love and courage in the face of persecution. Yes, you will be honored the same as the great prophets of old. Like them, you are now the salt of the earth and the light of the world. So, be courageous and bold so others will see the light and praise God as your Father in heaven.

Only it's not a fairy tale, of course!

See for yourself in today's New Testament Bible reading, Matthew 5:1–20.

*Lord, I want to re-embrace the Beatitudes
anew today. May they transform me.*

ARE YOU LIKE ABRAHAM?

And Abram believed the LORD, and the LORD
counted him as righteous because of his faith.
GENESIS 15:6 NLT

At about age seventy-five, Abram (Abraham) responded to the call of God on his life. Turning from his pagan past, he repented and put his trust in the one true God.

Here in Genesis 15, Abraham was resting in his large Bedouin-style tent to beat the fierce afternoon heat (compare 18:1) when the Lord appeared to him in a second vision. Taking Abraham outside, the Lord said, "Look up into the heavens and count the stars if you can. That's how many descendants you will have!" (15:5 NLT).

Of course, Abraham couldn't see any stars—the sun wasn't scheduled to set for a few more hours (see 15:12, 17). Yet Abraham knew the stars, as always, would appear in the sky that night. Just as surely, he believed that God's promise to make him the father of many peoples would come about—at the right time.

Because Abraham believed, the Lord declared him righteous (15:6). Not that Abraham became perfect overnight. Seven chapters later, however, Abraham demonstrates complete, unquestioning trust in God.

As a reward for his faith, God blessed Abraham abundantly—with many descendants, much land, ongoing protection, a great name, long life, and much more.

Lord, transform me. Like Abraham, I am the recipient of incredible
blessings when I believe You. How good that I can trust You, always.

SAYING THE LORD'S PRAYER ANEW

*"This is your Father you are dealing with, and he knows better
than you what you need. With a God like this loving you,
you can pray very simply. Like this: Our Father in heaven."*

MATTHEW 6:8–9 MSG

When you get ready to read or say the Lord's Prayer, what's most often on your mind?

Is it God the Father's role in your life—in eternal past? in your conception, birth, and life so far? in your destiny and certainty of living with Him forever?

Is it God the Father's infinite and eternal qualities—His sovereignty (greatness), providence (guidance and goodness), holiness (glory), love (graciousness), and mystery ("God alone knows")?

Is it God the Father's marvelous and amazing grace, mercy, care, compassion, love, joy, and peace as He relates to you?

Is it God the Father's deep and passionate love for you, His child?

Don't miss what He's saying to you right now: "I love you! I'm crazy about you! Open your heart wider and experience My love anew."

*Lord, transform me. Renew how I think and feel and respond
toward You when I pray, when I read Bible verses, when I read
each day's devotional. Help me know that You love me!*

OPPORTUNITIES FOR TRANSCENDENCE

*When I consider your heavens, the work of your fingers, the moon and
the stars, which you have set in place, what is mankind that you are
mindful of them, human beings that you care for them?*

PSALM 8:3–4 NIV

When is the last time you felt awe-inspired by the sheer beauty of
a sunset? By the magnitude and majesty of the night sky? By the
ocean's relentless lapping waves? By the immense grandeur of the Grand
Canyon or Rockies or Mississippi or Great Lakes or Appalachians?

Those awe-inspired feelings of transcendence can provoke a number
of mixed emotions, including exhilaration, thankfulness, and worship—and
also including fear, insignificance, and overwhelmedness.

Thankfully, the psalmist David can relate to many such feelings.

First, David is excited how much creation magnifies the Lord's fame.
If God crafted the universe by merely speaking the word, then there is
no limit to His greatness!

Second, David is thrilled how God can use anything for His glory,
honor, and praise. Even little children!

Third, David is humbled by God's special place for mankind here on
earth and later in heaven (and still later in the new heavens and earth).

Every man experiences moments of transcendence, when "awe-
inspired" becomes reality. Men will fly, drive, and walk long distances
in search of them.

After such moments, where does your heart turn? King David shows
the way.

*Lord, transform me. When I stand outside at night,
overwhelm me with thanksgiving to You.*

ARE YOU LIKE SARAH?

*The LORD kept his word and did for Sarah
exactly what he had promised.*
GENESIS 21:1 NLT

It isn't always easy to believe the fantastic promises of God.

For years Sarah had heard about the promised blessings to Abraham and his descendants. Tired of waiting, Sarah had even tried to hurry along the process herself by seeking a surrogate son. All she got for her trouble was more sorrow, distress, and pain.

As each year passed, perhaps Sarah felt less and less a part of God's plan.

Finally, God stepped through the curtain to reaffirm His promise to Abraham and to remind Sarah that she herself would be the mother of this blessed people. Even Abraham, who had taken a knife to his own flesh to show that he accepted God's covenant, laughed to think Sarah could mother a child. No wonder Sarah laughed too when she heard the angels predict her coming pregnancy.

As the baby grew within Sarah, God gave her plenty of time for her faith to grow as well. "How could it be?" became "Come, laugh and rejoice with me!" Part of Sarah still couldn't grasp what a marvelous thing God had done. A baby born from her own body. The promised son of Abraham.

Laughter of disbelief became laughter of delight!

*Lord, transform me. Like Sarah,
I know You will always keep Your promises.*

EMBRACING THE GOLDEN RULE ANEW

*"Therefore, whatever you want men
to do to you, do also to them."*
Matthew 7:12 nkjv

Almost everyone knows the Golden Rule, and knows that Jesus said it, but many aren't quite sure how to live it out.

Four centuries ago the KJV translated the Golden Rule this way: "Therefore all things whatsoever ye would that men should do to you, do ye even so to them." That wording, of course, might be a little hard to explain to family and friends.

One of the contemporary English Bibles does a great job of expressing the Golden Rule this way: "Here is a simple, rule-of-thumb guide for behavior: Ask yourself what you want people to do for you, then grab the initiative and do it for them" (Matthew 7:12 and Luke 6:31 msg).

Of course, Jesus isn't talking about paying for an extra coffee drink at Starbucks. That's nice, but not nice enough. Remember, Jesus is talking about the kingdom. If you are a citizen of God's kingdom, what is the most loving thing you can do for others?

The most loving thing you can do is to invite others to consider Jesus Christ's Good News. After all, in the past someone shared the Gospel with you. Now would be a great time to pay it forward in love.

*Lord, I want to embrace the Golden Rule anew.
Transform my heart. Then help me talk about the
love of Jesus with someone this weekend.*

ARE YOU LIKE ISAAC?

Isaac pleaded with the LORD on behalf of his wife, because she was unable to have children. The Lord answered Isaac's prayer, and Rebekah became pregnant with twins.

GENESIS 25:21 NLT

The young couple beamed as they stood in front of the small congregation, their precious new son in their arms.

On either side of them, their parents looked on with equal pleasure as the minister prayed for their new grandson and dedicated him and his family to the Lord. The baby squirmed and cooed, not realizing his tremendous heritage—his family on one side had served the Lord for four generations, on the other for five.

Isaac's heritage went back only one generation, but it would stretch physically and spiritually for scores of generations to come. Isaac passed on to his sons not just a hope and a prayer, but a real spiritual blessing.

Down through the centuries, Moses and later Jesus spoke of "the God of Abraham, Isaac, and Jacob." And that faith passes not just through physical families. Many a man and childless couple, although without physical descendants, have gained spiritual children by passing on their faith to others.

Today, all who believe in God are described in scripture as "children of Abraham," the man of faith. Isaac started passing along the blessing. You can do so as well.

Lord, transform me. Like Isaac, I want to bless generations to come by passing on a spiritual heritage to my family.

ARE YOU UNLIKE REBEKAH?

"Now, my son, listen to me. Do exactly as I tell you."
GENESIS 27:8 NLT

Sometimes it seems as if God purposely sets up obstacles to fulfilling His promises so He then can overcome them and build His people's faith.

Like Abraham and Sarah, Isaac and Rebekah were childless—a problem when you're supposed to be the parents of "many nations." Unlike Abraham and Sarah, Isaac prayed about their difficulty, and God allowed Rebekah to conceive.

Just as God gave Sarah the promise that she would have a son, so He gave a promise to Rebekah. This time, God promised that her youngest son would not only father a nation, but also rule over his brother. When it came to seeing that promise fulfilled, however, Rebekah became desperate and fell into the same trap that Sarah had fallen into.

The day for Isaac to bless his sons approached. These blessings were not "good luck" wishes but in a real sense would predict the destinies of the two sons. To ensure the right outcome, Rebekah used deceit in an attempt to gain what God had promised.

Rebekah believed God, but not enough to wait for Him to overcome what looked impossible. In contrast, you don't need to become desperate when God's methods and timing don't meet your expectations.

You can rest assured that God's promises *will* come true.

Lord, transform me. Unlike Rebekah, I do not attempt to obtain Your blessings through my own schemes.

ARE YOU LIKE MATTHEW?

While Jesus was having dinner at Matthew's house, many tax collectors and sinners came and ate with him and his disciples.

MATTHEW 9:10 NIV

Do you like going to banquets? Jesus did! He enjoyed the opportunity to meet new people and whet their appetite for the kingdom of God.

The Gospel accounts make it clear that Jesus loved to have others—friends, disciples, new converts, even religious leaders who opposed His ministry—throw parties for Him.

When Jesus invited Matthew to become one of His disciples, Matthew must have been shocked. Yet immediately he gave up his lucrative tax-collecting business and held a huge banquet that evening. The banquet wasn't in Matthew's honor—a "retirement" party of sorts. Instead, Matthew somehow knew Jesus wanted to meet his friends. So he invited them all over to his home.

Sure enough, the word about Matthew's party got out to that city's religious elite, who condemned Jesus. Jesus used their harsh criticisms, however, as an opportunity to demonstrate His love and compassion for the "scum" of the earth.

Like Matthew, you have work associates, friends, neighbors, and relatives who don't know the Lord yet. Some may be rather shady characters. But the Lord loves them and wants you to eat with them and find a way to introduce them to the Savior.

Lord, transform me. Like Matthew, I want to invite my friends to get to know You.

CHOOSING GOD'S WORD ANEW

*You, LORD, will keep the needy safe and will protect us
forever from the wicked, who freely strut about when
what is vile is honored by the human race.*

PSALM 12:7–8 NIV

Sometimes, things look hopeless. At least they did to David, who starts out this psalm with this lament: "Help, LORD, for no one is faithful anymore; those who are loyal have vanished from the human race." That's pretty pessimistic. Yet, it's true to how David felt at that time.

The second verse continues David's lament: "Everyone lies to their neighbor; they flatter with their lips but harbor deception in their hearts." Yes, that had happened to David repeatedly. Yet he didn't take things into his own hands.

In the next two verses, David asked the Lord to silence these hypocrites and evildoers. Thankfully, the Lord assured David that He would arise and act. In deep gratitude, David affirms the absolute trustworthiness of the Lord's words. Then he closes with the two verses quoted above.

What a contrast between the content, quality, and duration of deceitful, defiant, and doomed men over against God's perfect, unerring, and everlasting Word.

How have things looked to you in recent days? Hopeless? Or hope-filled? Or somewhere in between?

Like David, you can tell the Lord how you feel and ask Him to rise up and act.

*Lord, transform me. Like David, may I always
turn to You in honest, heartfelt prayer.*

ARE YOU LIKE JACOB?

*Then Jacob prayed, "O God of my grandfather Abraham,
and God of my father, Isaac. . . I am not worthy of all the unfailing
love and faithfulness you have shown to me, your servant."*

GENESIS 32:9–10 NLT

Maybe Jacob was originally from Missouri, the "Show Me" state. Raised to be the recipient of God's promises to Abraham and Isaac, Jacob wanted to see for himself that the Lord was at work in his life.

As a young man, he slept on a pillow of stone and dreamed of a stairway to heaven. When he awoke, he realized God's presence with him. Jacob responded by declaring that he would follow the Lord if God would show Himself faithful and bring Jacob back safely from a foreign land.

The Lord did bless Jacob and brought him back with tents bursting with children, and large flocks and herds grazing under the care of many servants. Jacob knew God had more than proven Himself, and he was prepared to worship Him alone. As always, the Lord gave His blessing and more.

One night, God came to test Jacob's true desires. After doing so, He changed his name from "Jacob, one who schemes" to "Israel, one who struggles with God."

Like Jacob, you can cling to the Lord, knowing that in Him alone you will find life and blessing.

*Lord, transform me. Like Jacob, I want to pursue Your
blessings and always recognize Your hand on my life.*

ARE YOU BOTH GIVING AND RECEIVING?

*"Accepting someone's help is as good as giving someone help.
This is a large work I've called you into, but don't be overwhelmed
by it. It's best to start small. Give a cool cup of water to someone
who is thirsty, for instance. The smallest act of giving or
receiving makes you a true apprentice."*

MATTHEW 10:42 MSG

God's kingdom and rule extends over everything in heaven and earth—not simply over emperors and kings, but over all of mankind.

This is clearly taught throughout the Old Testament writings, and in the teachings of Jesus Himself during His three and a half years of public ministry.

The implication is rather startling: Every human being on earth is a servant of God Most High. They are servants no matter how high or low, rich or poor, powerful or weak, proud or humble.

So it's crystal clear: Only redeemed believers and followers of Jesus Christ are "citizens" of God's kingdom. But all human beings everywhere are "servants" in God's kingdom.

What does this mean? Practically, whatever you're doing to serve others, please keep doing. But this coming weekend, switch things 180 degrees. Ask one of your not-yet-Christian neighbors or friends to serve you. Their service to you can open a door for their salvation.

*Lord, transform me. I'm more than happy to help others, but I hate to ask
for help. May my act of receiving bear eternal fruit in Your kingdom.*

ARE YOU HAVING DINNER WITH GOD?

God, who gets invited to dinner at your place?
How do we get on your guest list?
PSALM 15:1 MSG

Each year the queen of England invites 30,000 men and women to her four summer afternoon garden parties. Sorry, it's not possible to request an invitation by writing to Buckingham Palace. Instead, guests are nominated by a network of top leaders over Britain's major institutions.

So, if you have any friends high up the ranks in the British government, military, or church, you may want to run the idea by them. Of course, if the queen of England does invite you, be prepared to buy a new wardrobe and practice dozens of rules of etiquette meticulously.

What does it take to have dinner with God? First, you need to be a citizen of His kingdom. Second, you need to love the Lord with all your heart, soul, strength, and mind. Third, you need to know that Jesus counts you among His friends.

Thankfully, Jesus already is knocking on the door of your heart (Revelation 3:20). Jesus is waiting for you to swing the door open wide, embrace Him, and invite Him in!

Don't worry about what to wear. Jesus already has clothed you with His robes of righteousness and given you His Holy Spirit. So, what are you waiting for?

Lord, transform me. The greatest privilege is breaking
bread and sharing a cup with You. I'm ready and willing!

IN THE LORD ALONE

*You will show me the way of life, granting me the joy of your
presence and the pleasures of living with you forever.*
PSALM 16:11 NLT

As you read the book of Psalms, you don't want to miss one of its top themes.

That vital theme is: *Everything* you desire, want, and need is found in the Lord, and in the Lord alone. Why look anywhere else?

Without question, David lived out of this core conviction. You see that in the verse quoted above and *many* other verses included in the psalms of David. Yet at one point when David lost this vital focus, his heart wandered and he broke half of the Ten Commandments in one fell swoop. So it's crucial that you grab on and hold tightly to this core conviction.

Not surprisingly, David's fellow psalmists wrote about this major theme as well. In Psalm 73:25 (NLT), for instance, Asaph writes: "Whom have I in heaven but you? I desire you more than anything on earth." Powerful words, indeed.

Jesus said it best in Matthew 6:21 (NLT), "Wherever your treasure is, there the desires of your heart will also be." It's not enough to believe in God and heaven. You need to want the God of heaven, and Him alone!

*Lord, transform me. I want to live out of the reality that
everything I desire, want, and need is found in You.
Make this my daily conviction, I pray.*

ARE YOU UNLIKE THE PHARISEES?

Then the Pharisees called a meeting to plot how to kill Jesus.
MATTHEW 12:14 NLT

Talk about a bunch of hypocrites. The Pharisees said they believed in God, angels, miracles, the Ten Commandments, and the prophecies of old. They went so far as to reinterpret the scriptures and follow strict rules governing all manner of external behavior in order to look ultra-religious.

Yet Jesus warned, "Unless your righteousness is better than the righteousness of the teachers of religious law and the Pharisees, you will never enter the Kingdom of Heaven!" (Matthew 5:20 NLT).

Why such a harsh rebuke? It turns out the Pharisees in Jesus' day had placed their own rules above God's Word and looked down on everyone else. They were far more interested in their own power and prestige than in God's glory and honor.

When Jesus started going out of His way to break the minute "laws" invented and revered by these men, the Pharisees saw red. The more convincingly Jesus demonstrated His deity, the more bloodthirsty the Pharisees became.

Sadly, many religious hypocrites seek to wield power today. If someone isn't careful, he can end up focusing on the external aspects of Christianity.

Unlike the Pharisees, take God at His Word and daily choose to love Him with all your heart, soul, strength, and mind.

Lord, transform me. Unlike the Pharisees, I don't want to be a self-centered legalist, but sometimes I act that way. Please change me.

ARE YOU LIKE JOSEPH?

The LORD was with Joseph, so he succeeded in everything
he did as he served in the home of his Egyptian master.
GENESIS 39:2 NLT

Rejected, kidnapped, falsely accused. Sentenced to prison and left to rot. The outline of the script for Joseph's life sounds depressing, an almost sure formula for developing a bitter spirit toward God and others.

Instead, Joseph emerges above his circumstances confident in God's purposes and able to forgive those who had hurt him most. Amazingly, even in the worst of times, he never gives up on life. He never forgets God's promises. He never stops trusting God.

What hurts and betrayals have you suffered? How have other people hurt you deeply? Joseph's life demonstrates that nothing can separate you from God's love (Romans 8:38–39).

Like Joseph's youthful dreams (Genesis 37:5–11), you can have a sure vision of present spiritual blessings and future triumph through Jesus (Romans 8:18 and Colossians 3:1–4).

Like Joseph, you can remain steadfastly confident that whatever evil Satan or someone else may plot against you (Genesis 50:19–20), God will turn it around to bring good into your life and the lives of others (Romans 8:28).

You may have to wait out extremely difficult circumstances, but like Joseph you can commit to trust the Lord your God, always.

Lord, transform me. Like Joseph, I want to enjoy Your ongoing presence
and blessing in my life. And, I never want to stop trusting You.

ARE YOU FAITHFUL?

For I have kept the ways of the LORD;
I am not guilty of turning from my God.
PSALM 18:21 NIV

Every winter sport has longstanding traditions, guidelines, and rules. When it comes to cross-country skiing in Minnesota, make sure you buy a ski pass so you can ski on groomed trails in state parks or state forests, and on state or grant-in-aid trails. Sign your ski pass and be sure to carry it with you every time you go skiing.

When it comes to ice fishing in Idaho, make sure you have a current fishing license, cut a hole no more than ten inches in diameter, use no more than five fishing poles, and add no more than five hooks per line.

So what's required when it comes to the winter sport of staying faithful to the Lord your God? It's easy to start the year with the best of intentions. Don't quit now!

One purpose of this book is to encourage you to use Barbour's popular "Read Thru the Bible in a Year Plan." Miss fifteen minutes of sleep if necessary, but don't miss feasting on three portions of God's Word daily.

Do this and you'll enjoy more of God's blessings in more areas of your life than you ever thought possible!

Lord, transform me. May this be the year that I read the
whole Bible. This week, help me to catch up on my
readings in Genesis, Matthew, and Psalms.

THANKFUL FOR GOD'S GENTLENESS

You have given me the shield of your salvation, and your right hand
supported me, and your gentleness made me great.

PSALM 18:35 ESV

H ow would you describe the kind of person Jesus is?

Biblically, you could talk about Jesus as the Messiah, the Christ, the Anointed One. You could describe Him as the King of kings and Lord of lords. You could say He is God the Son, God's Son, and the Son of God.

Theologically, you could talk about Jesus as the second member of the Trinity, coequal with God the Father and God the Holy Spirit. You could talk about His infinite and eternal sovereignty (greatness), providence (guidance and goodness), holiness (glory), love (graciousness), and mystery ("God alone knows").

More importantly, how did Jesus describe Himself? You find the answer in a single verse, Matthew 11:29, where Jesus says He is gentle and humble (or lowly) in heart. And for both you can give much thanks!

The Lord could but speak the word and create the heavens and earth. So you don't want His full power to land on you. As King David wrote three thousand years ago, His gentleness is more than enough.

Lord, transform me. Too often I want to see Your power and fury, when
what I really need is Your gentleness. Gently speak to my heart today.
Guide me in the right paths to success in Your eyes, I pray.

THANKFUL FOR NATURE'S LESSONS

*God's glory is on tour in the skies, God-craft on exhibit across
the horizon. Madame Day holds classes every morning,
Professor Night lectures each evening.*

PSALM 19:1–2 MSG

If you're looking for daily moments of transcendence, you may want to head to Instagram and follow @astronomicwonders. On a slow day, its stunning images generate more than 1,200 likes. On many days, double that number. On the best days, triple or quadruple it.

When you look at the best new @astronomicwonders captured by NASA, and by an elite group of world-class photographers, it can take your breath away.

The atheist, however, shivers. In awe, yes, but also in the perception that Earth is a microscopic speck in a cold and heartless universe that neither knows nor cares about humanity. Brrr.

Conversely, the believer looks beyond what is seen to the One who is unseen. That unseen One both knows and cares about you in ways that stagger the imagination.

From eternity past, the Triune God planned creation, with man and woman as the lead characters in what would become the greatest story ever told.

Unlike the atheist, the believer has no need to fold his arms across his chest and shiver. Instead, he has every reason to lift his arms in praise to his creator, his heavenly Father, his heart's greatest joy and delight.

*Lord, transform me. The next time I see the stars,
I want to see You and smile in true worship.*

WHAT BLESSING BEST FITS YOU?

All these are the twelve tribes of Israel. This is what their father said to them as he blessed them, blessing each with the blessing suitable to him.

GENESIS 49:28 ESV

The phrase "with the blessing suitable to him" offers three practical insights.

First, God wants to bless you through your forefathers, and in turn He wants you to bless your children and grandchildren. These blessings are rooted in God Himself and flourish best in godly family trees. That doesn't mean that every branch is godly, but the more godliness, the better.

Second, God wants you to bless your children, nephews and nieces, and grandchildren in specific suitable ways. No two individuals have the same aptitude, the same potential, or the same opportunities. Yet each person is created in God's image with a specific calling on his life. So, the pressure is off. You can encourage each one to discover how God has made them to work and serve and bless others.

Third, God wants you to bless the children in your family spiritually as well. While aptitudes may differ, you want to lovingly and earnestly pray for the salvation and spiritual growth and maturity of every member of your family. How happy the man whose loved ones worship the Lord wholeheartedly and love others well.

Lord, transform me. This weekend, help me to bless at least one member of my family. Eventually, may I bless each one, I pray.

GETTING INTO EXODUS

*Eventually, a new king came to power in Egypt
who knew nothing about Joseph or what he had done.*
EXODUS 1:8 NLT

Today's Old Testament Bible reading bridges from the end of Genesis to the beginning of Exodus. This second book of the Bible reveals the amazing lengths to which God will go to save His less-than-perfect people. Along the way, get ready for some of the Bible's biggest stories.

Moses begins by describing how the emerging nation of Israel was enslaved by the Egyptians (chapter 1). He then records in dramatic detail how God called him to deliver the Israelites (chapters 2–6), how the Lord brought down a series of terrible plagues on the Egyptians (7:1–12:30), and how they escaped from bondage (Exodus 12:31–15:21).

In this book, Moses also records how the Israelites began complaining against the Lord (15:22–17:7) and how Joshua and others helped lead the people (17:8–18:27).

Moses then tells how he received the Ten Commandments and other laws of the Lord (chapters 19–31), how the people quickly began to rebel (chapters 32–33), and how God renewed His covenant with His chosen people (chapter 34).

Famous passages in the early chapters include God appearing to Moses in a burning bush (3:2–9) and revealing His covenant name (3:14).

*Lord, transform me. Transform my vision of who You are and the
mighty acts You performed to save Your people out of Egypt.
May I never doubt what You can do even today.*

JESUS SPEAKS— SOMETIMES WITH WORDS

But Jesus gave her no reply, not even a word.
MATTHEW 15:23 NLT

One day Jesus heads north with His disciples to the region of Tyre and Sidon. He specifically says He wants His presence kept secret. Yet a Syrian woman spots them down the street, runs up, and falls at the feet of Jesus. "Have mercy on me, O Lord, Son of David! My daughter is cruelly demon-possessed."

Jesus stands there looking at her—saying nothing.

The disciples can't stand quiet, so they start berating the Syrian woman. By the end, they're telling Jesus to send her away.

Jesus continues looking into the woman's eyes. No one has ever looked at her with such love and compassion. Before Jesus breaks His silence, He is speaking to the Syrian woman's heart. And, when He breaks His silence, the woman knows what Jesus has done and plans to do next.

Imagine if Jesus had started talking the moment the Syrian woman begged for His help. True, Jesus still would have healed her daughter. . . but everything else would have been lost.

In Jesus' eyes, it was more important to win and heal and bless the Syrian woman's heart. To grant her true heart's desire. To honor and respect her before her own people. And finally, to ensure that His disciples would never treat women and foreigners the same again.

Lord, transform me. Make me a listener,
a lover of souls, a man who treats others well.

ARE YOU LIKE MOSES?

Moses and Aaron went and spoke to Pharaoh. They told him,
"This is what the LORD, the God of Israel, says: Let my people go."
EXODUS 5:1 NLT

What did it feel like for Moses to reenter the palaces of Egypt after a forty-year absence? These halls had once been his home. He practically owned them. But now he approached the new Pharaoh as a stranger with a wild demand: "Release the Israelites to go and worship their God."

As a brash young prince of Egypt, Moses first attempted to use his own strength and position to identify with his people and bring them justice. As a seasoned old man, he first argued with God, then gave himself completely to the Lord. From that point on, his identity was as the friend of God (Exodus 33:17). None of the splendors of Egypt could ever capture his heart or eye again (Hebrews 3:5).

Like Moses, you live in an era of spectacular culture and extravagant resources. Worldly possessions and praise actively seek your attention and affection. But all your attention and affection belong to the Lord God. As you openly identify with Him, you will find that no cost is too great in order to gain God's friendship.

Lord, transform me. Like Moses, I want to value my relationship
with You far more than any temporal possession or fame.

TO YOU, WHO IS JESUS?

Simon Peter replied, "You are the Christ,
the Son of the living God."
MATTHEW 16:16 ESV

Halfway through the Gospel of Matthew, you start seeing Peter talking to Jesus in front of the other disciples. The first time around, Peter jumps out of the boat only to look at the waves and start sinking (14:28–31). The second time, he asks a good question (15:15).

The fourth time, Peter rebukes Jesus, only to get rebuked right back (16:22–23). The fifth time, he tries to delay the departure of Moses and Elijah (17:4). The sixth time, Peter and Jesus talk about paying taxes (17:24–27). The seventh time, he asks another good question (18:21). The final time, Peter denies the possibility that he would deny Jesus (26:33–35).

Mixed results, to say the least.

Yet the third time, Peter throws a beautiful spiral forty yards for a touchdown—thanks to his heartfelt obedience to the Holy Spirit's illumination (16:16).

Like Peter, your results are mixed. You don't always say the right thing the right way at the right time. Sometimes, you say the wrong thing in the worst possible way at the worst possible time.

Like Peter, don't shut up. Instead, strive for heartfelt obedience when the Holy Spirit speaks to your heart and mind.

Lord, transform me. Sometimes I do need to keep my thoughts to myself. Sometimes I need to listen and wait. Sometimes I need to speak boldly about You. Each time, guide me, I pray.

JESUS SHINES LIKE THE SUN

He was transfigured before them. His face shone like the sun,
and His clothes became as white as the light.

MATTHEW 17:2 NKJV

In many ways, the transfiguration of Jesus is a sneak preview of His bodily resurrection appearances and His eternal radiance and glory in heaven.

So what is your proper response to the transfiguration? Clearly, it's not fear. Instead, your proper response is belief and trust (1) in Jesus' divinity as God's Son and (2) in the new covenant that He offers through the Good News message of the Gospel. The more clearly your family members and friends see and understand these two proper responses, the more they will celebrate the Lord's love and friendship now—and forever.

The Good News message is deeply rooted in who God is, in His covenant with His people, in His judgment, in His great sacrifice, in the Day of Atonement, and in Passover. The Good News also is deeply rooted in who Jesus is, in His new covenant with His people, and in all He did for your redemption, reconciliation, propitiation, and justification.

When you speak about the Gospel with someone, remember the example of Jesus. Do so winsomely, with great compassion and love, from one happy heart to their own.

Lord, transform me. You told us, "You are the light of the world"
(Matthew 5:14 ESV). May I shine more brightly for
You both today and in coming days.

WHAT'S AHEAD FOR YOU?

Show me your ways, LORD, teach me your paths.
Guide me in your truth and teach me, for you are
God my Savior, and my hope is in you all day long.

PSALM 25:4–5 NIV

Does it feel as if 2020 is off to a fast or slow start? Either way, does it feel like you're headed in the right direction? More importantly, what does God think?

It's so easy to get swept up by the next thing and the next thing after that. Before you know it, another month has come and gone. Is God happy with the pace and direction of your life right now? (Yes, you can know which.)

Repeatedly throughout the Psalms, David and other inspired writers poured out their hearts to the Lord. Not surprisingly, they often asked God to teach and direct them along the right path, step by step.

How good when any man stops long enough to read scripture, pray and listen, and wait for the Holy Spirit to speak to his heart. True, not every impression is inspired divine revelation. Far from it. But if you read the Bible daily, you'll be able to differentiate between God's will and your own ideas.

Don't skip today's prayer. Instead, pray it more than once until it becomes your own heart's desire.

Lord, transform me. I don't want to waste another week, another month, busy but about the wrong things. Lead me, guide me, direct me each day.

GOD'S HEART FOR CHILDREN

*"And anyone who welcomes a little child like this on my behalf
is welcoming me. But if you cause one of these little ones who trusts
in me to fall into sin [or lose their faith], it would be better for
you to have a large millstone tied around your neck
and be drowned in the depths of the sea."*

MATTHEW 18:5–6 NLT

Sadly, it's very possible for a child to grow up in church, learn scores of Bible stories, sing lots of songs, memorize plenty of scripture verses, say all the right things, look good—very good—and yet experientially lose their faith. Sometimes, it's the individual's own choice. Sometimes, however, it's because of the sinful actions of adults the child should have been able to trust. Scripture couldn't be clearer that anyone who hurts a child or young adult is in grave danger of God's judgment.

The point Jesus is making is crystal clear: don't let your critical attitudes, your hasty and harsh words, your hypocritical actions, and your self-centered living end up soiling or stealing the God-given faith of a child.

This isn't about being perfect. Instead, you can rest assured that a child's faith grows, not diminishes, when you apologize to them sincerely.

*Lord, transform me. Transform the way I treat children.
May they experience Your love when I listen to and speak with them.*

THE TRIUMPH OF SILENCE

"The Lord will fight for you, and you have only to be silent."

Exodus 14:14 esv

I n the midst of historic battles and future prophecies, and in wise sayings and heartfelt psalms, you'll find moments of unexpected silence. One such moment occurs near the climax of the Exodus of the Israelites from Egypt in today's Old Testament scripture reading.

Shortly before the Lord's judgment on His enemies, He often tells His people to stand still and stay perfectly quiet. It's the proverbial calm before the storm of God's fury. You see this here and in Amos 5:13, Habakkuk 2:20, and Zephaniah 1:7, as well as in Revelation 8:1, where it says that heaven itself is silent for half an hour.

Similarly, before the Lord's salvation of His people, He often tells them to be silent. Psalm 62:1 (esv) says: "For God alone my soul waits in silence; from him comes my salvation." Lamentations 3:26 (esv) affirms: "It is good that one should wait quietly for the salvation of the Lord." Isaiah 30:15 (esv) adds: "For thus said the Lord God, the Holy One of Israel, 'In returning and rest you shall be saved; in quietness and in trust shall be your strength.' "

So, what's on your to-do list today?

Lord, I'm a man of action. I'm not a man who likes to sit still and rest quietly for long periods of time. Right now, I'm going to take a deep breath and wait on You.

ARE YOU LIKE MIRIAM?

*Then Miriam the prophetess, the sister of Aaron, took a tambourine
in her hand, and all the women went out after her
with tambourines and dancing.*
EXODUS 15:20 ESV

Miriam had seen the mighty God at work. First, when she was a young girl guarding her baby brother until the Lord answered prayer and brought a princess to rescue him. She then had seen her parents' faith rewarded as the princess returned baby Moses to his parents for a few more precious years. After years of waiting, she also watched as God struck the Egyptians with plagues to show His glorious power.

Now past her ninetieth birthday, Miriam experienced the Lord's complete deliverance as she and the rest of the Israelites marched through the Red Sea and turned around to see Pharaoh and his army swept away in the crashing waters. Age would not keep her from leading in the festival of worship that day. She gave all the glory to God and helped others do the same.

You too can give glory to God and help others to praise Him too. Opportunities abound, whether through music ministry, leading a small group Bible study, teaching a Sunday school class, or community outreach.

Don't keep it all to yourself. Tell others the good news: the Lord saves!

*Lord, transform me. Like Miriam, I want to
encourage others to praise God for His goodness.*

ARE YOU UNLIKE THE RICH YOUNG RULER?

Jesus looked at them intently and said, "Humanly speaking, it is impossible. But with God everything is possible."

MATTHEW 19:26 NLT

When the rich young man came to Jesus, he sincerely thought he wanted eternal life, and he asked Jesus what he could do to get it. Jesus felt genuine love for the man—so much so that He pinpointed the one obstacle that had to be removed first.

This particular man, like many other rich men, wanted to *do* something to gain eternal life. Money makes you feel like you can do anything, doesn't it? He had his financial portfolio and professional résumé all in order. Alongside his impeccable character qualifications, his résumé even listed all his favorite charities. That always looks good when closing a deal, doesn't it? But Jesus wasn't interested in dealing—He wanted the man's heart.

The man had indeed obeyed the everyday commands Jesus listed—but not the greatest command of all. He *didn't* love the Lord his God with all his heart and soul and strength. He *did* have other gods before the true God.

Unlike the rich young man, you can make the right choice. Let go of anything that keeps you from enjoying God's very best.

Lord, transform me. Unlike the rich young man, I don't want anything to come in the way of me following the Lord Jesus. Make me wholly devoted to You.

ACCEPTING GOD'S BOUNDARIES OF BLESSING

*And God spoke all these words, saying: "I am the LORD your God,
who brought you out of the land of Egypt, out of the house
of bondage. You shall have no other gods before Me."*

EXODUS 20:1–3 NKJV

How do you view the Ten Commandments? No, not the classic movie—instead, the real thing you can review in today's Old Testament scripture reading.

Culturally, people often view the Ten Commandments as God's idealistic yet impossible demands for the Jewish people long, long ago. Then, as now, people want to do their own thing, their own way, without anyone or anything interfering with their choices. If only they could see the Ten Commandments as God's boundaries of blessing.

After all, each of God's Ten Commandments protects you from serious error, terrible harm, unbearable heartache, and severe loss. Invest tens of thousands of dollars worshipping false gods? Bad idea. Work long hours seven days a week to get ahead? Another bad idea. Take a former neighbor to court on false charges and commit perjury? Super bad idea.

After nearly 3,500 years, every one of God's Ten Commandments is still relevant. All ten continue to offer God's rich blessings.

May you never tire of enjoying what God meant for your good.

*Lord, I'm prone to sin. No, I haven't committed murder,
but I've hated other men made in Your image. Now, more than ever,
I want to stay well within Your boundaries of blessing.*

ENJOYING GOD'S SPACIOUS PLACES

*I will be glad and rejoice in your love, for you saw my affliction
and knew the anguish of my soul. You have not given me into the hands
of the enemy but have set my feet in a spacious place.*

PSALM 31:7–8 NIV

I n scripture, "spacious" places symbolize the Lord's deliverance, salvation, and blessing.

You certainly see this in the psalms of David. In 2 Samuel 22:20 (NIV), he thanks God: "He brought me out into a spacious place; he rescued me because he delighted in me." In Psalm 18:19 (NIV) he thanks God again: "He brought me out into a spacious place; he rescued me because he delighted in me." In Psalm 31:8 David says it yet again, as you saw above.

When the Lord first appears to Moses, God describes how He wants to bless His people, the ancient Israelites: "So I have come down to rescue them from the hand of the Egyptians and to bring them up out of that land into a good and spacious land, a land flowing with milk and honey" (Exodus 3:8 NIV).

Sadly, the Israelites squandered what God gave them. In Nehemiah 9:35 (NIV), eight Levites under Ezra's direction confess: "Even while they were in their kingdom, enjoying your great goodness to them in the spacious and fertile land you gave them, they did not serve you or turn from their evil ways."

*Lord, the warning is clear. I never want to
take You or Your blessings for granted.*

TRUSTING GOD'S PERFECT TIMING

But I trust in you, Lord; I say, "You are my God."
My times are in your hands.
PSALM 31:14–15 NIV

Wise men worth reading and heeding. . .

"I am convinced that the answers to every problem and issue of life for both time and eternity are resolved through a correct understanding of God." *David Needham*

"There are times when the most important thing we can do is to do nothing. It is that aspect of patience which is to wait until God's time and then move only in accordance with His specific command." *John W. Lawrence*

"He who waits on God loses no time." *Vance Havner*

"It is impossible for a believer, no matter what his experience, to keep right with God if he will not take the trouble to spend time with God. . . Spend plenty of time with God; let other things go, but don't neglect Him." *Oswald Chambers*

"We ought to see the face of God every morning before we see the face of man. If you have so much business to attend to that you have no time to pray, depend on it, you have more business on hand than God ever intended." *D. L. Moody*

"Live near to God, and the things of time will appear little to you in comparison with eternal realities." *Robert Murray M'Cheyne*

Lord, I want to be a wise man. I want to trust in You more.
Truly, my times are in Your hands.

NEVER LOSE YOUR HOPE IN GOD

Be strong and take heart, all you who hope in the LORD.
PSALM 31:24 NIV

Throughout the Psalms, David uses a traditional pattern for prayer to God that Moses, Nehemiah, Hezekiah, Daniel, Ezra, and others used throughout Bible times. This pattern has four distinct elements.

Look up. This is what believers often call praise and worship, especially when your words echo what God has said is true about Himself.

Look down. In confession and repentance, admit how you have failed and fallen short of God's glory because of how you have disobeyed Him. All great men of God, no matter how badly they've failed God, have learned to confess their sins. Keep short accounts and thank God for His forgiveness.

Look up again. Thanksgiving arises out of your faith, hope, and love for God, again based again on what God has said. How often men neglect this essential element of prayer in their eagerness to tell God what they're thinking. Instead, thank God for what He has told you in His Word.

Look down again. Cry out for God to act as He has promised He will for believers. Don't cry out for God to do what you alone want, need, and desire. Instead, humbly ask God to do what scripture says God already wants to do.

Lord, transform me. Transform my prayers. May I echo the words of the psalmists and prophets, following their examples as I pray to You.

ARE YOU UNLIKE THE SADDUCEES?

That same day Jesus was approached by some Sadducees—
religious leaders who say there is no resurrection from the dead.
MATTHEW 22:23 NLT

Talk about a bunch of rich fools. The high priest and his fellow Sadducees acted like Jewish aristocrats. They ruled the temple and ran the Lord right out the door. They denied some of the most basic teachings of scripture—life after death, heaven, hell, angels, demons, miracles (Acts 23:8)—to the point of casting doubt on God Himself. No wonder Jesus harshly rebuked them and said, "Your mistake is that you don't know the Scriptures, and you don't know the power of God" (Matthew 22:29 NLT).

After Pentecost, the Sadducees were very disturbed that Peter and John were claiming, on the authority of Jesus, that there is a resurrection of the dead. They arrested the two leading apostles (Acts 4:1–3) and later threw the whole lot—including Matthew—into jail (Acts 5:17–18). The apostles must have seen the irony when God sent an angel to perform a spectacular miracle that threw the Sadducees into a fit.

Like the Sadducees, you can be tempted to doubt the supernatural details of God's Word. Yet if God is God, nothing is impossible!

Unlike the Sadducees, stand in awe of the Lord, gladly acknowledge His mighty power, and heed His every word.

Lord, transform me. Unlike the Sadducees, I never want
to become a skeptic, doubting You and Your Word.

WHY JESUS BLASTED RELIGIOUS HYPOCRITES

"So you must be careful to do everything they tell you. But do not do what they do, for they do not practice what they preach."

MATTHEW 23:3 NIV

Jesus missed no opportunities to harshly criticize the religious hypocrites of His day, especially the scribes, Pharisees, Sadducees, and ruling family of high priests, as well as the everyday priests and Levites. With them, Jesus definitely is not nice.

Of course, how do you know Jesus wasn't a hypocrite? First, He clearly and correctly defined what hypocrites say and do. In contrast, Jesus fulfilled every requirement of the Old Testament and lived out every requirement of the New Testament.

Besides, Jesus would have admitted if He were a hypocrite, His enemies would have pointed out His hypocrisies at every turn, and His disciples definitely would *not* have given up everything to follow Him until each was cruelly martyred.

If Jesus wasn't a hypocrite, then why wasn't He nice? And why did He launch so many harsh verbal hand grenades at the hypocrisies of the religious leaders of His day?

Each carefully designed event (statements, actions, or miracles) was intended to spark fierce responses within them for or against God. Within "them" as a group *and* individually.

The Lord doesn't want anyone to perish, but all to come to repentance (2 Peter 3:9).

Lord, transform me. Unlike Jesus, I can be a hypocrite.
Please help me live out what I believe. No more Mr. Show.

NEVER GIVE UP

"And this gospel of the kingdom will be preached in all the world as a witness to all the nations, and then the end will come."

MATTHEW 24:14 NKJV

Not everyone goes to heaven. Then again, don't assume that someone who has died—and who knowingly rejected the Good News for years—went to hell. Never say such words. Only God knows that.

Instead, pray for God to reveal whether that person trusted Jesus Christ before the very end. Then, trust that your loved one is in the hands of a just and merciful God.

One man rejected the Gospel his whole life. His father had been a circuit preacher, but he wanted nothing to do with God or church (though he still could quote Psalm 23). On his deathbed, the man read a final letter (plea) from a step-granddaughter, Renée, and trusted Jesus Christ two days before his passing.

The other step-grandfather even more adamantly rejected Christ his whole life. When he died, Renée and her husband told their children what's stated above. A few days later a step-grandson (whom Renée hadn't met before) said he too was a Christian and had led Grandpa to Christ the day before he died.

How very good that, no matter what, the Lord never gives up.

Lord, transform me. It's hard to imagine certain people ever coming to faith. Thank You that You never give up on them. Help me to prayerfully do the same.

ARE YOU UNLIKE AARON?

*So Aaron said, "Take the gold rings from the ears of your wives
and sons and daughters, and bring them to me."*

EXODUS 32:2 NLT

Peer pressure. Do you ever really outgrow it? Aaron experienced such great pressure to please other people that even a meal in the bright presence of God didn't deter him from giving in soon thereafter.

It probably wasn't that Aaron lost his faith in the Lord God. So what went wrong with Aaron? Left in charge of the Israelites for a mere forty days, Aaron couldn't hold to what he knew was true over against what the people wanted.

The Israelites wanted a god they could see, not a God cloaked in dark clouds and lightning (Exodus 19:16–18). They wanted a religion of wild parties, not a situation where they must wait to hear from God. And who knows what happened to that Moses guy, anyway?

Aaron didn't lose the priesthood for his part in the Israelites' idolatry, but he did lose an opportunity to lead the people closer to their one true God.

You certainly can sympathize with others as they wrestle with the unexplained parts of life and God's mysterious ways. But, unlike Aaron, never give in to the pressure to remake God just to make them feel better.

*Lord, transform me. Unlike Aaron, I do not give
in to the pressure of others to redefine You.*

STOP DREAMING ABOUT EASY STREET

Many are the afflictions of the righteous,
but the LORD delivers him out of them all.
PSALM 34:19 ESV

God, and God's principles, and life's difficulties, haven't changed over time. David's psalms aren't just stories about someone who lived a long time ago. They're stories about you and your life too.

The apostle Paul said it well: "For whatever was written in former days was written for our instruction, that through endurance and through the encouragement of the Scriptures we might have hope" (Romans 15:4 ESV).

The great paradox of life is that suffering and humility are necessary steps to God's best in your life. You see that in Romans chapter 5, in James chapter 1, in 1 Peter chapters 1–5, and many other scripture passages, including today's New Testament scripture reading.

That God's preparation and training program for you includes hardships and trials is a very unpopular and countercultural message. You would much rather enjoy a nice, comfortable lifestyle perpetually free of pain and suffering. But you might as well face reality.

In David's psalms, you don't hear God's perspective much at all, but His fingerprints are everywhere. They help you see God behind the scenes, at work in and through the narrative of your life. Because the reality is, God is always doing something bigger than you can see.

In the meantime, stop dreaming about Easy Street.

Lord, transform me. Transform my dreams. May I see Your
fingerprints scattered everywhere throughout my life.

PUT WHAT GOD GIVES YOU TO GOOD USE

"To one he gave five bags of gold, to another two bags, and to another one bag, each according to his ability. Then he went on his journey."

MATTHEW 25:15 NIV

Throughout the wisdom literature of the Old Testament, especially in Psalms and Proverbs, "gold" refers to the tremendous value of God's words and wisdom, and His commands and instructions.

Today's New Testament scripture reading is the fourth time Jesus talks about "gold" during His public ministry. This final time is shortly before His arrest, flogging, and crucifixion. So Jesus uses "gold" to communicate something very important about God's kingdom.

In His parable, Jesus speaks about three men of differing abilities. Two of the men wisely used the bags of gold entrusted to them. In turn, their master rewarded both men the same way. The third man hid his bag of gold out of fear, had nothing to show after such a long time, and therefore faced his master's worst possible judgment against him.

God is not impressed when you give your resources back to Him, for they are His anyway. Even the third man knew that (Matthew 25:26).

Instead, God wants you to use your resources—your heart and soul, your time and attention, your abilities and talents, your resources and wealth—for His glory.

Lord, transform me. Help me to be usable.
All I am and have is nothing without You.

HOW TO LOVE THE LORD WHOLEHEARTEDLY

The Israelites completed all the work, just as GOD had commanded. Moses saw that they had done all the work and done it exactly as GOD had commanded. Moses blessed them.
EXODUS 39:42–43 MSG

Today your wife may want a heartfelt Valentine's Day card and a beautiful bouquet of flowers. More importantly, do you know what she wants every other day of the year? Yes, your wholehearted love, respect, and gracious manner with her.

Even more importantly, do you know what God wants every day of the year? Yes, your wholehearted love, obedience, and worship. That's what makes today's Old Testament Bible reading so incredible.

Repeatedly, you discover that God's people did two things. First, they gave generously for the construction of the Lord's tabernacle. Second, they carefully did all that the Lord had commanded.

On the last day of his own life, Moses longed for these good old days. He told the people: "What do you think GOD expects from you? Just this: Live in His presence in holy reverence, follow the road he sets out for you, love him, serve God, your God, with everything you have in you, obey the commandments and regulations of GOD that I'm commanding you today—live a good life" (Deuteronomy 10:12–13 MSG).

In your own life and experience, don't waste these days!

Lord, transform me. Transform my heart, soul, strength, and mind. May I live sold-out for You all my coming days.

REJOICING WHEN GOD DWELLS AMONG MEN

*Then the cloud covered the Tabernacle, and the glory of the Lord
filled the Tabernacle. Moses could no longer enter the Tabernacle
because the cloud had settled down over it, and the
glory of the Lord filled the Tabernacle.*

Exodus 40:34–35 NLT

The glory of the Lord looks more dazzling than anything you've seen in this universe. When the cloud came down atop Mount Sinai, God's people trembled. Months later, when the Lord's glory left Sinai and filled the brand-new tabernacle, everyone trembled again.

Four hundred years later, God's people trembled once more when the Lord's dazzling glory left the tabernacle and filled Solomon's newly dedicated temple (1 Kings 8:10–11 and 2 Chronicles 7:1–2). Fast-forward a few more centuries. Just as God had warned repeatedly, His judgment ensued.

Accordingly, the Lord's dazzling glory in the temple slowly departed from the Holy of Holies to the entrance of the Holy place, and from there to the outer gate of the temple area, and from there to a mountain, and from there apparently back to heaven (Ezekiel 8:4, 9:3, 10:4, 10:18–19, and 11:22–23). But that's not the end of the story.

Don't miss the exclamation point of history: "Look, God's home is now among his people! He will live with them, and they will be his people. God himself will be with them" (Revelation 21:3 NLT). How dazzling that will be!

Lord, transform me. Give me a new vision of dwelling with You in glory.

GETTING INTO LEVITICUS

The LORD called Moses and spoke to him from the tent
of meeting, saying, "Speak to the people of Israel."
LEVITICUS 1:1–2 ESV

Today's Old Testament Bible reading explains what happened next after the Lord's glory filled the newly constructed tabernacle. This third book of the Bible answers the tough question, "Since the Lord is so holy, what must I do to worship Him properly?"

Unlike the first two books of Moses, Leviticus contains only a handful of narrative accounts. It's primarily a handbook the Israelites used to know how best to worship the Lord.

In chapters 1–27, it's easy to see that sacrifices played a very important role in Old Testament worship, as did festivals. In fact, the Lord instructed Israelite families to celebrate at least three festivals each year. These festivals served as tangible reminders of the Lord's covenant with the Israelites.

Many aspects of the Levitical system of worship illustrate one's need of God's cleansing and forgiveness. Several key aspects clearly foreshadow the saving work of the promised Savior.

Famous passages in Leviticus include:

- instructions about various sacrifices (1:1–7:38)
- Moses consecrates Aaron and his sons (8:1–9:24)
- "Be holy because I am holy" (11:44–45, 19:2, 20:7, 20:26, 21:8)
- instructions about sexual purity (18:6–23)
- "Love your neighbor as yourself" (19:18, 19:34)
- the year of jubilee (25:8–55)

Lord, transform me. Give me a new vision of Your holiness.
Thank You so very much for clothing me in Christ's robes of righteousness.

ARE YOU LIKE PETER?

Suddenly, Jesus' words flashed through Peter's mind:
"Before the rooster crows, you will deny three times that you
even know me." And he went away, weeping bitterly.

MATTHEW 26:75 NLT

From the time you were a kid, you've been told: "Three strikes and you're out." Thankfully, God's kingdom operates on an entirely different basis. You can never let God down one too many times. If you love Him and own up to your sins, confessing them and asking for His forgiveness, God keeps right on forgiving you and putting you back in the game.

If anyone has ever understood the marvel of God's goodness to keep giving second chances, it was the apostle Peter. In the course of a single evening, Peter denied Jesus Christ three times: first to a maid, then in front of a couple of her friends, then before an entire group of bystanders. Yet after His resurrection, Jesus made a point of repeatedly reassuring Peter that He still had great things in store for this very human, less than perfect disciple.

Later in life, Peter was quick to remind his fellow believers that Jesus Christ "personally carried our sins in his own body on the cross so we can be dead to sin and live for what is right" (1 Peter 2:24 NLT).

Lord, transform me. Like Peter, I know that no matter
how often I let You down, You won't give up on me.

ARE YOU UNLIKE PILATE?

"Don't you hear all these charges they are bringing against you?"
Pilate demanded. But Jesus made no response to any
of the charges, much to the governor's surprise.
MATTHEW 27:13–14 NLT

What's your greatest claim to fame? Besides Jesus, it's said that no other man's name is spoken more often in churches around the world every Sunday than Pontius Pilate. That's because he is mentioned by name in the Apostles' Creed.

Why all the attention? History portrays Pilate as a rash, capricious, and ultimately ineffective Roman provincial governor. At his greatest hour of testing, Pilate failed miserably by condemning to death the world's only innocent man—God's Son, Jesus Christ.

Each of the Gospel writers records this trial at length. Ironically, they almost make it sound as if Pilate is on trial, not Jesus. And for good reason. If Pilate committed one more blunder, he knew Caesar might throw him forcefully out of office, disgraced.

Despite his better judgment, Pilate bowed to the political will of the chief priests and sentenced Jesus to merciless flogging and crucifixion. In a futile attempt to save his own neck, Pilate washed his hands, effectively signing away the rest of his life in bitter exile.

When the pressure was the greatest, Pilate listened to everyone— except his conscience, his wife, and the Truth.

Lord, transform me. Unlike Pilate,
I want to embrace Your truth wholeheartedly.

ARE YOU LIKE JOSEPH OF ARIMATHEA?

As evening approached, Joseph, a rich man from
Arimathea who had become a follower of Jesus,
went to Pilate and asked for Jesus' body.
MATTHEW 27:57–58 NLT

The cast of characters changes from one Gospel to the next—except for John the Baptist, Mary, the apostles, the Pharisees, and Pilate. And somebody named Joseph of Arimathea, who appears on the stage for a brief moment, then exits, never to be heard from again.

Scripture says Joseph was from a village in the hill country northwest of Jerusalem. It says he was rich, "an honored member of the high council. . .[who] was waiting for the Kingdom of God to come" (Mark 15:43 NLT), "a good and righteous man" who "had not agreed with the decision and actions of the other religious leaders" (Luke 23:50–51 NLT) and "who had been a secret disciple of Jesus" (John 19:38 NLT).

As far as one can tell, Joseph had no idea he was fulfilling the prophecy that the Messiah's body would be "buried. . .in a rich man's grave" (Isaiah 53:9 NLT).

To one degree or another, most Christians find it hard to be outspoken about their faith in Jesus Christ. You certainly are not alone when you feel nervous, hesitant, or afraid. But like Joseph, gather your courage and obey the Holy Spirit's promptings to honor and glorify Jesus Christ.

Lord, transform me. Like Joseph of Arimathea,
I don't hide my faith in the Lord Jesus.

ARE YOU LIKE MARY MAGDALENE?

*Early on Sunday morning, as the new day was dawning, Mary
Magdalene and the other Mary went out to visit the tomb.*
MATTHEW 28:1 NLT

Before her deliverance, Mary Magdalene experienced a never-ending nightmare at the hands of demons. Not overwhelming life circumstances, but seven wicked spiritual beings who invaded her body and tormented her spirit. Mary found no way of escape—until the day she met Jesus.

When Mary came face-to-face with Jesus, He immediately cast out the demons and she awoke to the glories of His salvation. She never faced those demons again. Instead, Mary became one of a handful of women disciples who stayed close to Jesus. She traveled with Him, supported Him financially, stood by and wept at His crucifixion, and saw Him first after His resurrection.

How many demons bind lost people in horrible nightmares today? Millions suffer from true demonic possession or from the demons of alcoholism, drugs, suicidal depression, and extreme insecurity about the future.

Mary came to Jesus not for a quick fix to her nightmares but for complete freedom and lifelong dependence and relationship.

Jesus still delivers people from nightmares today. No nightmare is too awful. He casts them all away. Like Mary, you can come to Him for complete salvation today.

*Lord, transform me. Like Mary Magdalene,
I believe You can deliver me from any nightmare.*

WHO IS KING OF YOUR LIFE?

Jesus and his companions went to the town of Capernaum.
When the Sabbath day came, he went into the
synagogue and began to teach.

MARK 1:21 NLT

Most of the time, you aren't privy to what's going on in the spiritual realm. Yet never forget: you are engaged in a war on a much larger scale than you can imagine.

After recruiting His first disciples, Jesus takes them to the synagogue in the city of Capernaum, where that unseen war became visible for a brief moment. When a demon-possessed man tries to tell Jesus what to do, He immediate rebukes the evil spirit and tells *him* what to do. To everyone's astonishment, the demon has to obey what Jesus says.

The reality is, everyone has to obey Jesus. Some may shake and scream. Some may try to tell Jesus what to do. But in the end, everyone has to obey Him. The question isn't, "Is Jesus the Lord of all?" The question is, "Have you acknowledged that fact in your own life?"

One day everyone in heaven and on earth and under the earth will have to bow the knee and proclaim that Jesus is Lord to the glory of God the Father (Philippians 2:9–11). How much better to gladly acknowledge His place in the universe, and in your life, here and now.

Lord, transform me. Every day, in every way,
in every sphere of life, I want to follow You.

IF JESUS DISAPPEARS

Now in the morning, having risen a long while before daylight,
He went out and departed to a solitary place; and there He prayed.
And Simon and those who were with Him searched for Him.

MARK 1:35–36 NKJV

Have you ever wondered how Jesus convinced Peter, Andrew, James, John, and others to drop everything, leave it all behind, and start following Him—with no stated destination, spelled-out itinerary, or promise of safe passage and return?

Exactly how did Jesus pull that off? You see the answer in today's New Testament scripture reading. First, Jesus came to their town. Second, He hung around with them for a number of days. Third, without warning, He disappeared.

Peter and the others looked for Jesus everywhere. Finally, they found Him away from town and in the wilderness, walking stick in hand, ready for a long day's journey.

"Don't you know everyone has been looking for you?" Peter asked.

Jesus' reply, in essence, was this: "Yes, but we need to be going. I have many other towns to visit." It was clear there was no point trying to convince Jesus to come back. He was already standing up and starting down the road.

In that instant, Peter and the others had a decision to make. Jesus wasn't laying out various options. By His very actions, He was issuing a command.

Lord, transform me. I sometimes wonder where You are in my
life. Instead, prompt me to start following You anew.

LOVING THE UNLOVABLE

"If You are willing, You can make me clean."
MARK 1:40 NKJV

I n ancient Israel, you could be wealthy, well married, with a house full of children and yet. . .if you became leprous, you instantly and permanently lost your lovely wife, your dear family, your luxurious villa, and the blessing and well-being of everyone else you knew and loved. From that moment on, and for the rest of your days, you were a sickly, and often impoverished, exile.

In Bible times, among the Jewish people few diseases provoked more fear than leprosy. You not only lost everyone and everything, but you eventually became disfigured and hideous. . .the walking dead.

Yet Matthew, Mark, and Luke all record the story of a leprous man who runs up to Jesus, falls on his face, and humbly yet desperately begs Jesus to heal him. The disciples cringe, yet Jesus isn't afraid of lepers.

Instead, Jesus touches the leper. He heals him. He sends him ahead to testify to the priests and Levites: "Look, I've been healed. I can enter the temple again and offer my sacrifices with joy and singing. I'm with my family again. Let's sacrifice the spotless lamb and feast!"

Lord, transform me. May I never doubt Your love for the unlovable.

ARE YOU UNLIKE JUDAS ISCARIOT?

Then he appointed twelve of them and called them his apostles. . .
[including] Judas Iscariot (who later betrayed him).

MARK 3:14, 19 NLT

The history of the nineteenth and twentieth centuries contains numerous stories of men and women who formed their own religious cults to make a fortune from gullible souls. Judas had dreams of fame and riches as grand as those of any charlatan. And he saw Jesus as his sure ticket to achieving them.

From the first time he "borrowed" a little money from the apostles' fund to the moment he pocketed thirty pieces of silver, Judas was looking out for his own best interests. When he objected to a woman's lavish outpouring of perfume on Jesus, for instance, it wasn't because Judas really cared about the poor. What Jesus saw as an act of worship, Judas calculated as a loss of funds to pilfer.

As Jesus approached Jerusalem and began predicting His sufferings, Judas counted the cost—and decided to cash in while he could. With ease, Satan entered Judas's heart and propelled him to cut a deal with the leading priests and then plot a way to betray Jesus.

Even when later Judas was filled with remorse, he never turned back to God in repentance. He simply regretted the tragic turn of events and took what appeared to be the easiest way out.

Lord, transform me. Unlike Judas, I do not follow
You out of selfish, ulterior motives.

ARE YOU READY AND RECEPTIVE?

"But to those who can't see it yet, everything comes in stories,
creating readiness, nudging them toward receptive insight.
These are people—whose eyes are open but don't see a thing,
whose ears are open but don't understand a word,
who avoid making an about-face and getting forgiven."
MARK 4:11–12 MSG

D on't skim today's New Testament scripture reading. All twenty verses are packed with practical truths.

Throughout this Gospel's first three chapters, Mark shows a marked progression in the size of the crowds coming out to see and hear Jesus. The exclamation point is today's first verse, which speaks of a huge crowd in the thousands. (This doesn't mean that Jesus won't continue to draw huge numbers. Just the opposite. From this point forward, He continues to draw the masses.)

In verses 2–9, Jesus presents one of His most famous parables—the parable of the soils. In verse 10, the masses have left and the followers of Jesus, including the apostles, ask Jesus to explain this parable. Then you have the two verses quoted above. In the very next verse, Jesus says: "Do you see how this story works? All my stories work this way." Then Jesus explains the parable in verses 14–20.

Don't rush through verse 20. In it, Jesus commends those who "hear the Word, embrace it, and produce a harvest." That's the man you want to be!

Lord, transform me. May I always long to hear
and embrace Your Word.

LOVE YOUR NEIGHBOR AS YOURSELF

*"The foreigner residing among you must be treated
as your native-born. Love them as yourself."*

LEVITICUS 19:34 NIV

I t's easy to forget how readily Jesus loved, well, *everyone.*

Jesus loved Jew and Gentile, men and women, youth and little children. He loved married and unmarried, rich and poor, zealot and tax collector, rebel and political insider.

If Jesus loved everyone, that's fine. Most Christians actually are okay with that.

What messes things up? Realizing Jesus calls you to do the same.

Proof? Choose to live, and embrace living, in a diverse community. Where your neighbors hail from dozens of countries and speak a plethora of languages.

Where your neighbors are Protestant, Catholic, Russian Orthodox, Greek Orthodox, Eastern Orthodox, Latin Pentecostal, Asian Presbyterian, Jewish, Muslim, Buddhist, Hindu, Sikh, Shinto, animist, agnostic, atheist, and "none of the above."

Where your neighbors are registered Democrats, Republicans, and Independents. Where they are super rich, upper middle class, middle class, lower middle class, lower class, and homeless.

One man whose family did just this remarked: "Yes, we know… we have all kinds of neighbors. We actually want it that way. We want our children to be able to grow up and know, in their heart of hearts, that they love *everyone.*"

Just like Jesus.

*Lord, transform my vision of "neighbor."
Stretch my heart to love every person I know and meet.*

"BE HOLY IN ALL YOU DO"

"You are to be holy to me because I, the LORD, am holy."
LEVITICUS 20:26 NIV

Sometimes the Bible says something so important that it says that truth or command repeatedly. That's certainly the case with today's key verse, which is the fifth time the Lord makes this statement in ten chapters (see also 11:44, 11:45, 19:2, and 20:7).

Some may be tempted to think: *But that was then. This is now. Holiness is impossible. Besides, the Lord forgives all my sins.*

Really? Listen to the apostle Peter's emphatic words: "Therefore, with minds that are alert and fully sober, set your hope on the grace to be brought to you when Jesus Christ is revealed at his coming. As obedient children, do not conform to the evil desires you had when you lived in ignorance. But just as he who called you is holy, so be holy in all you do; for it is written: 'Be holy, because I am holy.' Since you call on a Father who judges each person's work impartially, live out your time as foreigners here in reverent fear" (1 Peter 1:13–17 NIV).

After love, holiness is the penultimate hallmark of the followers of Jesus Christ. It doesn't mean that you never sin. It does mean you keep short accounts with God. It means you forsake old ways of living. It means you focus on heaven. It means you seek God's "Well done!"

Lord, transform me. As You have said, I want to be holy.

ARE YOU LIKE JAIRUS?

*Then a leader of the local synagogue, whose name was Jairus,
arrived. When he saw Jesus, he fell at his feet.*

MARK 5:22 NLT

J airus held his twelve-year-old daughter's trembling hand as his wife cooled the girl's forehead. He and his wife both knew the horrible truth. They were about to lose their precious daughter.

Just then, Jairus heard a commotion and stepped outside. A large crowd was gathering along the shore in front of the village. It was Jesus! In desperation, Jairus threw aside all decorum and pushed his way forcefully through the crowd. Falling at Jesus' feet, Jairus pleaded with the Lord to heal his daughter.

Jesus agreed and started toward Jairus' home—but then stopped for what seemed like an eternity. Then came the worst news a father ever could hear. Jairus fell to his knees in grief, only to feel Jesus' hand upon his shoulder. "Get up, Jairus," Jesus said. "Don't be afraid. Just trust me." Slowly, Jairus stood up and started walking back, half in a daze, to his house. Then the sounds of wailing started to fill the air. "Don't stop, Jairus," Jesus said. "Just believe."

Later that night, after kissing their daughter good night, Jairus and his wife fell into each other's arms and wept great tears of joy.

Jesus now calls you to believe.

*Lord, transform me. Like Jairus,
I always want to believe You can do miracles.*

HAVE YOU FULLY REPENTED?

*So the disciples went out, telling everyone they
met to repent of their sins and turn to God.*

MARK 6:12 NLT

What did Jesus and early Christians mean when they used the word *repent*? The New Testament presents ten important aspects of repenting.

First, it means you reject and turn away from something (sin). Second, it means you accept and turn toward Someone (the Lord). Third, it means you believe in Jesus Christ and His Good News (Mark 1:15). Fourth, it means you receive the Lord's forgiveness of your sins (Mark 1:4). Fifth, it means you become a citizen of God's kingdom (Mark 1:15 again). Sixth, it means the angels in heaven celebrate your conversion (Luke 15:10). Seventh, it means you are willing to be baptized as a believer (Acts 2:38). Eighth, it means you receive the Holy Spirit within your heart (Acts 2:38). Ninth, it means you prove you have changed by the good you do (Acts 26:20). Tenth, it means you continue to turn from sin back to the Lord (Revelation 3:3).

So do all ten aspects of repenting resonate with you? If yes, great! If no, stop everything and talk it over with the Lord right now.

Don't let it be said of you: "If only he had fully repented."

---

*Lord, I want to fully repent and keep turning back to You. With Your help,
may that be my daily experience in the days, weeks, and months ahead.*

TRANSFORMED BY REST

"You have six days each week for your ordinary work, but the seventh day is a Sabbath day of complete rest, an official day for holy assembly. It is the LORD's Sabbath day, and it must be observed wherever you live."

LEVITICUS 23:3 NLT

Why did God command His people to set aside a specific day for rest? Most importantly, what do you think God could do in your life with one day set aside for rest?

Think about all the ways that your calendar fills up. You surely have plenty of obligations that may include work, caring for a family member, helping your kids with homework, or the chores and projects that pile up around the house. The question, "Why a Sabbath?" suddenly becomes, "Who has time for a Sabbath?"

The striking nature of God commanding His people to rest may have a message for you today. What are you missing from God that could come from a weekly Sabbath? Perhaps the message of a Sabbath is to place greater faith in God right now. Then again, this may be an opportunity to rely on others in your faith community. Regardless, the Sabbath is your chance to receive a blessing from God today.

Lord, open my eyes to the ways I can observe the blessing of Your Sabbath in faith. May I turn my worries and fears over to You and fully enjoy the rest You offer Your people.

JESUS IS FULL OF COMPASSION

*Jesus saw the huge crowd as he stepped from the boat, and he had
compassion on them because they were like sheep without
a shepherd. So he began teaching them many things.*

Mark 6:34 nlt

J esus recognized how draining it could be to meet the spiritual and
physical needs of others, and so He modeled rest and restoration for
His followers. However, He also responded to the needs of others with
compassion, even when He had reached His human limits.

You will encounter many different needs and kinds of people each
day, but are you aware of what motivates them? What drives people to
act the way they do?

Today's scripture shows that Jesus didn't respond to people based
on how exhausted He felt. Rather, He saw that the people seeking Him
were desperate for direction. His compassion was rooted in His ability
to identify with their inner struggles.

Are there opportunities for you to ask what's motivating certain
people or what's behind their actions? It could be that an angry person is
driven by a deep wound from the past or a person who struggles to trust
has been betrayed by someone who should have been reliable. Ministry
can flow out of compassion and the act of relating to the stories of others.

*Jesus, give me eyes to see and ears to hear the stories and struggles
of others. May I serve them with mercy and generosity
even when I have grown weary.*

GOD DWELLS AMONG THE OBEDIENT

*"I will make my dwelling among you, and my soul shall not abhor you.
And I will walk among you and will be your God, and you shall
be my people. I am the LORD your God, who brought you out of the
land of Egypt, that you should not be their slaves. And I have
broken the bars of your yoke and made you walk erect."*
LEVITICUS 26:11–13 ESV

God desires to dwell among His people, but sometimes He needs to offer reminders of what He has done in the past, letting His people know that their freedom comes from God's work in their lives, not from indulging their own desires or bowing to the wishes of others.

What has God done in your life to help you live in freedom? Are there ways you have seen God's provision for you? These are the moments God wants you to remember, keeping them before your mind as you face new challenges. The faithfulness of God in the past is what can transform fear into faith today.

Just as the people of Israel continued to face difficult situations and choices—where they had to weigh the direction of God against their own desires and wisdom—the defining moment in your life may come down to what you remember.

*Lord, I am grateful for Your presence and provision in my life.
May I remember the ways You have been faithful so
that I will be guided by faith in You.*

WHERE DO YOU TURN FOR HELP?

God is our refuge and strength, an ever-present help in trouble.
Therefore we will not fear, though the earth give way and the
mountains fall into the heart of the sea, though its waters roar
and foam and the mountains quake with their surging.

PSALM 46:1–3 NIV

When was the last time your life was disrupted? Is there something that you fear today? The writer of the Psalms provides a picture of global cataclysms, natural disasters that would cause the courage of anyone to melt. While the earth shakes, sources of comfort and trust fall to pieces, and new threats emerge, God remains ever-present to help.

There is no condemnation for reacting to troubling situations with fear, but fear isn't the place to remain. The difference today is where you turn. Do you look for comfort, strength, or protection in the many distractions, pleasures, or material items around you? Whether you turn to a stocked bank account or an escape from reality, the appropriate response to frightening circumstances is a resolution to trust in the strength of God.

God is present in His beloved creation, and He is with you, His beloved child. He will not abandon you. Every other source of comfort and protection will dissipate, crumble, or slip away. Only God remains.

God, You alone stand immovable in this disruptive and frightening world.
May I turn to You alone in faith throughout the fearful seasons of life.

PREEMPTIVE LOVE FROM THE FATHER

Then a cloud overshadowed them, and a voice from the cloud said,
"This is my dearly loved Son. Listen to him." Suddenly, when they looked
around, Moses and Elijah were gone, and they saw only Jesus with them.

MARK 9:7–8 NLT

J esus knew that suffering awaited Him if He made His customary trip to Jerusalem, and so He turned to God the Father in prayer before beginning His journey. What could the Son of God receive in His darkest moment? The Father simply affirmed His love for the Son.

As you seek to imitate the journey of Jesus, taking up your own cross, counting the cost daily, and surrendering yourself to the plans of God for your life, perhaps you need to imagine yourself in this scene. You have taken up a costly journey, the future is unknown, and there may be plenty to fear. What would you imagine God the Father saying to you at this moment when turning away certainly feels much easier than pressing on?

How would you respond if you heard God the Father call out, "You are My beloved son!"? Whether you have failed or succeeded, the love of the Father is reaching out to you today. What if that is enough for the challenges you face today?

Father, You adopted me into Your family and showed
me the same love that You give to Jesus, Your Son.
May I rest in the security of that love today.

A HOLY CALLING

"Bring the tribe of Levi near, and set them before Aaron the priest, that they may minister to him. They shall keep guard over him and over the whole congregation before the tent of meeting, as they minister at the tabernacle."

NUMBERS 3:6–7 ESV

Perhaps the calling of the tribe of Levi may appeal to you if you're in a season of searching, uncertainty, or confusion over your calling. A clear, direct command from God may sound like the perfect thing. You just need to serve where God has called you at the tabernacle, and that's that, right?

With the many choices, options, careers, calls, and vocations that appear before you today, perhaps it may help to step back and ask where God has placed you now. Is there one thing that God has set before you that requires your full attention and faithfulness?

You may not know what your calling or career will be for the rest of your life, let alone for the next five years. Those big picture questions can take time to sort out. If you are seeking God's transforming power and faithfulness in your life, then the best place to start may be right where you are.

Lord, You know me better than I know myself. Guide me to the people, places, and tasks where I can serve You and others best.

MEDITATE ON GOD'S UNFAILING LOVE

Within your temple, O God, we meditate on your unfailing love.
Like your name, O God, your praise reaches to the ends of the earth;
your right hand is filled with righteousness. Mount Zion rejoices,
the villages of Judah are glad because of your judgments.

PSALM 48:9–11 NIV

The Psalms encourage you to surrender to God's judgments and plans, but you may be right to ask: "What kind of God am I surrendering to?" Surrender is no easy matter. Do you trust God's judgments more than your own? What will happen if you leave your own paths behind and pursue God's judgments and plans instead?

The people of Israel offer a helpful starting point in your meditations: God's unfailing love. This is the God who continued to send prophets to His people even when they were unfaithful. And then when all appeared lost, God sent His beloved Son to save His people from their sins. This is a trustworthy God who is worthy of your best hopes and plans.

If trusting God is a challenge, perhaps the place to begin is considering what's on your mind today. Are you considering the ways God's love has been manifested in your life? If not, then that may explain why it's hard to trust God during this season.

Lord, You have proven Yourself faithful and just.
May I rest in Your unfailing love today.

TRANSFORMED TO LEAD BY SERVING

*"Whoever wants to be a leader among you must be your servant,
and whoever wants to be first among you must be the slave of
everyone else. For even the Son of Man came not to be served but
to serve others and to give his life as a ransom for many."*

Mark 10:44–45 nlt

What does a great leader look like? At times people may think of the person who draws the attention of others when she walks in the room, the athlete who guides a team to a championship, or the confident CEO who takes charge of a meeting. In the eyes of Jesus, the greatest leader among His followers will be the one who understands service. Those who sacrifice themselves for the sake of others will be the ones who have understood the message of Jesus best and follow His example of leadership.

If you don't aspire to be a leader, that doesn't leave you off the hook to serve others. The model of Jesus' life is one of self-sacrifice and service. The purpose of Jesus' life revolved around giving His life as a ransom to serve others, and so the challenge of Jesus is to ask how you can make sacrifices for the sake of others and yield your desires to God.

*Jesus, You led the way by giving up Your life for others.
Help me to let go of my own desires so that I can serve others freely.*

SAVE AWE FOR GOD, NOT WEALTH

*Do not be overawed when others grow rich, when the splendor of
their houses increases; for they will take nothing with them when
they die, their splendor will not descend with them. Though while
they live they count themselves blessed—and people praise you
when you prosper—they will join those who have gone before them,
who will never again see the light of life.*

PSALM 49:16–19 NIV

H ave you ever made the mistake of believing that wealth determines
how blessed you are? It's tempting to believe that those who are
rich have been blessed by God, but the psalmist offers a reminder that
wealth is not a blessing, for it cannot last from this life into the next and
it may even keep you from being present for God.

If anything, it's possible that wealth is more of a curse than a blessing
if it keeps you from serving God or recognizing God's presence in your life.
The splendor of today will fade soon enough, and when those possessions
crumble, what will be left?

The true blessing for you today is to recognize that God is present
with you in times of plenty and times of struggle. At the end of your life,
the one thing that lasts will be the investment you've made in God.

*Lord, You know what will last, and I trust that You can bring me
safely home to You one day. May I let go of what perishes
so that I can forever treasure Your love.*

WHAT BELONGS TO GOD?

*When they handed it to him, he asked, "Whose picture and title
are stamped on it?" "Caesar's," they replied. "Well, then," Jesus said,
"give to Caesar what belongs to Caesar, and give to God what
belongs to God." His reply completely amazed them.*

MARK 12:16–17 NLT

What belongs to God in your life? While the earth and everything in it belongs to God, Jesus challenged His listeners to stop looking for religious technicalities and traps to prove one's devotion to God. Every act of religious devotion can be used as a way to determine who is in and who is out, but the heart of the matter is whether you have given yourself completely to God or to a system of rules.

This passage offers a challenge to look at your heart rather than the standards of others. Can you approach God in confidence and hope that you are fully surrendered to God's ways? Those trying to trick and trap others are more concerned about who belongs to them than what belongs to God.

This invitation from Jesus isn't an easy word for today. Could Jesus completely change how you live your faith? It's a possibility, but on the other side there is freedom from condemnation and a simple invitation to live in the freedom of surrender to God.

Jesus, Your wisdom disrupts and amazes me. Give me grace to focus on my devotion to You rather than placing more boundaries around others.

MOVING AT GOD'S SPEED

At the command of the LORD the people of Israel set out, and at the command of the LORD they camped. As long as the cloud rested over the tabernacle, they remained in camp. Even when the cloud continued over the tabernacle many days, the people of Israel kept the charge of the LORD and did not set out.

NUMBERS 9:18–19 ESV

I srael recognized that they would only experience God's guidance, blessing, and protection if they resolved to only move with the cloud. Even though they longed to venture into the promised land, they had to entrust themselves to God's direction for their lives.

When is it hard for you to wait on God's timing? Have you ever felt that you've rushed ahead without God's guidance, provision, or protection? It can be humbling to admit that you don't know what's best for yourself. However, the story of Israel may provide the reminder that it's far worse if you move forward without God's power and leadership. If you try to move forward without God's transforming presence in your life, then you may have difficult days ahead.

Perhaps a time of waiting for the Lord looks like seeking the counsel of someone at church or relinquishing your desires for a particular outcome in your life. The delay may be agonizing, but God's presence is worth waiting for.

Lord, I trust that You will show me when to move forward and that Your timing is perfect.

GOD'S LOVE DETERMINES HIS MERCY

Have mercy on me, O God, according to your unfailing love;
according to your great compassion blot out my transgressions.
Wash away all my iniquity and cleanse me from my sin.

PSALM 51:1–2 NIV

You may not be able to argue the case for your own virtue or perfection before God, but the reality is that your transgressions aren't something that you can hide. Even if you are painfully aware of your sins and you feel shame before God, today's psalm has a message of hope and encouragement.

Powerless though you may be, God is prepared to show mercy to you based solely on His unfailing love. There is nothing you can bring to the table. There is no condition you have to meet in order to prompt God to love you or to show you mercy. You only need to seek His mercy in humility. As you recognize God's compassion and mercy, you can drop every other pretense or plan to blot away your sins. The transformation from fear and shame to cleansed and confident is God's work that you can only receive.

Make no mistake that God's love and mercy is a serious matter. God is under no obligation to save anyone, but His love and delight in mercy prompt Him to continue reaching out, even to those who have rejected His mercy.

Lord, I am not worthy of Your mercy and love, but I come to You in confidence today because You have chosen to cleanse me of my sins.

BEWARE CARELESS WORDS

*"Not so with my servant Moses. He is faithful in all my house.
With him I speak mouth to mouth, clearly, and not in riddles,
and he beholds the form of the LORD. Why then were you
not afraid to speak against my servant Moses?"*

NUMBERS 12:7–8 ESV

Miriam and Aaron had spoken against Moses, criticizing his Cushite wife and claiming that they had the same authority to speak on God's behalf. God's judgment put an end to both of their claims against Moses, and they offer a reminder that careless words and criticism can lead to unforeseen consequences.

Far from giving every leader a free pass from criticism, this passage specifically addresses the times you may be tempted to think more highly of yourself or to unjustly attack a person in authority. Even more broadly, careless criticism rarely leads to the results that you may imagine. Careless words can lead to division and an even lower opinion of your wisdom and insight.

By the time God was finished exposing the pride of Aaron and Miriam, they had no illusions about themselves. Before speaking up, consider whether you may be blinded by your own illusions. Have you considered yourself more qualified or more connected to God than someone else? If so, proceed cautiously.

*Lord, grant me the wisdom and knowledge to speak constructively
and helpfully, never assuming I am wiser or more
knowledgeable than warranted.*

COULD YOU EVER FAIL?

"No!" Peter declared emphatically. "Even if I have to die with you,
I will never deny you!" And all the others vowed the same.

Mark 14:31 nlt

If Peter could have imagined the worst thing he could ever say, it would surely have to be a denial of Jesus. Having been the one disciple blessed with the Spirit's insight into the divinity of Jesus as the Christ or promised Messiah, a denial was a significant fall.

Today's success or profession of faith is not a guarantee of continued faithfulness in extremely trying circumstances. It's hard to see Peter's denial unfold in the pages of Mark's Gospel, and so it may be even more troubling to imagine yourself making a similar denial in your own life.

Perhaps you haven't denied Jesus with the blatant words of Peter, but you've denied Jesus in other ways. Maybe you have jumped into your day without any awareness of Jesus or you have made decisions that run counter to the values and morality Jesus taught. There are many ways to deny Jesus that don't involve saying, "I don't know you."

You can take hope today that Jesus loved Peter and included him in His beloved community of disciples, knowing full well that Peter would deny Him. Even after Peter's failure, Jesus welcomed him back with open arms and the gift of the Holy Spirit.

Jesus, I thank You for Your mercy and affirmation
that overcome my denials and failures.

WHO IS MY NEIGHBOR?

"For the assembly, there shall be one statute for you and for the stranger who sojourns with you, a statute forever throughout your generations. You and the sojourner shall be alike before the Lord."

NUMBERS 15:15 ESV

While the Lord blessed Israel with a land of their own, this land was supposed to bless and benefit immigrants and migrants who wandered throughout the land, whether in search of work, refuge, or pasture. Rather than treating immigrants as second-class citizens, the Lord viewed them as equals in His presence, welcoming them to present pleasing offerings.

Boundaries aren't just a matter of national borders today. Boundaries can exist in your heart and in your views of other people. Perhaps you have a subtle tendency to view others as less important or you simply aren't aware of the needs and challenges that immigrants may face. Treating one group differently than another runs counter to the approach that God mandated for the people of Israel. Mercy and freedom to worship is guaranteed for all, and so you are invited to consider how you can view the "sojourner" of today with similar mercy.

You may not get to choose who your neighbor is or where your neighbor comes from, but you can choose how to respond to who shows up in your neighborhood.

Lord, help me to see the needs in my community so that I can serve others and ensure they have equality and mercy.

HOW TO RESPOND TO GOD'S PROVISION

Surely God is my help; the LORD is the one who sustains me.
Let evil recoil on those who slander me; in your faithfulness
destroy them. I will sacrifice a freewill offering to you;
I will praise your name, LORD, for it is good.

PSALM 54:4–6 NIV

How should you respond to those who attack and slander you? Besides endeavoring to live a holy and blameless life in the first place, today's psalm offers a few helpful clues about responding to a difficult situation with slander or accusations. Rather than rushing to defend yourself, begin by acknowledging that God is your help and your refuge. You will never find peace if you seek affirmation and security in the opinions of others.

In addition, slander itself can be self-defeating, recoiling back on those who verbally attack others. A slanderer is exposed by his actions, and so your best defense is to let the slander to be seen for what it is. Responding in kind will hardly help anyone.

Finally, while there may be situations where a clear, fact-based response to slander may be required, focus your energy on the goodness of God. Praise God for His love and goodness, for it is on God's goodness that you rise or fall, not the slander of someone else.

God, You are good and trustworthy, lifting up and
affirming Your people when they trust in You.

NO LONGER SEPARATED FROM GOD

Then Jesus uttered another loud cry and breathed his last. And the
curtain in the sanctuary of the Temple was torn in two, from top to
bottom. When the Roman officer who stood facing him saw how he
had died, he exclaimed, "This man truly was the Son of God!"

MARK 15:37–39 NLT

Saint Patrick, whose feast we observe today, was celebrated because he returned to Ireland, where he had been enslaved as a young man, to preach the Gospel. Patrick risked his life to convert the people who had threatened his life, and he spent his remaining days advocating for the people of Ireland. In many ways, he imitated his Savior, who sacrificed His life in order to unite people with God.

If you have any doubts about the power of Jesus, His observers in the Gospels can help put some of them to rest. Even as He died, crying out to God with one final breath, the soldiers recognized that Jesus was surely divine. The torn temple veil offers yet another clue to His significance and connection to God.

You have been reunited with God through the death of Jesus. This is a gift that you can freely accept today, approaching God the Father in faith. It's important enough that Saint Patrick risked his life to share it.

Jesus, I trust that You have broken down every
barrier between God and humanity.

JESUS IS AHEAD OF YOU

"Now go and tell his disciples, including Peter, that Jesus is going ahead of you to Galilee. You will see him there, just as he told you before he died." The women fled from the tomb, trembling and bewildered, and they said nothing to anyone because they were too frightened.

MARK 16:7–8 NLT

Although the women were terrified at the sight of the angel, they received a message of good news and comfort: Jesus was alive and would be going ahead of them. The next step wasn't up to them. They only had to find Jesus.

For the challenging and discouraging moments of your life, it's understandable that you may grow fearful and uncertain about the next step. Perhaps you may even know what you should do, but following through leaves you weak in the knees.

Imagine for a moment that Jesus is already ahead of you on the road that stretches before you. If you can focus on Jesus, then the details will fall into place. It may not end up the way you expect or even desire, but you will find peace and security if you stay close to Jesus. He's ahead of you and will show you the way.

Jesus, I trust that You know what is best for me and how I can best serve others. Guide me and give me strength to take the right steps forward today.

WHERE GOD'S TRANSFORMATION BEGINS

"And he will turn many Israelites to the Lord their God. He will be a man with the spirit and power of Elijah. He will prepare the people for the coming of the Lord. He will turn the hearts of the fathers to their children, and he will cause those who are rebellious to accept the wisdom of the godly."

LUKE 1:16–17 NLT

Where did God want to begin the transformation of His people? Rather than taking over the palace of Herod or the religious halls of power at the temple, God chose the more obscure, easily overlooked places. Besides empowering John the Baptist for his ministry in the wilderness, the Lord saw John's ministry having a generational impact.

When the people of God turn away from Him, a part of the problem can be traced back to the dedication of parents in the discipleship of their children, and God was particularly concerned about fathers. Is there something that distracts you from the calling God has placed in your life? Perhaps your heart is turned toward something other than your children or the place where you need to serve the most.

The impact of fathers dedicating themselves to the flourishing and spiritual growth of their children will result in them being prepared to receive the Lord and to accept the wisdom of godly teachers. This devotion of fathers has a far-reaching impact.

Jesus, open my eyes to the many ministry opportunities around me today.

SPEAK ONLY WHAT GOD COMMANDS

*And the angel of the Lord said to Balaam, "Go with the men,
but speak only the word that I tell you." So Balaam
went on with the princes of Balak.*

Numbers 22:35 esv

While Balak commanded Balaam to speak curses over the people of Israel, Balaam had limitations that he never anticipated, because the Lord prompted him to only shout blessings over the people of Israel. Although this is an extreme situation, even involving a talking donkey, the seriousness of blessings and curses shouldn't be overlooked.

Your words carry a significant impact, and the blessings and curses you extend to others are noted by the Lord. God desires to see His people thrive and grow, and so He is eager to help those who will bless them and help them thrive. On the other hand, working against the purposes of God will surely lead to frustration, at best.

Is there something that God is prompting you to say today? Is there any reason why you may not be willing to say it? Your circumstances may end up prompting you to say it whether you want to or not. Such a situation may end up being more of a blessing than a curse in the long run.

*Lord, open my ears to the messages You want me to share and give me
the boldness and resolution to deliver them without fear.*

GOD WILL BRING JUSTICE

Do you rulers indeed speak justly? Do you judge people with equity?
No, in your heart you devise injustice, and your hands mete out violence
on the earth.... Then people will say, "Surely the righteous still are
rewarded; surely there is a God who judges the earth."

PSALM 58:1–2, 11 NIV

How do you use your influence and power each day? It's clear that some believe there will be no consequences for their choices, either shrugging their shoulders at injustice or working to advance their own ends regardless of the impact on others. The Psalms are full of laments that call on God to take notice of injustice and evil in the world. The psalmists watched far too many devise evil schemes and then work toward ill-gotten gains without apparent consequence.

Does God still notice the violence and injustice in the world? Is there any benefit to being righteous, following God's commands and ensuring that all are treated with equity and justice?

The consequences may not come today, but the Psalms are a reminder that you will one day need to give an account of your actions. God will come to judge the earth, giving to each person according to what they had done. It may be tempting to live each day without a thought of tomorrow, but your choices for justice and holiness will one day be called to account before God.

Lord, may I use my influence for justice
and may I walk in holiness today.

WHERE IS THE SPIRIT LEADING?

That day the Spirit led him to the Temple. So when Mary and Joseph
came to present the baby Jesus to the Lord as the law required,
Simeon was there. He took the child in his arms and praised
God, saying, "Sovereign Lord, now let your servant
die in peace, as you have promised."
Luke 2:27–29 nlt

Simeon had spent his life waiting on the Lord and listening to the direction of God. The daily rewards of holy living may not have seemed apparent. Was it worthwhile to seek God when it appeared the people of Israel would remain subjugated under Roman rule?

The blessing of God for faithfulness and listening for God's voice each day may not come to you on your timetable, but it will come. Most importantly, the daily actions of faithfully remaining attentive to God will prepare you to respond to God when the time is right. There will be plenty of distractions in your life, so you may well miss God's provision when it comes. Jesus reminded His followers to be watchful, and Simeon offers a helpful example of someone who remained attentive for God's salvation.

What could this kind of "watching" look like for you today? Do you need a moment of silence? Is there something you need to say in prayer? The Holy Spirit is present to lead you if you are willing to listen.

Lord, open my eyes to the ways You're working around me,
and grant me ears to hear Your voice.

PLANNING FOR THE FUTURE

So the LORD said to Moses, "Take Joshua the son of Nun, a man in
whom is the Spirit, and lay your hand on him. Make him stand
before Eleazar the priest and all the congregation,
and you shall commission him in their sight."

NUMBERS 27:18–19 ESV

Are you aware of the challenges that await the next generation of Christians? Part of the calling of Moses was to look beyond his own role and into the future. Who would continue to lead Israel after he passed away?

There are ways you can begin to affirm others today, pass along what you have learned about following Jesus, and help them take their God-led role among God's people. Publicly affirming others can also help give them confidence among those they lead.

It may be humbling or even troubling to acknowledge that your own efforts and plans aren't going to last forever. At a certain point, you will need to pass the baton along to someone else. Your faithfulness matters a great deal, but at a certain point, you will need to ensure that future generations learn something from your faithfulness and can continue.

Is there someone you know who needs your affirmation today? Are there ways you can encourage others to pursue God even after you are gone?

Lord, help me to make time to encourage others and to
build up the faith of those who will follow after me.

WHAT DOES REPENTANCE LOOK LIKE?

John replied, "If you have two shirts, give one to the poor. If you have food, share it with those who are hungry." Even corrupt tax collectors came to be baptized and asked, "Teacher, what should we do?" He replied, "Collect no more taxes than the government requires."

LUKE 3:11–13 NLT

You may feel sorry for a personal failure or for harming someone unintentionally, but righting a wrong and choosing a new path is essential for repentance and getting right with God. John made it clear to his audience that they could no longer make the same choices and enjoy the same level of comfort and status if they wanted to change their ways.

Part of counting the cost of discipleship is the process of repentance, and sometimes it can be quite humbling. At a certain point, you have to acknowledge that the path you've chosen isn't acceptable to God and may even be harming your neighbors.

On the other side of repentance, there is a greater opportunity for being at peace with yourself and with others. There will be no need to hide your deeds in shame, no guilt to bear over your choices, and freedom to approach God with confidence and joy.

Lord, help me to see myself with honesty and clarity so that I can repent of my sins and receive the abundance of Your mercy.

ARE YOU PREPARED FOR TRIALS?

*"I will give you the glory of these kingdoms and authority over them,"
the devil said, "because they are mine to give to anyone I please. I will
give it all to you if you will worship me." Jesus replied, "The Scriptures
say, 'You must worship the LORD your God and serve only him.' "*

LUKE 4:6–8 NLT

At the moment of His trial in the wilderness, Jesus was ready to answer Satan with the scriptures that had become a vital part of His life. Even with the temptation to avoid His looming death and humble ministry, Jesus remained grounded in the truth about God rather than giving in to the promises of Satan.

The slow work of transformation and holiness may be difficult to observe on a day-to-day basis. There may not be too many dramatic moments of deliverance or manifestations of God's presence. However, attention to the teachings of scripture and the truth about God will have a payoff one day. It may not happen right away, but it will certainly happen when an unexpected trial or temptation arises. The time you spend before God will help you stand when trouble comes.

How can you make space this week to grow in your reliance on God's strength and wisdom?

*Jesus, You overcome Satan with the truth of Your Word.
Help me see the power and beauty of Your words so
that I can rely on You in times of trial.*

WHAT DO YOU DEPEND ON?

*Hear my cry, O God; listen to my prayer. From the ends of
the earth I call to you, I call as my heart grows faint;
lead me to the rock that is higher than I.*

PSALM 61:1–2 NIV

Have you ever wondered if God hears your prayers? Have you doubted whether God is attentive to your needs? This is a common theme in the Psalms, as the writer struggles to reconcile God's power with the dangers and injustices that come each day.

The answer to such struggles in the Psalms is to call out to God and patiently wait on the Lord. Don't stop calling out to God even if you grow weary and fearful. While circumstances may suggest otherwise sometimes, God remains as the rock that His people can depend on in their time of need.

The life of faith can be challenging when the promises of scripture don't match your circumstances. Perhaps today you are even relating to the words of this Psalm: "Lead me to the rock." You may need to reach out to someone else for help and guidance to seek God's strength and support. You surely can't stand on your own, and so today may be the day to ask for help to stand on the solid ground of God's promises.

*Lord, I trust that You are the steady, unmovable rock in my life.
Expose the false sources of hope and security in my
life so that I rely on You alone.*

WHAT DOES RISKY FAITH LOOK LIKE?

So they went up to the roof and took off some tiles. Then they lowered the sick man on his mat down into the crowd, right in front of Jesus. Seeing their faith, Jesus said to the man, "Young man, your sins are forgiven."
LUKE 5:19–20 NLT

The faith that Jesus praised wasn't content to sit back and wait. Risky faith that leads to life transformation risks personal reputation and the criticism of others in order to reach its end. The men who sacrificed their reputations and even their financial well-being for the sake of their friend show that risky faith can also be put into action for the benefit of others. Seeing the needs of their friend, they placed their hope in getting him to Jesus. No obstacle could keep them from seeking Jesus.

Is there someone in your life who needs your support? Is there a way that you can "carry" this person to Jesus in faith? Is there anything holding you back at this time?

The kind of risky faith that Jesus commended sought ways to overcome obstacles for the sake of others and had a kind of desperate confidence in the power of Jesus. Today may be a good time to ask if you've underestimated Jesus.

Jesus, help me become aware of the needs around me and grant me the faith to act and pray boldly on behalf of others.

TRUST IN GOD AT ALL TIMES

*My salvation and my honor depend on God; he is my mighty
rock, my refuge. Trust in him at all times, you people;
pour out your hearts to him, for God is our refuge.*

PSALM 62:7–8 NIV

What does it feel like to trust in God always to the point that your honor depends on God alone? It's easy to let other priorities and sources of comfort or support get in the way of depending on God and living by faith. Even if God has proven faithful in one situation, that doesn't mean the next challenge will be a walk in the park.

Perhaps the place for you to begin to take refuge in God is to pour out your heart to God. Let God know about your fears, desires, doubts, and anxieties. You can only rest completely in God if you are completely honest with God. As you let go of your deepest worries, you will begin to seek God's healing and support so that you can find God's direction for the future.

Turning to God as your refuge is a slow transformation process. You may even need to experience failure and struggle for a season before you learn what it means to trust in God at all times.

---

*Lord, I trust that You are a present refuge for me. Give me the grace
to let go of every other source of comfort so that I can
pour out my heart to You in faith.*

REMAIN FAITHFUL WITHIN THE FAMILY

*"Only take care, and keep your soul diligently, lest you forget the
things that your eyes have seen, and lest they depart from
your heart all the days of your life. Make them known
to your children and your children's children."*

DEUTERONOMY 4:9 ESV

The care of your soul is of the utmost importance for your own spiritual well-being and salvation today as well as for the future salvation of your children. Daily attentiveness to prayer, scripture, and obedience will bear fruit over time, and it will go on for generations as your children learn from your example. Each of the ways you have experienced God's provision and care will offer reassurance to your children and encourage them to remain near to God throughout their lives.

Perhaps the story of God's provision in your family or among others close to you has proven critical in your faith. If not, don't underestimate how much a story of God's faithfulness can mean to the people in your family or community. God's provision in your life can strengthen your faith and the faith of others for the long haul. Remembering is a central discipline in the story of scripture, and making space for it will bear fruit for years to come.

*Lord, open my eyes to the ways You are present in my life, and may
I live in faith today so that I can testify to You and Your provision.*

A REASON TO FORGIVE GENEROUSLY

"Do not judge others, and you will not be judged.
Do not condemn others, or it will all come back against
you. Forgive others, and you will be forgiven."

LUKE 6:37 NLT

Jesus knew that the imperfect judgment of people would only prompt more judgment and antagonism. Those who withhold forgiveness and mercy will be far less likely to receive it from others.

If there is any reason that may motivate people to be more merciful, forgiving, and gracious, it may be this truth that mercy begets mercy and grace begets grace. If you hope to be treated mercifully in your moment of need, then consider how you treat others.

However, an even more urgent truth about mercy and forgiveness holds true for those who follow Jesus. Receiving the mercy and forgiveness of God will radically change your capacity to show mercy and grace to others. If you are judgmental or struggle to forgive, then it is likely that you have not received the mercy and grace that is freely yours from God the Father. Jesus sought to break the destructive cycles of judgment and unforgiveness by offering God's love and grace to all who were willing to receive it.

Do you need to receive God's forgiveness and grace today?

Jesus, thank You for accepting me and saving me long before
I was born. May Your grace transform the way I interact with others.

KEEP GOD'S WORDS BEFORE YOU

"And these words that I command you today shall be on your heart. You shall teach them diligently to your children, and shall talk of them when you sit in your house, and when you walk by the way, and when you lie down, and when you rise."

DEUTERONOMY 6:6–7 ESV

How many different advertisements do you think you see in a day? How often do you watch a show, read a story, or hear a report about someone who is acting contrary to the ways of God? Even just being in the company of people opposed to God's commands can become discouraging and disorienting.

The solution of God is to keep the words of His commands always before His people and to encourage them to make His teachings a regular part of their lives. They should make a point of keeping the teachings of scripture in front of them, discussing them, and even considering them when they rested at home.

There isn't one way to do this, but consider how you are most likely to be mindful of scripture and God's commands. Christians have used fixed hour prayer for centuries, and even Daniel and Peter clearly observed set times to pray each day. Perhaps a podcast, journal, or book can help you continue to meditate on scripture's message today.

Lord, help me consider ways I can keep Your commands before my eyes so that I will carefully obey them.

HOW NEGATIVES BECOME POSITIVES

*Remember how the LORD your God led you all the way in the
wilderness these forty years, to humble and test you
in order to know what was in your heart.*

DEUTERONOMY 8:2 NIV

Have you ever wondered if reflecting on a negative event could make it positive?

That's what Moses told God's people to do—to remember the forty years they were humbled in the wilderness. He wanted them to understand that to make a genuine contribution in a person's life, humility has to be humanized—negative events have to be remembered.

Remembering personal lessons in humility can help you transform your experience too. It can help you find God in places you have forgotten—in your surf and turf (Deuteronomy 8:3, Luke 4:4) and in your lakefront property and financial security (Deuteronomy 8:12–13).

It was remembering his failures that gave John the Baptist the humility to step down so Jesus could step up (Luke 7:28), that gave David the humility to glory in God (Psalm 64:10), that gave Moses the humility to center his leadership on the Lord (Deuteronomy 8:11). Each of these individuals rejoiced in remembering how God led them "all the way" through the humbling events of their lives, and you can too.

*Lord, help me to spend time today thinking through an event You used
in my past to humble me and teach me what was really in my heart.*

THE LEGACY THAT LASTS

That is why the Levites have no share or inheritance among their fellow Israelites; the LORD is their inheritance.

DEUTERONOMY 10:9 NIV

Are you going to inherit a classic car, a painting by Caravaggio, a vintage book, some land or money?

Maybe you've inherited some things already.

An inheritance can provide you with things to celebrate and talk about. Even those without parents understand the happiness an inheritance can provide. So what kind of inheritance are you leaving?

The Levites were an Old Testament family who refused to worship a golden calf their relatives had made while Moses was receiving the Ten Commandments. Because of their love for God, the Lord gave the Levites more than the inheritance of their relatives—He made Himself their inheritance.

You could leave a car or a painting or you could leave those things and something more. Moses wrote: "Fix these words of mine in your hearts and minds. . . . Teach them to your children, talking about them when you sit at home and when you walk along the road, when you lie down and when you get up" (Deuteronomy 11:18–19 NIV).

Living "these words" in the ordinary moments of every day will help you leave the kind of legacy that lasts.

Lord, help me to model Your words to those who come after me so that I can leave the kind of legacy that matters.

PARTY WITH PURPOSE

"There you and your families will feast in the presence of the Lord your God, and you will rejoice in all you have accomplished because the Lord your God has blessed you."

Deuteronomy 12:7 NLT

Have you ever been at a party and wondered, "What in the world am I doing here?" Perhaps the frivolity seemed pointless. Maybe meandering through the events of the evening made you feel empty.

In the Old Testament, God invited people to celebrate their accomplishments. He did this because parties where He's the focus are the most meaningful. The same is true today.

When your party's theme involves celebrating all that God has done during a particular season of life, the food and festivities suggest a deeper significance. You feel energized instead of exhausted.

God asks you to party because it prepares you for future experiences with Him. David wrote that God clothes the hills "with gladness" (Psalm 65:12 NIV). Luke wrote that when Jesus brought a girl back to life, they were "astonished" (Luke 8:56 NIV). Gladness and astonishment are two intoxicating aspects of your experience when you spend time celebrating what God has done—when you party with a purpose.

Lord, help me to plan a party with family and friends that celebrates the extraordinarily good things You do!

OPENHANDED, OPENHEARTED

At the end of every three years, bring all the tithes of that year's
produce and store it in your towns, so that. . .the foreigners,
the fatherless and the widows who live in your towns may come
and eat and be satisfied, and so that the LORD your God
may bless you in all the work of your hands.
DEUTERONOMY 14:28–29 NIV

Twenty-two billion dollars. That number certainly pleases God.

It's roughly the amount of money spent by the federal government on the fatherless each year. How that money's spent is debatable, but there is no debating the fact that generosity toward the fatherless, widows, and foreigners clearly pleases God.

Moses continues this teaching in the next chapter: "Do not be hardhearted or tightfisted. . . . Rather, be openhanded" (Deuteronomy 15:7–8 NIV).

Jesus demonstrated this openhanded, openhearted generosity when He cured Mary, Joanna, Chuza, Susanna, "and many others." In turn, those women demonstrated the same generosity when they supported Jesus and His disciples "out of their own means" (Luke 8:2–3 NIV). David wrote about openhanded and openhearted generosity when he said that believers should make their praise more than a last-minute overture: "Sing the glory of his name; make his praise glorious" (Psalm 66:2 NIV).

The time and rehearsal it takes to "make" His praise glorious confirms the critical importance of a generous life.

Is your life openhanded, openhearted?

Lord, lead me to someone who needs my
open hand and open heart today.

A PECULIAR PRIORITY

"This festival will be a happy time of celebrating with your sons and daughters, your male and female servants, and the Levites, foreigners, orphans, and widows from your towns. For seven days you must celebrate this festival to honor the LORD your God."

Deuteronomy 16:14–15 NLT

E very world culture has its own ideas about what constitutes a waste of time.

In materialistic cultures, activities that do not promote wealth "waste time." These cultures use metaphors like "Time is money" and "You're killing time" to promote materialism—"As if you could kill time, without injuring eternity," Thoreau said. For the Christian, eternity always trumps money.

So the question becomes, what do you "spend" your time on? In Deuteronomy, God wanted His children to "spend" seven days being happy, celebrating His goodness. Certainly, this would be a "waste" of time, though, in a culture where "time is money."

Was coming to Jesus to touch His cloak a waste of time for the woman who had been bleeding for twelve years? Was asking to have his daughter brought back from the dead a waste of time for Jairus (Luke 8:41–56)? Was traveling to the temple to fulfill vows made when the psalm writer was in trouble a waste of time (Psalm 66:13–14)?

Does spending seven days happily feasting to worship God seem like a peculiar priority?

Lord, on this Palm Sunday, help me to evaluate my ideas about worship and happiness and time today.

A CITY OF REFUGE

*"Then you must set apart three cities of refuge in
the land the LORD your God is giving you."*

DEUTERONOMY 19:2 NLT

God established cities of refuge to protect people from the judgments of others.

If a man committed a crime by accident, God did not want him punished as if he had committed the crime with forethought. God knew that for a variety of reasons humans condemn each other far too quickly. Sometimes those who judge are motivated by jealousy, other times by self-interest, and other times by a desire to see someone humbled. People jump to the wrong conclusions for all the wrong reasons.

The cities of refuge provided a place for people to run for protection. The cities welcomed the fearful, the wronged, and the misunderstood.

God is all about refuge. In Luke 9 the wronged and misunderstood came to Jesus who welcomed and fed them. When the writer of Psalm 66 concludes, "Praise be to God, who has not rejected my prayer or withheld his love from me!" (66:20 NIV), it is clear he found refuge in the same accepting and loving God.

Are you a person of refuge? Are you like an established city where wronged and misunderstood family members, neighbors, friends, and coworkers can find protection? The world still needs places and people of refuge.

*Lord, help me make myself available to someone
who needs a place of refuge today.*

PURGING

You must purge the evil.
DEUTERONOMY 21:21; 22:21, 22, 24 NIV

God does not require the purging listed in today's passage for two major reasons.

First, cultural practices no longer produce the horrific social conditions and other reasons for the destruction outlined in Deuteronomy.

Second, according to Hebrews 8:13 (ESV), believers are under a new covenant: "In speaking of a new covenant, he makes the first one obsolete."

Still, God's purposes for purging still work to protect His children. Purging is important because evil behaviors mess with God's good gifts and pervert every pleasure (Psalm 67).

In Luke 9:41 Jesus called the unbelieving crowd who came to test Him "perverse," because their unbelief affected the healing of a demon-possessed child. This is partly why unbelief will also be purged at the final judgment.

Finally, when Paul talks about putting away the old self (Ephesians 4:31), he is reminding believers to work at *purging* inappropriate behaviors.

Is there a behavior you need to work toward purging today?

*Lord, help me find the right encouragers to help me with
the purging process. Help me choose one behavior
I can work toward "putting away" today.*

BRINGING HAPPINESS

"A newly married man must not be drafted into the army or be given any other official responsibilities. He must be free to spend one year at home, bringing happiness to the wife he has married."
DEUTERONOMY 24:5 NLT

Bringing happiness is a priority for every Christian.

Married men are singled out in today's key verse. The poor treatment of wives in the cultures surrounding God's people at that time demanded drastic change. Still, the principle of bringing happiness belongs to all believers.

Bringing happiness requires the kind of humility Jesus was talking about when He said, "It is the one who is least among you all who is the greatest" (Luke 9:48 NIV). Most people are fine with getting up in the morning and thinking about what might make them happy. What's difficult is getting up and having your first thought be about the happiness of your wife, a coworker, a family member, or neighbor. Humility helps with that.

Some of the loneliness people experience comes because they long for the kind of person who brings happiness, the kind of person who sings with the love and humility of the psalmist, "May *they* be happy" (Psalm 68:3 NIV, emphasis added).

Passover is a *time* to spread happiness, because it celebrates God's "passing over" and sparing the lives of those who obeyed Him in Egypt (Exodus 12).

Lord, teach me to search for less happiness
for myself than I give to others.

I CAN HEAR YOU!

"The LORD heard our voice."

DEUTERONOMY 26:7 NIV

One of the most common frustrations a counselor hears is, "He doesn't listen."

When confronted, the offender will often reply, "I do listen. I hear every word."

Why the disconnect?

Listening requires the kind of mature love that moves a person to leave his own world to enter another's—a love that does more than hear words—the kind of love God demonstrated when Jesus entered earth's atmosphere to serve humanity (Philippians 2:5–8). This kind of love is difficult in a self-saturated world.

Moses reminded his listeners that when they cried out for help, it was the Lord who heard them (Deuteronomy 26:7). Listening isn't a luxury. So often, it's the road to experiencing love.

If you learn to listen the way God listens, your life will make a difference. In hearing like He hears, you'll love like He loves. Listening will help you know, like He knows, what to give people, how to refresh them and how to provide for their needs (Psalm 68:7–14).

Lord, help me listen in a way that helps people hear Your love.

PROSPERITY'S PROBLEM

*You did not serve the LORD your God joyfully
and gladly in the time of prosperity.*
DEUTERONOMY 28:47 NIV

The expression "out of sight, out of mind" often applies to how believers treat God—especially in their prosperity.

Prosperity should increase a Christian's joy and bring about the kind of gladness that celebrates God. Instead, it often obscures like window glare, blinding the prosperous from seeing Him.

Jesus' disciples certainly knew spiritual prosperity. They knew the joy and gladness His words and miracles produced. He said to them: "Blessed are the eyes that see the things you see. For I tell you that many prophets and kings wanted to see what you see but did not see it" (Luke 10:23–24 NIV).

Although their eyes were "blessed," this prosperity eventually impaired their vision too. They began to see themselves ruling with Jesus rather than serving with Him. They became, at times, like those who passed by the wounded man, when they could have been like the Samaritan who stopped to help. Even on Good Friday, when He died for their sins, they chose self-preservation over consecration.

The solution to prosperity's problem is to thank God, like the psalmist who wrote, "Praise be to the Lord, to God our Savior" (Psalm 68:19 NIV).

*Lord, help me to see You, to serve You joyfully
and gladly—especially in my prosperity.*

IN THE LITTLE THINGS

Choose life so that you and your children will live.
And love GOD, your God, listening obediently to him,
firmly embracing him. Oh yes, he is life itself.
DEUTERONOMY 30:19–20 MSG

Rarely does a person wake up and say, "I think I will choose death today." Equally as rare, though, is the person who wakes up and says, "I will choose life."

Choosing life involves behaviors that are easy to describe but harder to do. Moses said that choosing life involved listening obediently to God (Deuteronomy 30:20). Simple to describe. Harder to do.

In Luke 10, two sisters had to decide what choosing life was going to look like. Martha was distracted by the busyness applauded in her culture, but Mary chose to sit and listen to Jesus. Accordingly, Mary chose life (10:38–42).

Like so many, Martha worked hard to do the great things valued by her culture, instead of the little things valued by her God. Mother Teresa, who ministered to lepers in India for decades, said, "We do no great things, only little things with great love."

Similarly, the psalmist wrote about how a little family in Israel, not a great family, led the worshippers in procession: "Praise God, all you people of Israel; praise the LORD, the source of Israel's *life*. Look, *the little tribe* of Benjamin leads the way" (Psalm 68:26–27 NLT, emphasis added).

Lord, help me to choose life by honoring You in the little things.

WIDE-EYED AWE

"Gather the people together—men, women, children,
and the foreigners living among you—so they can listen
well, so they may learn to live in holy awe before GOD."

DEUTERONOMY 31:12 MSG

Those who pretend to be the masters of their own fates find the Christian faith scary, even foolhardy. For them, it's more comfortable to know things and explain away apparent mysteries, including the resurrection.

Even those who should have believed in Jesus' miracles found putting their faith in Him difficult. He cautioned them, "Everybody's looking for proof, but you're looking for the wrong kind" (Luke 11:29 MSG).

What kind of proof should they have been looking for? The kind that accepts miracles. The kind of faith that enables people to live in wide-eyed wonder.

Later Jesus used a metaphor to explain: "If you live wide-eyed in wonder and belief, your body fills up with light. If you live squinty-eyed in greed and distrust, your body is a dank cellar. Keep your eyes open" (Luke 11:34–36 MSG).

The life of wonder is the life characterized by the holy awe that Moses wrote about (Deuteronomy 31:12), and the life the psalmist sang about: "You, God, are awesome in your sanctuary" (Psalm 68:35 NIV).

Lord, thank You for the reality of Jesus Christ's resurrection.
Help me see You at work in the world around me.
Thank You for still doing miracles today.

LIKE EVERLASTING ARMS

"The eternal God is your refuge,
and underneath are the everlasting arms."
DEUTERONOMY 33:27 NIV

When you volunteer your personal time and money, your behavior agrees with the character of God and you become a refuge to those who are struggling. When you work to stop injustice, your behavior mirrors God's attributes and you become more like Him.

When you become a place of refuge for the people and family around you, when you become like His everlasting arms to the anxious or afraid, then your life aligns more with the character of the eternal God.

In Luke 11:42, Jesus tells the religious rulers that, although they give a tenth of their prosperity, they deny justice. Jesus warns them not to live like this. It provides no benefit to anyone, and it argues against God's character.

Whenever a believer feels like David, "I am worn out calling for help" (Psalm 69:3 NIV), it is critical to listen and to meet that need, to become a refuge to him like God's everlasting arms.

Lord, help me become a place of refuge for those who are
struggling. Help me become like Your everlasting arms
for a worried or anxious family member or friend.

THE CRUX OF COURAGE

"Be strong and courageous. Do not be afraid; do not be discouraged, for the LORD your God will be with you wherever you go."

JOSHUA 1:9 NIV

How would you feel about taking over for a boss who was loved so much that people spent thirty days mourning him after he died? How would you feel about leading an entire industry with a million employees and their dependents into a new country?

That's what Joshua did, and that's why God told him, "The LORD your God will be with you." Jesus told His followers the same thing when He compared His care for them to the care He has for sparrows: "Not one of them is forgotten by God. . . . Don't be afraid" (Luke 12:6–7 NIV).

King David wrote, "But I pray to you, LORD, in the time of your favor; in your great love, O God, answer me with your sure salvation" (Psalm 69:13 NIV). David knew who to go to when he was afraid. So did Joshua and those who followed Jesus.

What is the crux of your courage? Who do you go to when you're facing circumstances that seem impossible?

*Lord, help me to live and lead with
You at the center of my courage.*

ANSWERS FOR ANXIETY

*"In the future when your descendants ask their parents,
'What do these stones mean?' tell them. . . . So that all the peoples
of the earth might know that the hand of the LORD is powerful."*

JOSHUA 4:21–22, 24 NIV

Having crossed the Jordan River at flood stage on dry ground, Joshua instructed the people to build a monument of twelve stones as a memorial to the miracle.

That pile of stones continually encouraged God's people to temper their anxieties with trust.

Jesus supported this kind of anxiety reduction when He said that life was about more than food and clothes. He said that when people prioritized His kingdom, their other needs were met as well. Then He added, "For where your treasure is, there your heart will be also" (Luke 12:34 NIV).

Longings of the heart provide the deeper answer for anxiety. Long for money, you'll be stressed. Long for popularity, you'll be worried. Long for success, you'll be anxious. Long for God, you'll be filled.

From the center of his angst, King David wrote, "I looked for sympathy, but there was none, for comforters, but I found none" (Psalm 69:20 NIV). He discovered that when the world around you can't answer the need, God can.

The Lord provided rest from anxiety for Joshua, His own disciples, and King David. He can do the same for you!

*Lord, help me find answers for my anxieties in learning
to long for Your kingdom rather than my own.*

THE GOD WHO REBUILDS

But the people of Israel broke faith in regard to the devoted things,
for Achan the son of Carmi, son of Zabdi, son of Zerah, of the tribe
of Judah, took some of the devoted things. And the anger
of the LORD burned against the people of Israel.

JOSHUA 7:1 ESV

God told His people to follow His instructions carefully as they moved into the promised land, but Achan stole from God and hid the goods.

When Joshua called the people together to ascertain who had sinned, the Spirit pointed out Achan from the tribe of Judah.

Can you hear the gossip and slander months later? "You shouldn't date her; she's from *that* clan" or "What do you expect? Isn't he from Judah's Carmi clan?" Achan's disobedience impacted the whole group. Disobedience always does.

Jesus told a similar story about a disobedient manager who abused his employees and partied while the owner was away. The manager's end and Achan's are surprisingly parallel (Luke 12:41–48). But their end is not your end, nor was it the end for Judah.

Later, David wrote: "God will save Zion and rebuild the cities of Judah.... And those who love his name will dwell there" (Psalm 69:35–36 NIV).

God, the divine fixer-upper, rebuilds for anyone who loves Him.

Lord, help me see and be grateful for the ways You rebuild my life.

BOLT BY BOLT

"Do not be afraid or discouraged."

Joshua 8:1 NLT

On April 17, 1970, the crippled Apollo 13 carrying astronauts James Lovell, John (Jack) Swigert, and Fred Haise landed safely in the Pacific Ocean.

No one will ever know the personal discouragement these astronauts battled. But three of the movie industry's most compelling actors were able to show how they made it back to Earth by rebuilding components one bolt at a time.

Have you felt lost in space? You try to improve your marriage, your family, your business, and you try to return to God, but failure sucks out all the oxygen?

Joshua knew discouragement. After a failed battle, God told him, "Do not be afraid or discouraged" (Joshua 8:1 NLT). So, like the astronauts, Joshua didn't give up or in, and he landed safely in the promised land.

Jesus' followers knew discouragement too. In Luke 12, Jesus clearly explained that His coming to earth would separate family members, and it did. As a result, some became discouraged and walked away. Others rebuilt their families and stayed the course.

In Psalm 70, the writer shares an answer for discouragement: "May those who long for your saving help always say, 'The Lord is great!' " (70:4 NIV). That's where Joshua's courage, the disciples' courage, and every believer's courage comes from—bolt-by-bolt reflections on how great God is!

*Lord, help me battle discouragement by rebuilding my
trust in Your greatness, one component at a time.*

ONE-OF-A-KIND DAYS

*There has never been a day like it before or since,
a day when the LORD listened to a human being!*
JOSHUA 10:14 NIV

When the book of Joshua lay completed, the Bible says there still had never been a day like the day described in Joshua 10. Not for Adam, for Noah, or for Moses. It was Joshua's one-of-a-kind day. The day the sun stood still.

But what about since?

Jesus healed many in His day, like the woman in Luke 13. Did that day compare to Joshua's? Did it compare to the day the sun stood still?

It did for her.

Because He wasn't interested in impressing the religious leaders or the cultural elite, Jesus listened and responded to the needs of people who needed miracles.

He still does.

And every time He listens and responds, that individual shares some of Joshua's incredible day—the day when God listened to a human being.

Psalm 71 also demonstrates that God listens. He hears and responds to the prayers of those who retreat to Him. "In you, LORD, I have taken refuge. . . . Turn your ear to me and save me" (71:1–2 NIV).

God will do just that. He will allow you to experience a Joshua kind of day. He will turn His ear to you and save you, if you retreat to Him.

Why? Because that's who He is: the God who listens to human beings.

*Lord, thank You for hearing me and for helping
me experience one-of-a-kind days.*

PEOPLE OF THE PRIESTHOOD

But to the tribe of Levi, Moses had given no inheritance; the LORD,
the God of Israel, is their inheritance, as he promised them.

JOSHUA 13:33 NIV

The apostle Peter wrote, "But you are a chosen people, a royal priesthood, a holy nation, God's special possession, that you may declare the praises of him who called you out of darkness into his wonderful light" (1 Peter 2:9 NIV).

Ever thought of yourself as a priest? God does.

God gave property as an inheritance to all of Jacob's descendants, except Levi's sons. To them He gave Himself (Joshua 13:33). There may have been times when the Levites wished they could have been other than a family of priests, but in their hearts they knew they had inherited more than the rest. So did you.

The priest brought the sacrifices to God—you bring yourself (Romans 12:1).

The priest entered the presence of God through the "narrow door" once a year—you can every day (Luke 13:24).

The priest led God's people in proclaiming His "mighty acts" (Psalm 71:16), so do you.

Like the Levitical priesthood, you traded land for the Lord. When all the people around you inherit temporal things, you inherit an eternal relationship with the One who made you. What better inheritance could you ask for?

Lord, thank You for the honors and privileges that
come with having You as my inheritance!

HOLE OR WHOLE?

*"I was forty years old when Moses the servant of the LORD sent me
from Kadesh Barnea to explore the land. And I brought him back a
report according to my convictions, but my fellow Israelites who
went up with me made the hearts of the people melt in fear.
I, however, followed the LORD my God wholeheartedly."*

JOSHUA 14:7–8 NIV

Mathematician Blaise Pascal's famous writings—about humans possessing a God-shaped vacuum that can be satisfied only by God Himself—divides human beings into two types: those who live hole-heartedly or wholeheartedly.

The religious leaders in Luke 14 were the hole-hearted kind. Rather than allowing God to fill them with the indescribable happiness that resulted each time Jesus healed someone, they despised Him for not following their rules. They had tried to fill the hole with self-righteousness and the praise of men (14:1–15).

Hole-hearted living leads to missed blessings, like the blessings of the promised land Caleb's fellow Israelites missed when they worried about their lack of ability rather than trusting God's abilities (Joshua 14:7–8).

Wholehearted living is what Pascal wanted for his readers; it's what Joshua wanted for the Israelites; it's what Jesus wanted for those He healed; it's what the psalmist wanted for "the next generation" (71:17–18); and it's what God wants for you!

Lord, fill the God-shaped vacuum in my soul with You!

YOU CAN

Joshua said to the tribes of Joseph . . . [,] "Though the Canaanites have chariots fitted with iron and though they are strong, you can drive them out."
JOSHUA 17:17–18 NIV

Sports psychology demonstrates that positive thinking impacts performance, but what a person can do is not the reason behind Joshua's optimism—the Lord is.

The psalmist demonstrated the same understanding when he wrote, "My tongue will tell of your righteous acts all day long, for those who wanted to harm me have been put to shame and confusion" (71:24 NIV). The writer isn't the one who put those who wanted to hurt him to shame—the Lord is.

He'll do for you what He did for Joseph's descendants and the writer of Psalm 71. His unlimited power secures every promise. Maybe you're facing a new business, a difficult relationship—the circumstance doesn't matter. The reason you can trust God is because He's already demonstrated His power and His love for you.

In the parable about guests invited to a banquet, the same people who had been told by the religious leaders they could never come to heaven's feast heard Jesus say, *now you can* (Luke 14:23). You are one of those people, one of the "uninvited" God chose to save. He has already done the impossible in you and He wants you to know He still will.

Lord, teach me to trade "I can't" for "You can."

THE LAW OF LOVE

*"Then the elders are to admit the fugitive into their city
and provide a place to live among them."*

JOSHUA 20:4 NIV

L aws protecting the fugitive have been necessary since Adam and Eve left the garden of Eden.

These early laws may have been disseminated through the first families or the priesthood of Melchizedek, but eventually principles such as "innocent until proven guilty" showed up in ancient legal codes including Hammurabi's.

It is clear from the Lord's words to Joshua that God wanted the innocent fugitive to be welcomed, that He wanted His people to learn the law of love.

It is the law the psalmist wrote about, "Give your love of justice to the king, O God, and righteousness to the king's son. Help him judge your people in the right way" (Psalm 72:1–2 NLT).

It is the law Jesus talked about in the parable of the lost sheep: "In the same way, there is more joy in heaven over one lost sinner who repents and returns to God than over ninety-nine others who are righteous and haven't strayed away!" (Luke 15:7 NLT).

This is the law of love: a legal code more concerned about welcoming the repentant fugitive than getting revenge. Is it easy for you to offer refuge when you've been wronged by a colleague, family member, or friend?

*Lord, teach me to welcome those who need forgiveness,
to operate from the law of love.*

DESERTERS

*"For a long time now—to this very day—you have not
deserted your fellow Israelites but have carried out
the mission the LORD your God gave you."*

JOSHUA 22:3 NIV

When the younger brother returns to his family in the story of the prodigal son, the older brother, instead of welcoming him, walks away (Luke 15:28).

Although this is uncommon in the Christian community, believers desert each other for a variety of reasons: envy, shame, bitterness, apathy.

The psalmist says that God is different. God will not desert the "needy who cry out, the afflicted who have no one to help" (Psalm 72:12 NIV). He's not a deserter.

Joshua commended three of the tribes of Israel for not deserting their fellow Israelites (Joshua 22:1–3). Their commitment and courage rest immortalized in his book.

Have you felt like deserting lately? Maybe deserting your church because of the lack of winsome and strong leaders, maybe a struggling friend because he takes up too much of your time, maybe a relative who makes life unbearable, maybe an employer because he takes credit for your ideas? Are these reasons to walk away?

Semper fidelis, a motto of every US Marine, is Latin for "always faithful." How powerful the testimony of the church is when believers refuse to desert, when they, like every good soldier, rush in while the rest of the world walks out.

*Lord, create in me the courage to stick
things out, to be always faithful.*

CHOICES

"Choose for yourselves this day whom you will serve. . .
But as for me and my household, we will serve the LORD."
JOSHUA 24:15 NIV

Joshua's statement represents a choice you make every day when you get out of bed. It's also a choice that makes you.

Jesus warned about one area of choice: "No one can serve two masters. Either you will hate the one and love the other, or you will be devoted to the one and despise the other. You cannot serve both God and money" (Luke 16:13 NIV). You choose whom you serve.

In Psalm 73 Asaph wrote about how some "lay claim to heaven" (73:9 NIV) with their mouths but leave the people around them "dismayed and confused" (v. 10 NLT). This hypocrisy is always a choice. Usually it starts with one small, seemingly insignificant concession—a white lie, the rounding of a financial amount in your favor, a few minutes of laziness at work, a thirty-second peek at a website.

Serving God starts with one small, seemingly insignificant choice as well—not withholding information when it inconveniences you, rounding a financial amount in someone else's favor, working a few minutes overtime for free, installing accountability software. Every choice makes you.

"Life is a matter of choices, and every choice you make makes you."
John C. Maxwell

Lord, help me make the right choices today, choices that
will help make me the man You want me to be.

WHO LISTENS?

*Then the Lord raised up judges, who saved them out of the hands
of these raiders. Yet they would not listen to their judges but
prostituted themselves to other gods and worshiped them.*

Judges 2:16–17 niv

At an open-casket funeral, would you listen or flee if the corpse sat up and started talking?

Jesus told the story of a dead man who asked Abraham to warn his family so they could avoid his suffering in Hades. Abraham replied, "Moses and the prophets have warned them. Your brothers can read what they wrote" (Luke 16:29 nlt).

The man thought, "If they hear from a dead man, they'll listen." But, Jesus explained with powerful foreshadowing, "If they do not listen to Moses and the Prophets, they will not be convinced even if someone rises from the dead" (16:31 niv).

The Old Testament believers struggled to listen too. Even when God sent judges and blessed the nation through them, the people turned away and invested their energies elsewhere.

Have you taken the time lately to think about the pastors and mentors God has sent to share His Word with you? Do you listen?

The psalmist listened. He wrote, "You guide me with *your counsel*, and afterward you will take me into glory" (73:24 niv, emphasis added).

*Lord, help me listen today to Your Word as I read it
and as it comes to me through Your messengers.*

THE RESCUER

But when the people of Israel cried out to the LORD for help,
the LORD raised up a rescuer to save them.
JUDGES 3:9 NLT

Twice in Judges 3 and several times in the following chapters, God's people succumbed to the following pattern: *The people sin—God hands them over—the people suffer—the people cry out to God—God sends a rescuer.*

God follows the repeated pattern of disobedience with a repeated pattern of rescue. He hears the cries of His people.

In Luke 17, Jesus hears ten lepers cry out "have mercy on us," so He does. Although He's aware that only a sidelined Samaritan will thank Him, the Lord rescues the other nine who also cried out to Him (17:14, 18). It's part of who He is.

In Psalm 73, Asaph recognizes God as the lone rescuer: "Whom have I in heaven but you? I desire you more than anything on earth" (73:25 NLT).

Rescuing is part of what God does. If you picked up this book because you've found yourself in the "suffering" stage, remember—like Old Testament believers, the ten lepers, and Asaph—you have a rescuer!

Lord, thank You for always rescuing me!

WHEN THE WEAK BECOME STRONG

"But LORD," Gideon replied, "how can I rescue Israel?
My clan is the weakest in the whole tribe of Manasseh,
and I am the least in my entire family!"

JUDGES 6:15 NLT

Reading the beginning of the story of Gideon is like reading a psychological summary of an insecure man with trust issues. Not exactly a high-level candidate for organizational leadership.

But despite his lack of attractiveness to headhunters in contemporary organizations, God uses Gideon. He even patiently waits for Gideon to address his weaknesses.

God often uses the weak of this world. When He does this, the individual He chooses experiences the unmistakable and unforgettable power of God in and through his routines. Gideon certainly did. So can you.

After sharing the parable of the Pharisee and tax collector, Jesus says that "those who humble themselves will be exalted" (Luke 18:14 NLT). In the next paragraphs, He adds that the kingdom of God belongs to those who humble themselves, like the tax collector, to those who come to Him the way little children come.

The psalmist Asaph expresses the same humility. While questioning God, he compares himself to sheep—not lions, tigers, or bears (Psalm 74:1).

Your areas of childlikeness and weakness are often the best places for God to show His power and strength. Will you let Him today?

Lord, I open my areas of weakness for You to use as You see fit.

HEROIC LEADERS

During that night the Lord said to Gideon. . . "If you are afraid to attack, go down to the camp with your servant Purah."
Judges 7:9–10 niv

E ven though the Lord promised to give the enemy into Gideon's hands, He added the statement quoted above.

God knew Gideon's fears, so He provided a helper. Much like the earlier story of the fleece where God allowed Gideon to test Him twice, here God takes into account Gideon's character, especially his anxiety. Inspirational leaders minister to the weaknesses of the people they serve.

The same shows up in the story of the young ruler. Jesus told him to sell his possessions. He did so knowing this ruler's security was in his wealth, so He responded to the man's real need. Perceptive leaders minister to the real needs of the people they serve.

The psalmist Asaph prayed: "How long will the enemy mock you, God? Will the foe revile your name forever? Why do you hold back your. . . right hand?" (Psalm 74:10–11 niv). In response, God demonstrates that heroic leaders sacrifice their right to be respected in order to allow people to express their emotions appropriately.

Whether you're leading a family or a Fortune 500 company, you need inspirational, perceptive, and heroic leadership skills.

Lord, help me minister to the weaknesses of the people I serve, to understand their real needs, and to allow them to express their emotions appropriately.

IT TAKES A BIG MAN?

*Gideon and his three hundred men, exhausted yet keeping
up the pursuit, came to the Jordan and crossed it.*

JUDGES 8:4 NIV

Having defeated tens of thousands with three hundred men, Gideon demonstrated to his Israelite brothers that God can do great things with a small group of men.

In the story of Zacchaeus, a despised tax collector, Jesus demonstrated how He can use a man small in stature to show the transforming power of personal faith (Luke 19:3).

In the parable that follows the story for Zacchaeus, Jesus shows that even small amounts of money can be used to show a person's true character (Luke 19:17).

A small group of soldiers? A small tax collector? A small number of coins? What value can these have to God?

They can show a world obsessed with great mythical powers, that the same God who is more powerful than any monster or myth (Psalm 74:13–14) often uses the "things the world considers foolish in order to shame those who think they are wise" (1 Corinthians 1:27 NLT).

The small things in your life may be the very things God uses to show the world around you His incredible power. It doesn't take a big man to change the world; it takes a big God.

*Lord, help me remember that You can use any small
detail in my life today to change the world.*

THE GOD WHO FEELS

He [God] could bear Israel's misery no longer.
JUDGES 10:16 NIV

Every time God's people experienced misery that came from following their own hearts, God felt the agony. This is because He reveals Himself as the God who feels.

Luke wrote that when Jesus approached Jerusalem, He knew its afflictions and sorrows and wept over it (19:41).

The psalmist appeals to this same compassion in God when he cries out, "Do not forget the lives of your afflicted people forever" (Psalm 74:19 NIV).

Are you like God in your compassion? Do you feel the misery of the people around you? Have you wept over your family and friends? God does.

When a believer strays from the faith and suffers from the resulting misery, you can speak—through his denial or shame-spawned facade—with words that communicate your willingness to listen with sympathy.

When people you love share their deepest sorrows, you can openly weep like Jesus.

When a coworker loses a loved one, you can put the date in your calendar and remember to send a card each year on the anniversary.

You can minister to a world full of hurting people when you pattern your life after the God who feels.

Lord, help me learn from Your example how to become a man who feels deeply about the people around me, and help me to respond to these feelings with activities that show I have not forgotten people's afflictions.

WORTHY OF THE PROMOTION

No one from the east or the west or from the desert can exalt themselves.
It is God who judges: he brings one down, he exalts another.

Psalm 75:6–7 niv

In just about every kind of workplace, men try their best, hoping to get a promotion to a higher-paying, more prestigious job. Everyone has heard the story of a guy who started out in the mailroom and worked his way through the ranks to become the departmental vice president.

Good for that guy!

But today's key verse strongly suggests that in God's kingdom work, it is He who puts people on the pathway to promotion. Your part in that arrangement is to do what He has for you to do today and to do it well.

Jesus once told the story of a servant who had served his master particularly well. When the master learned of the servant's work, he told him: "Well done, good and faithful servant! You have been faithful with a few things; I will put you in charge of many things. Come and share your master's happiness!" (Matthew 25:21 niv).

God chooses whom He wants to promote. When you show yourself faithful in doing what He has given you to do, you prove yourself worthy of additional assignments.

Loving Father in heaven, help me remember the importance
of faithfully doing what You have asked me to do here
on earth—leaving the rewards up to You.

SEEKING WISE COUNSEL

*Then Manoah prayed to the LORD: "Pardon your servant, Lord.
I beg you to let the man of God you sent to us come again
to teach us how to bring up the boy who is to be born."*
JUDGES 13:8 NIV

M any men have a tough time breaking down and admitting they don't have the knowledge or the wisdom they need to handle certain situations. Most of us would rather cling to that oh-so-Western ideal of rugged individualism than to humbly ask for help.

King Solomon offers this bit of wisdom in the book of Proverbs: "Plans fail for lack of counsel, but with many advisers they succeed" (15:22 NIV). Being king of Israel during its zenith of wealth, power, and influence, Solomon had personally experienced the benefits of wise counsel. It's hard to imagine one man, even one as wise as Solomon, accomplishing what he did without a high-quality team of advisers.

Fast-forward to the year 2020. Life today is complicated, and it's often difficult to know which of the many decisions you can make is best. Each man needs wise, godly counsel.

So use your own learning and wisdom when that's enough to make a good decision. Also have the humility and wisdom to know when to reach out for godly counsel.

*Father God, keep me humble enough to know when it's wise to move
forward on my own and when I should seek out godly counsel.*

GIVING OF WHAT YOU HAVE

He also saw a poor widow put in two very small copper coins.
"Truly I tell you," he said, "this poor widow has put in more than
all the others. All these people gave their gifts out of their wealth;
but she out of her poverty put in all she had to live on."

LUKE 21:2–4 NIV

The Bible has a lot to say about giving. It talks about giving to God's commission to take the Gospel message to the world, giving to individuals in need, and giving with a joyful heart. God has called you to give generously and even sacrificially.

Sacrificial giving requires a special kind of faith. It requires you to believe in and trust God to meet your own needs and your family's needs—especially when times are tight. *Without* that kind of faith, you'll do what is natural to all men and hang on to what you have so that you can meet your obligations. *With* that kind of faith, you give of what little you have, knowing that God sees your sacrifice and then meets your needs in ways only He can.

Father in heaven, I know You want me to be a generous man.
So even when times are tight for me financially, give me the courage
to give of what I have, knowing that it blesses others and
that it leads to blessings for my family and me.

GUARDING THE HEART

"But take heed to yourselves, lest your hearts be weighed down
with carousing, drunkenness, and cares of this life,
and that Day come on you unexpectedly."

LUKE 21:34 NKJV

King Solomon wisely said, "Above all else, guard your heart, for everything you do flows from it" (Proverbs 4:23 NIV). A thousand years later, Jesus put some meat on the bones of Solomon's warning, telling you that your focus on the cares of this world, if you're not careful, can weigh down your heart.

God knows your heart, and He knows that you're prone to doing things, thinking things, and looking at things that can weigh down your heart and keep you from pure fellowship with Him. That's why He's so committed to transforming your thinking so that it focuses on Him first—ahead of your own fleshly desires and even ahead of the legitimate cares of this world you must deal with daily.

What kinds of things take your focus off God? If it's a particular sin, take the time to confess it and turn away from it. If it's your worldly responsibilities, put them in His able hands so they don't distract you from what's most important.

Gracious Father, many things in this world have the potential to weigh down my heart and cause me to stray from You. You've saved me and transformed me, so help me show my gratitude by fervently guarding the new heart You've placed within me.

REMEMBERING GOD'S AMAZING WORK

Then I thought, "To this I will appeal: the years when the Most High stretched out his right hand. I will remember the deeds of the LORD; yes, I will remember your miracles of long ago."

PSALM 77:10–11 NIV

During a particularly difficult time, have you ever found solace in thinking back on better times? If so, then you can probably identify with what Asaph was going through when he wrote Psalm 77.

In the first nine verses, Asaph writes about his responses to "the day of my trouble" (NKJV). He can't find comfort anywhere and becomes so miserable that he can't eat or sleep. He wonders if he will ever again see God's favor. He cries out, and God gives him a reprieve from his sorrows when he remembers the days when the Lord very clearly was at work in the lives of His people.

People often warn against the dangers of "living in the past," but today's scripture passage shows you that you can find assurance and encouragement during difficult times—by remembering the times when you knew and could feel God at work in your life.

Mighty God, thank You for giving me examples of Your amazing deeds— both in the lives of those I read about in Your Word and in my own life and the lives of those close to me. Remind me of these things, especially when I'm enduring difficulties and pain.

IN TIMES OF CRISIS

*When he rose from prayer and went back to the disciples, he found them
asleep, exhausted from sorrow. "Why are you sleeping?" he asked them.
"Get up and pray so that you will not fall into temptation."*

LUKE 22:45–46 NIV

Times of crisis can bring out the best in each of us—or they can reveal our deepest weaknesses. Jesus had given His apostles a simple command: Wait and pray while I go and pray (Luke 22:39–41). But when He returns, He finds them sleeping—certainly not praying.

You probably know the rest of the story. After Jesus is arrested, His disciples scatter. Later that evening, one even denies knowing Him!

In a moment of crisis, they failed miserably.

It's easy to wonder how Jesus' followers, who had spent three years seeing Him perform amazing miracles and deliver life-changing teaching, could abandon Him. But think about how you usually respond to your own crises. Yes, in such times you don't think—at least not clearly!

There's nothing you can do to avoid the crises. They are a part of life in this fallen world. How you prepare for those things will determine whether you stand or fall. And how do you prepare? By doing just as Jesus had commanded His friends: you pray!

*Loving Father, please energize and strengthen me when it's time
for me to seek You and bring my thanks, my requests,
even my complaints to You.*

A GODLY LEGACY

I will open my mouth with a parable; I will utter hidden things,
things from of old—things we have heard and known, things our
ancestors have told us. We will not hide them from their
descendants; we will tell the next generation the praiseworthy
deeds of the LORD, his power, and the wonders he has done.

PSALM 78:2–4 NIV

Many fathers work hard, hoping they can leave their children some kind of earthly inheritance. But there's a more important inheritance Christian men should leave for their children: a legacy of faith. It's the kind of faith that shows itself in a commitment to God and His written Word. That's a legacy your children can take from their homes growing up to their own adulthood and on into eternity.

Of course, it's important on a purely personal level to live the life God calls you to live. But God also calls you to leave a legacy to your children and to the rest of the next generation (and others to follow). He wants you to leave a legacy of faith, a legacy of godly living, and a legacy of love for God and His Word.

How can you begin working to leave your children that kind of inheritance?

Father in heaven, show me how I can leave my own children, as well as
their children, an inheritance of godliness and love for Your Word.

SOME NEEDED SELF-AWARENESS

But the other criminal rebuked him. "Don't you fear God," he said,
"since you are under the same sentence? We are punished justly,
for we are getting what our deeds deserve. But this man
has done nothing wrong."

Luke 23:40–41 niv

In the pivotal moment in all human history, the Creator of the world hung nailed to a wooden cross between two criminals. One mocked Jesus and the other—painfully aware that he was receiving his just punishment—spoke the words recorded above.

Then a true miracle happens. This self-admitted criminal turned to the Lord and said, "Jesus, remember me when you come into your kingdom" (Luke 23:42 niv). The Savior answered, "Truly I tell you, today you will be with me in paradise" (23:43 niv).

There's a universal truth in the criminal's words: "We are punished justly, for we are getting what our deeds deserve." Every man deserves God's judgment and punishment. That's the bad news.

The good news is that, when you recognize your unworthiness for God's eternal kingdom, you can place your faith in the One who died and was raised from the dead. One day you too will be with Him in paradise.

God of grace and forgiveness, thank You for being a God who delights in
saving even the worst of sinners. Never let me forget that You delight in
transforming those who come to You in desperate need of Your mercy.

REMEMBERING

They forgot what he had done,
the wonders he had shown them.
PSALM 78:11 NIV

Have you ever spent time with your family looking at old scrapbooks, watching old vacation videos, or talking and recounting pleasant memories from the past? Doing so can be a wonderful way to strengthen family bonds.

It's good to do the same thing with your Father in heaven. In scores of scripture verses (ten in Deuteronomy alone), God encourages His people to not forget the amazing things He had done for them in the past. He encouraged and challenged the people to remember His goodness so that they wouldn't be tempted to turn away from Him. The same thing is true today.

Take the time to recall and revel in God's goodness to you over the years. Think about the moment He saved you and made you part of His eternal family. Remember the times He has helped you out of terrible jams. And consider those amazing instances when it was obvious He had moved on your behalf as a direct result of prayer.

Doing these things can strengthen your faith. And they can also give you good reasons to smile.

Perfect God, never let me forget the amazing things You have done
for me, starting with making me one of Your own. That way,
I'll have the faith to believe You and trust You and ask
You to do the things I know You want to do.

KNOWING YOUR PLACE

*John answered them, saying, "I baptize with water, but there stands
One among you whom you do not know. It is He who, coming after me,
is preferred before me, whose sandal strap I am not worthy to loose."*
JOHN 1:26–27 NKJV

Today's key verses feature the words of a man who was part of God's plan of bringing salvation to the world. They're also the words of a man who knew his place within that plan. As a result, he was able to point people to Jesus as the Savior they desperately needed.

John's humility and knowledge of his role makes him a great example Christian men should follow every day. John had accumulated a large following by this time, and some believed that he might be the long-awaited Messiah. But John knew his place in God's grand plan of salvation, and he told his followers that he was only God's messenger to point others toward Jesus.

That's really God's calling for each of us, isn't it? He gives you specific gifts and talents, as well as a calling and sometimes a following, and He wants you to use everything He gives you to point others to Jesus.

*Father in heaven, I want to be a part of Your plans for bringing others
into Your kingdom. As You direct, remind me to remain humble,
knowing that the work isn't about me. Instead, it's all about Jesus.*

CONDITIONAL PROMISES

*"If you return to the LORD with all your hearts, then put away
the foreign gods and the Ashtoreths from among you, and prepare
your hearts for the LORD, and serve Him only; and He
will deliver you from the hand of the Philistines."*
1 SAMUEL 7:3 NKJV

Any wise father knows some of his promises to his children should be unconditional ("I will always love you!") and some should be conditional ("If you clean your room, you can go to the movies with your friends").

Many of God's promises are conditional, meaning you must do your part before He will do His. For example:

- "Delight yourself also in the LORD, and He shall give you the desires of your heart" (Psalm 37:4 NKJV).
- "Trust in the LORD with all your heart and lean not on your own understanding; in all your ways submit to him, and he will make your paths straight" (Proverbs 3:5–6 NIV).
- "If you abide in Me, and My words abide in you, you will ask what you desire, and it shall be done for you" (John 15:7 NKJV).

When you read God's promises of blessing in the Bible, make sure you also take special note of what He expects of you before He fulfills them.

*Generous Father, thank You for keeping Your promises. Help me purge
from my life anything that keeps me from enjoying the things You've
promised to do for those who serve and follow You faithfully.*

GOD'S UNDERSTANDING NATURE

Yes, many a time He turned His anger away, and did not stir up
all His wrath; for He remembered that they were but flesh,
a breath that passes away and does not come again.

PSALM 78:38–39 NKJV

A big part of being a good father is recognizing your children's considerable limitations. That's especially true when it comes to them understanding *how* they're to behave and *why* they're to behave that way. No loving, compassionate dad would expect his seven-year-old son to behave anywhere close to the way a full-grown man would (1 Corinthians 13:11).

God's love for you is a lot like that. He understands you, and He knows you are severely limited—in your wisdom, thinking, and ability to live in a way that meets His standards of holiness. And while the Lord will never compromise His standards, He has compassionately and mercifully reached down. He's reached down to flawed men He knows are incapable of doing anything in their own power to reach Him.

This truth is humbling because it reminds you of your own smallness. Then again, it is cause to praise God for sending His Son to do what you could never do for yourself.

Father in heaven, thank You for knowing me and understanding me
far better than I know or understand myself. It's only because
of Your love and understanding that I have the blessed
privilege of knowing You and living for You.

LIFTING UP JESUS

"And as Moses lifted up the serpent in the wilderness, even so must the Son of Man be lifted up, that whoever believes in Him should not perish but have eternal life."

JOHN 3:14–15 NKJV

Men today will turn to just about anything as a remedy for their loneliness, guilt, and lack of purpose—including money, status, alcohol, sex, sports, gambling, and gaming.

As a follower of Jesus, you have the antidote to guilt, sin, and separation from God, and He calls you to share the story of His gift of salvation with those who need to hear it.

In today's scripture passage, Jesus likens Himself to a bronze snake Moses had held up in the wilderness so that the people of Israel could be healed of snakebites (Numbers 21:4–9). To hold Him up in front of hurting, lost sinners, then, is to help them see healing and deliverance from the work of the serpent back in the garden of Eden.

God has provided your source of healing, forgiveness, and salvation, and His name is Jesus. When desperately needy and hurting people cross your path, have the courage to lift Him up above anything or anyone else.

God in heaven, please bring people into my life who need to hear Your message of salvation. And when I talk with them, help me to lift up Jesus.

A PRIVILEGE AND RESPONSIBILITY

"As for me, far be it from me that I should sin against the LORD by failing to pray for you. And I will teach you the way that is good and right."

1 SAMUEL 12:23 NIV

The words of the prophet Samuel above are an important challenge to all Christian men to pray regularly about all things, and especially to pray for one another.

Samuel was addressing his own people who had sinned terribly against God, including essentially turning against Him when they demanded a king to rule over them. Yet Samuel assured them that God had not rejected them and challenged them to serve Him and not turn away into idolatry (1 Samuel 12:20–22). Then Sam3uel promises that he would pray for them, for to do otherwise would be a sin against God.

It's very important to God that you come to Him in prayer. Prayer is a wonderful privilege, but it's also a responsibility. He wants you to come to Him with requests for yourself, your family, your Christian brothers and sisters, for those who need Jesus, and for anything else He lays on your heart.

When your heart feels burdened over an issue or situation, talk it over with God, who *wants* to hear from you.

Father, thank You for the gift of prayer. Remind me daily that You want me to come to You regularly to talk with You and quietly listen to You.

WORSHIPPING FROM THE HEART

Jesus said to her, "Woman, believe Me, the hour is coming when you will neither on this mountain, nor in Jerusalem, worship the Father. You worship what you do not know; we know what we worship, for salvation is of the Jews. But the hour is coming, and now is, when the true worshipers will worship the Father in spirit and truth; for the Father is seeking such to worship Him."

JOHN 4:21–23 NKJV

Are you the kind of worshipper God seeks? In today's scripture passage, Jesus tells a Samaritan woman that God seeks those who would worship Him "in spirit and in truth." That, He told her, is what true worship is all about.

When you think of the word *worship*, your mind may be tempted to go to what you do at church before the preacher delivers the sermon. And while those things are legitimate forms of worship, you can safely conclude that Jesus had something more in mind here.

The kind of worship God loves most is the worship that comes from a heart focused solely on Him. It's not just the kind of worship you do at church, but also the worship you offer Him every day—as you love Him with every part of your being and as you surrender yourself fully to Him.

Loving Father, may I worship You with every part of my being. May I live a life of fully surrendered love and worship for You.

OUTWARD APPEARANCES

But the LORD said to Samuel, "Do not consider his appearance
or his height, for I have rejected him. The LORD does not look
at the things people look at. People look at the outward
appearance, but the LORD looks at the heart."

1 SAMUEL 16:7 NIV

You probably don't need to reread today's key verse to know that people with an attractive physical appearance (men and women alike) have many advantages in this life. It's just part of fallen human nature that you somehow equate having "the look" with important qualities that have nothing to do with personal appearance.

But it's not like that with God. He doesn't care what men look like or how tall they are or what they've accomplished in this life. He concerns Himself only with what is in your heart and mind—definitely *not* with what you look like.

The verse quoted above stands as a challenge for you to do two things. First, you should make sure you never judge or evaluate anyone, including yourself, based on physical appearance. Second, you should evaluate your own heart to make sure you are focused on pleasing God in every area of your life.

Righteous God, thank You for looking into my heart and for knowing
me better than I know myself. Search my heart today and let
me know if there is anything that displeases You.

SLAYING GIANTS

Then David said to the Philistine, "You come to me with a sword, with a spear, and with a javelin. But I come to you in the name of the LORD of hosts, the God of the armies of Israel, whom you have defied."

1 SAMUEL 17:45 NKJV

Men tend to highly respect physical and emotional strength, intelligence, know-how, wisdom, and other things you believe make a man a *real* man. While those are all good qualities, those who want to accomplish great things for God's kingdom must remember that you can't do a single thing without Him.

The young shepherd boy David understood this as he faced off with a giant warrior named Goliath. There's some debate about Goliath's size, but you know that his armor alone weighed 175 pounds. To say the least, Goliath was a man's man, and his awesome size and weapons made this match-up a "no contest."

Except. . .

David knew from the beginning that this confrontation wasn't going to end well for Goliath. He knew that for one very good reason: he was fighting in the name of his mighty, all-powerful God. It was indeed a no contest, but not the way Goliath thought it would be.

What giant do you face today? How can you defeat him?

Mighty God, thank You that—while I can't accomplish anything for You in my own strength—with You I can do anything You call me to do.

WHO AM I?

So David said to Saul, "Who am I, and what is my life or my father's family in Israel, that I should be son-in-law to the king?"

1 SAMUEL 18:18 NKJV

King Saul, Israel's first monarch, feared that his days as king were numbered. As a result, he deviously offered the man God had chosen as his successor, young David, an irresistible prize—his oldest daughter's hand in marriage. The only caveat: the young king-to-be would have to routinely slay the dreaded Philistine soldiers in hand-to-hand combat.

David's response to Saul's offer (above) demonstrated his humility. The Bible is abundantly clear that God loves humility and hates human pride. Humility keeps you on track with what God wants to do in and through you, while pride scuttles what could have been something great.

Can you think of an example of how pride has kept someone from a great blessing from God? Has that ever happened to you?

How can you keep a humble heart so that you can receive everything God has for you?

Begin with the prayer below.

Father in heaven, Your written Word says You resist the proud and bless those who are humble. I don't want to miss anything You have for me, so please help me. Help me check myself when I am tempted to think more highly of myself than I should.

TEST QUESTIONS

When Jesus looked up and saw a great crowd coming toward him,
he said to Philip, "Where shall we buy bread for these people
to eat?" He asked this only to test him, for he already
had in mind what he was going to do.

John 6:5–6 niv

Remember how your schoolteachers and college professors would pose tough questions and you were pretty sure they already knew the answers? It's a method of teaching as old as teaching itself, because it challenges students to think and seek out answers for themselves.

In today's scripture passage, the Great Teacher asked one of His disciples how to feed thousands of hungry people. They had no food with them, and they probably didn't have enough places close by to buy bread for everyone.

Then again, Jesus knew what He was going to do and how He was going to do it. Before He acted, though, Jesus used this opportunity to teach His friend an important truth about faith and about who his Provider really was.

When you look at something you know God wants you to do, and then ask how, you're in the place where God can teach you a little more about trusting Him.

Lord, thank You for having Your plans for me all mapped out.
When I wonder how I'm going to act on those plans, teach me
to trust in You more and then to act on what I know.

YOUR SOURCE OF NOURISHMENT

Jesus said to them, "Very truly I tell you, it is not Moses who has given you the bread from heaven, but it is my Father who gives you the true bread from heaven. For the bread of God is the bread that comes down from heaven and gives life to the world."

JOHN 6:32–33 NIV

Experts on the subject will tell you that in order for a man to be properly nourished, he needs the right mixture of proteins, carbohydrates, dietary fats, vitamins, and minerals. Life is busy, though, and you have a difficult time making sure you consume a healthy diet.

While properly nourishing your body can be a little complicated, nourishing your soul is as simple as knowing Jesus Christ, the Bread of Life sent directly from heaven, in a personal way. Jesus is your source of life and abundance. He is with you and will be each and every day.

When God sent His Son to this world to live, die, and then be resurrected, He provided you with everything you need. He provided everything you need to live a life that pleases Him before you spend all of eternity with Him in heaven. Let Him fully nourish your soul today.

God my provider, I want to learn to be more grateful for the many blessings You so generously pour out on me. Thank You most of all for sending the true Bread of Life who fulfills me in every way.

KEEP FOLLOWING

*"You do not want to leave too, do you?" Jesus asked the Twelve.
Simon Peter answered him, "Lord, to whom shall we go? You have
the words of eternal life. We have come to believe and
to know that you are the Holy One of God."*

JOHN 6:67–69 NIV

J esus had come to a point in His ministry when many who had followed Him turned away and went back to their old lives. As He had said it would, the seed of His word had fallen among thorns and weeds that choked out the new plants (Matthew 13:7). As a result, thousands left Him and went their own way.

The thorns Jesus referred to could be the cares of this life or the distractions of worldly pleasures and goals. Those things existed two thousand years ago, and they're still around today.

Life presents all sorts of distractions and temptations that, if you're not careful, can untrack you from following Jesus Christ with your whole heart. He came to earth to speak the words of eternal life and offer Himself, even to the point of death, so that you could follow Him forever.

What distractions or temptations are you battling today? How can you overcome them? Begin with this prayer. . .

---

*Jesus, I live in a time and place where many have left You and turned to
other things. Please alert me when the world or the devil tries to divide
my heart and distract me from following You with my whole heart.*

WHEN YOU SEE INJUSTICE

"How long will you defend the unjust and show partiality to the wicked? Defend the weak and the fatherless; uphold the cause of the poor and the oppressed. Rescue the weak and the needy; deliver them from the hand of the wicked."

PSALM 82:2–4 NIV

Of all the tough questions the skeptic can ask about the Christian faith, probably the most difficult is, "If God is so good, then why does He allow so much suffering in the world?"

That's a tough question for even the most learned Bible scholar to handle, for it forces believers to ponder the nature of a God who created the world and who self-identifies as love itself. The world is filled with oppressive levels of poverty, war, slavery, and many other evils. Evil people use and exploit the vulnerable and the weak for their own benefit.

And God cares.

God cares so much that He has called Christian men to both pray and take action. He calls you to stand up to and oppose those who hurt or exploit others (see Proverbs 31:8–9 and Psalm 82:3, for example).

What action can you take to care for the helpless, feed the hungry, or free the enslaved?

Generous Father, I am grieved when I hear horrible stories of abuse and exploitation. Show me how I can stand up for those who can't stand up for themselves, and then strengthen me so I can take action.

WHEN GOD SEEMS SILENT

O God, do not remain silent; do not turn a deaf ear,
do not stand aloof, O God.
PSALM 83:1 NIV

At the end of World War II, the following was found scrawled on the wall of a Nazi concentration camp.

I believe in the sun even when it's not shining. I believe in love even when I don't feel it. I believe in God even when He is silent.

For a person suffering the horrors of a concentration camp, it probably would be very easy to question where God was. Yet an anonymous believer found the inner faith to continue believing in God, even though He seemed so far away.

Today's scripture shows you that many before have struggled during times of difficulty, when it seemed as though God wasn't listening and wasn't answering. It also shows you that when you're suffering and it feels as though God doesn't care, He still hears you as you talk to Him about your difficulties and register your complaints.

Life is truly difficult sometimes, and you may find yourself occasionally questioning whether God cares about your struggles. In turn, God invites you to come to Him and cast your cares on Him, for He truly cares about you (1 Peter 5:7).

Father God, Your Word promises me that You desire to hear me.
Remind me daily of that wondrous fact, especially
during those times when You seem so far away.

A SOURCE OF CONFIDENCE

David inquired of the LORD, "Shall I pursue this raiding party?
Will I overtake them?" "Pursue them," he answered. "You will
certainly overtake them and succeed in the rescue."

1 SAMUEL 30:8 NIV

Most have been there: you feel a burden or have a plan to do something you believe needs to be done, but you want assurance that God approves. What can you do to move forward confidently knowing you're doing God's will?

Today's scripture is King David's prayer seeking God's go-ahead to pursue an enemy who had committed atrocities against a city called Ziklag. David wanted to pursue the enemy forces, so he asks God a very specific question. He asks whether a military venture against the raiders would be successful. God's answer was a very clear yes, so David launched the campaign. In the end, it was one of David's finest hours.

None should launch out on big, life-altering ventures without first seeking God's approval. God promises to hear your prayers and to act on your behalf. That includes giving you approval for plans that are His will for you.

Lord, please guide me and direct me as I seek Your will in every
area of my life. Let me know when I'm headed in the right
direction, when I should stop, or when I should wait.

ALL GOOD THINGS FROM GOD

For the LORD God is a sun and shield; the LORD will give grace and glory;
no good thing will He withhold from those who walk uprightly.
O Lord of hosts, blessed is the man who trusts in You!

PSALM 84:11–12 NKJV

The writer of Psalm 84 was a man who understood what he needed to do to put himself in position to receive the best God so freely offers. He understood that God was his source of provision and protection, but he also understood that God's promises of blessing are contingent on one simple thing: walking as God wanted him to walk and trusting Him for everything.

That all sounds so simple, doesn't it? And yet it's so easy for you to turn to other sources for protection and security. But only God can give you everything you need to live the abundant life Jesus promised those who follow Him.

A man who consistently follows God and lives as He wants him to live is a blessed man, a man who will receive God's very best. There may be no greater promise in the Bible than that!

Lord, it's sometimes difficult for me to fully grasp the fact that You
want to bless me with all I need to serve You and live a life that
glorifies You. Remind me daily to cling tightly to You so
that I can be in position to receive all You have for me.

HE'S LISTENING!

"We know that God does not listen to sinners.
He listens to the godly person who does his will."
JOHN 9:31 NIV

Have you ever wondered if God really listens to you? Sure, you know the Bible promises that He listens to His people's prayers. Then again, have there ever been moments when you doubted this promise applies to *you*?

If so, then take another look at today's scripture as well as the promises listed below.

- "As for me, I call to God, and the LORD saves me. Evening, morning and noon I cry out in distress, and he hears my voice" (Psalm 55:16–17 NIV).
- "For the eyes of the Lord are on the righteous and his ears are attentive to their prayer" (1 Peter 3:12 NIV).
- "The LORD is far from the wicked, but he hears the prayer of the righteous" (Proverbs 15:29 NIV).

Our God is the personification of perfect love. He listens to the prayers of His people, simply because listening means loving. If you start thinking He doesn't want to hear from you, stop. Ask yourself if you're where you need to be in your relationship with God so that He will hear you. After all, He's still right where He's always been.

Father in heaven, thank You for hearing me when I come to You
in prayer. Keep me from wandering, even in what seem like
small ways. That way, I can approach Your throne with
confidence, knowing that You will hear me.

GOD WITH YOU

*David then took up residence in the fortress and called it the City
of David. He built up the area around it, from the terraces inward.
And he became more and more powerful, because the
LORD God Almighty was with him.*

2 SAMUEL 5:9–10 NIV

The biblical story of David is an amazing one. He rose from humble beginnings to a position of great power and prestige in the ancient world. Yet David didn't grow in power because of his own wisdom and strength, let alone because he was perfect in all his ways (in fact, he was far from it). He grew in his power for one reason: God was with him.

God may not have planned to make you a powerful person, a famous person, or a rich person. But He has plans for those He loves, and you can place yourself in the middle of those plans when you put yourself in the place where He wants you to be.

How can you know that God is with you? What can you do to make sure He stays with you today and always?

*Gracious heavenly Father, more than anything else, I want to know
that You are with me in all I do and everywhere I go. Show me how
I can stay in the place where You want me to be so that I
may enjoy everything You have for me in this life.*

A PLACE OF SECURITY

"My sheep listen to my voice; I know them, and they follow me.
I give them eternal life, and they shall never perish;
no one will snatch them out of my hand."

JOHN 10:27–28 NIV

Today's scripture reading contains amazing promises for those who have been transformed by the work of Jesus Christ on the cross. None of them is as important and life-changing, though, as the promise of eternal life. This is a promise to those Jesus calls His sheep. He not only promises you eternal life, but He also promises security.

At some point in life, a man of faith will suffer bouts of insecurity, even wondering if it's possible to lose his place in God's eternal kingdom. But here, straight from the Savior's mouth, is the double assurance: "They shall never perish; no one will snatch them out of my hand."

Do you ever worry that the devil will tempt you beyond what you can endure, and that he will win a victory over God by taking you away from the Savior? If you have, you're not alone. Then again, you can rest assured that if you belong to Jesus, He will hold you securely in His hand, always and forever.

Lord Jesus, thank You that I can be secure in You. Remind me daily that
no one or nothing can take me out of Your hand.

AN UNDIVIDED HEART

Teach me your way, LORD, that I may rely on your faithfulness;
give me an undivided heart, that I may fear your name.

PSALM 86:11 NIV

Jesus told His disciples something that resonates with many today: "Do not set your heart on what you will eat or drink; do not worry about it. For the pagan world runs after all such things, and your Father knows that you need them. But seek his kingdom, and these things will be given to you as well" (Luke 12:29–31 NIV).

Was Jesus saying that you shouldn't concern yourself with providing for yourself and your family? Not at all! The Bible warns that a man who doesn't care for his family is "worse than an unbeliever" (1 Timothy 5:8 NIV).

Jesus' point echoed the words of King David in today's scripture verse. Yes, a godly man works to care for himself and his family, but he doesn't allow those tasks to distract him from God. Instead, he relies on God's faithfulness so that he can keep his heart from becoming divided.

The things you must do in this world can distract you from your relationship with your heavenly Father. So God calls you to set your heart on Him and His eternal kingdom first—and then allow Him to meet your needs here on earth.

Father in heaven, as I tend to my responsibilities here on earth,
help me stay focused on what's most important to You.

GOD'S TIMING

When Mary reached the place where Jesus was and saw him,
she fell at his feet and said, "Lord, if you had been
here, my brother would not have died."

JOHN 11:32 NIV

Jesus raising His friend Lazarus from the dead is one of His greatest, most memorable miracles. It powerfully demonstrates God's power over death. It also teaches you a great lesson regarding His timing in doing the things He does.

When Lazarus's sister Mary first met Jesus after her brother's death, she voiced a measure of faith while protesting that if He'd only come sooner, Lazarus would still be alive. When you read this account, you can almost feel her grief at the loss of her brother. You can imagine her disappointment that Jesus waited so long before coming.

In the end, Mary and her sister, Martha, saw God glorified when Jesus brought their brother back to life. Not only that, many others witnessed this miracle and came to faith in Him.

Are you facing a situation where you need a miracle, but think God has failed you? If so, hold to your faith and wait. It's possible that the Lord has planned an even greater miracle, one that benefits you, glorifies God, and brings others to faith.

Sovereign God, I know that Your timing is not always my timing.
Please sustain my faith as I wait for You to intervene
on my behalf in a way only You can.

A COMMITMENT TO PRAISE GOD

I call to you, LORD, every day; I spread out my hands to you.
PSALM 88:9 NIV

If you're honest with yourself, you have to admit that Psalm 88 is a gloomy piece of writing. In it, the psalmist first praises God for saving him and then presents a series of sorrowful laments. In the midst of his complaints, the writer presents a moment of hope in today's scripture quotation.

Today's psalm is not an easy read, but it can challenge you to praise and thank God in easy and difficult times alike. True, it's not easy to praise God when you're going through difficulties. But when you praise Him and reach up to Him, even when you don't feel like it, He'll strengthen and encourage you. He may even teach you some wisdom in the midst of your trials.

What does your walk with God look like when your life is difficult, when it seems like He's disappeared in the midst of your troubles? Do you find yourself withdrawing and trying to handle your problems on your own? Or do you spread out your hands to Him, praise His name, and ask Him to bless you through everything?

Merciful Father, when I'm going through tough times, I don't usually feel like praying or praising Your name. Strengthen me during those times, and help me remember that You always deserve my praise.

MAKE THIS FOLLOWER WILLING

*"I tell you the truth, unless a kernel of wheat is planted in the soil
and dies, it remains alone. But its death will produce many new
kernels—a plentiful harvest of new lives. Those who love their life
in this world will lose it. Those who care nothing for
their life in this world will keep it for eternity."*

JOHN 12:24–25 NLT

Plant a wheat kernel and it will move from dormancy to death. It seems unfair, harsh, and hopeless.

Oddly, this transition is a cause for joy because new life breaks the soil's crust. One lifeless wheat kernel makes it possible for a hundred new kernels to grow.

As one who follows Jesus Christ, you intentionally plant seeds in the thinking of those who don't follow yet. Your greatest hope is that the seeds will cause new life to grow. Yes, some seeds are plucked. Some don't develop deep roots. Some blow away. Still, never stop sowing!

The verses above ultimately describe the transformation of Jesus from death to life, from crucifixion to resurrection, and from the one planted seed to a remarkable harvest.

Jesus always is your perfect example—and He gives you the seed.

*Dear God, You made plants grow from the death of a lone seed.
You made new hearts grow from the death of Your Son. You made
transformation possible from the death of self and a
willingness to follow. Make this follower willing.*

COME HOME

Your love has always been our lives' foundation,
your fidelity has been the roof over our world.
PSALM 89:2 MSG

The *foundation* of your spiritual life is God's love. The *roof*? His faithfulness. God keeps you both steady and protected. He secures your future so you can be assured that whatever happens today doesn't summarize your life story.

Now? You can face the spiritual equivalent of earthquakes and tornadoes with confidence. *There's more.* God wants you to stop believing that if things are going to get done it will be due to your own effort, planning, and personal experience.

It is true God gives you skills. It's also true that work is something He wants you to do. But trouble visits when you attempt to replace God *in life's management office.* Make your plans, but God has veto power (Proverbs 16:9).

Throughout biblical history men who trusted God often (not always) stopped consulting Him like they once did. Many ultimately chose a path leading away from the *foundation and roof* of God's love and faithfulness. The *fraternity of the walkaway* includes mighty King Solomon and Judas Iscariot, to name but two.

God always works to remind you of the place where love and faithfulness invite you home.

Dear God, You are faithful. I'm not. You love. I grip seeds of
bitterness. You stay. I consider walking away. Thank You for
being all that I'm not so I can learn to be more like You.

RADICAL KINDNESS

When [Jesus] had washed their feet. . .he said to them,
"Do you understand what I have done to you?"
JOHN 13:12 ESV

They didn't understand. How could they? It was customary for someone to clean the dust from the feet of guests when they arrived in a home. They were guests. Someone failed in their role of hospitality.

Yet Jesus got a basin and towel to clean the feet of the men He would use to change the world. Perhaps the disciples were embarrassed. The last person they thought should assume this *servant role* was Jesus. You can almost sense a feeling of awkwardness in the room as the one they called *Master* was doing something no one else was willing to do.

Peter resisted the cleansing, but Jesus gently yet firmly washed his feet.

You will never become what God has in mind for you by resisting His help. That help can often seem like something you should be able to do yourself, but you haven't. You might think someone else should have done it for you, but they can't. Romans 2:4 (MSG) says, "In kindness [God] takes us firmly by the hand and leads us into a radical life change."

Life change is transformation. Transformation begins with the kindness of God. God's kindness was once delivered through a basin and a towel. Don't resist the servant Savior.

Dear God, by Your kindness draw me close,
do what I can't, and show me Your way.

LIFE CHANGE

*Jesus said to him, "I am the way, the truth, and the life.
No one comes to the Father except through Me."*
JOHN 14:6 NKJV

L ife change. Everyone wants it and many go to great lengths to find it. Some discover the true source of life change, yet fail to believe.

You might have explored self-help methods that revolve around behavior modification, multiple steps to success, or finding a different network of friends. These methods never bring lasting life change.

It may be possible to improve personal interactions, find a new job, or identify new people who will like your social media posts. Then again, if you want to find God there is a single way, a simple truth, and an abundant life. *Jesus.*

You can look for it elsewhere. *Maybe you have.* You can believe something else. *Maybe you did.* You can accept a substitute. *Maybe you are.* At some point the *imposter's well* will run dry and your questions will be met with an indifferent shrug.

You need to be saved from the penalty of sin, separation from God, and life without direction. Jesus offers the way, truth, and life that leads to real transformation.

*Dear God, there are many paths, but only one leads to You. There are
many beliefs, but only one absolute truth. Life is only existence
without Your purpose. I come to You in the name of Your Son,
Jesus. Help me accept Your way, truth, and life.*

LIFE IN THE REARVIEW MIRROR

God guaranteed his covenant with me,
spelled it out plainly and kept every promised word.
2 SAMUEL 23:5 MSG

David, Israel's most famous king, was nearing the end of His life. The king had a lot of years to review and time was not on his side.

He could have lamented poor choices, impulses, and personal example. He could have focused on his personal achievements, adventurous life, and *winner-take-all battle* with the giant, Goliath. He could have. *He didn't.*

David spent most of his final words recounting the *faithfulness of God*. He called Him a rock, fortress, and deliverer. He recalled the bad days and the God who made them good. He saw the value of following the God of both mercy *and* justice.

The list of those who had negatively impacted King David was long, but his last moments were spent remembering the goodness of God instead of the imperfections of man.

If this resonates with you as an *I-want-that-too* kind of life, take courage! Always remember the goodness of God. It will bring the contrast needed to see a value far greater than bitterness, revenge, or an unforgiving spirit. *This* thinking changes a man.

Dear God, between now and the moment my life is over, I have the
opportunity to live without regrets, revenge, and reactionary living.
May my life be so changed between now and that day that
people will think of You when they remember me.

ONE FULL SPONGE

"There is so much more I want to tell you, but you can't bear it now. When the Spirit of truth comes, he will guide you into all truth. He will not speak on his own but will tell you what he has heard."

JOHN 16:12–13 NLT

J esus would soon be betrayed and face false charges. He would be killed. There would be a resurrection too, but the things His disciples *didn't know* captured Jesus' focus and attention.

If the disciples' minds were spongelike, then they were oversaturated. They had learned much, but there was still more to learn. The time had come for Jesus to initiate God's great *rescue plan*. The disciples wouldn't understand, though they had been told. As Jesus prepared for His death, the disciples entertained confusion.

Are you puzzled when you read the Bible? It may seem that the connections you hoped to find by reading the Bible are hard to decode. Jesus could have been talking to you when He said that you might not be able to understand everything in one reading of His Word. God's Spirit closes the knowledge gap by teaching, leading, and guiding. The Holy Spirit helps you understand more of the nature of God so you can become more like His Son.

Dear God, since Your Spirit lives with me, help me attend master classes in Your wisdom. Help me pay attention. Help me understand what You want me to know most.

A NEW KING IN TOWN

[David] ordered, "Gather my servants, then mount my son Solomon on my royal mule and lead him in procession down to Gihon. When you get there, Zadok the priest and Nathan the prophet will anoint him king over Israel. Then blow the ram's horn trumpet and shout, 'Long live King Solomon!' You will then accompany him as he enters and takes his place on my throne, succeeding me as king."

1 KINGS 1:34–35 MSG

King David needed to name his replacement. In failing health, David heard news that his son Adonijah claimed to be the new king. This move did not sit well with David.

Some sons were older, considered more handsome, and had a better claim to the throne. Yet Solomon was David's clear choice.

The new king would have to learn fast. When God offered to give Solomon what he wanted most, he chose wisdom above riches and fame (1 Kings 3:1–15).

The great transition for Solomon wasn't when David made him king. Instead, it was when God gave him the wisdom to lead.

The same is true for you. You begin your transformation when God gives you the tools needed to become a new creature. Seek His wisdom, follow His lead, and obey His commands.

Dear God, I can't transform myself. I can't save myself. I can't earn a pass into Your presence. Transform me through the gifts of Your grace, wisdom, and presence.

NEVER OVERLOOKED

"As you sent me into the world,
so I have sent them into the world."

JOHN 17:18 ESV

Nothing escapes Jesus' attention. He will never be *king of the uninformed*. Jesus knew the troubles and persecutions His disciples would face once He returned to God. All the more, He needed them to know they were receiving a commission from His heavenly Father, who wanted to use them to shake the Roman empire.

Jesus knew that as His disciples were increasingly transformed, they would be more and more useful in helping change the hearts, minds, and lives of those who never met Him face-to-face. Jesus longed for the societal changes that would bring His wisdom and purpose to the top of mankind's list of choices.

The world changed because Jesus obeyed. The world continues to change because the followers of Jesus obey.

You are moving from what you were to what you will become. This *chain of change* relies on your link to Jesus. God made you to be different from others because His plan for mankind doesn't borrow from man's natural thinking. *God's* wisdom can't be explained by *your* wisdom. Stop trying to compare two things that aren't comparable.

Dear God, help me remember that the transformation of Your Son
from Messiah to Savior, Teacher to Redeemer, and Master to Lord is
a brilliant example of the fact that You want to change me too.
May others catch a glimpse of the faithfulness You inspire.

CONFIRMED. ESTABLISHED.

Let the beauty and delightfulness and favor of the Lord our God be
upon us; confirm and establish the work of our hands—yes,
the work of our hands, confirm and establish it.

PSALM 90:17 AMPC

Positive transformation is defined by the standards of God. Accept the standards of self-help and you might discover change. You can accept the standards of your worst influence and identify change. You can hold tight to tradition and be subject to change. You can even be transformed by the influence of unforgiveness. Transformation means change, but not all change is good.

When you choose God's standards you will desire His approval and favor. You will want to see your efforts become something bigger than your best dream. Ideas, plans, and hopes can be transformed into a life you can be pleased with because the end results are in line with what pleases God.

Spend time making sure you're happy, and the satisfaction you experience will be short-lived. Spend too much time making other people happy, and they may come to believe this is your full-time job. Spend time pleasing God, and you will be satisfied. What's more, those closest to you will experience a love from you that pushes past temporary happiness to long-term joy and security.

Dear God, establish what I do because I am doing it for You.
Help me find joy, peace, and courage when I do
the things You made me to do.

FICKLE AND FAITHLESS

They slapped him in the face.

JOHN 19:3 NIV

Cheers billowed over Jerusalem like smoke from a fire. The crowd shouted, "Hosanna! Blessed is he who comes in the name of the Lord! Blessed is the king of Israel!" (John 12:13 NIV).

As the days passed the voices grew silent and then surly. The minds of the masses were transformed negatively. The once adoring crowd shouted insults at the Messiah. They demanded His death. Their enthusiastic worship turned to bitter scorn.

The people were comfortable watching Roman soldiers slap the face of Jesus. How had this man become so despised, so rejected?

You never would have turned your back on Jesus, right? This event is an example of why Jesus came. Like the fickle crowd, you were born in need of the grace made possible when Jesus died for the sins of deserters.

You can follow God and act like He's the enemy, say you want to be more like Christ and act like you're unteachable, or sing *God-songs* and never let the words speak life to your spirit.

God does not force transformation. He offers it. If you refuse to cooperate, you could find yourself singing praise one moment and denying you know Him the next.

Dear God, help me resist negative transformation. I want to know You more and introduce You to others. I want to learn from You and let it positively alter what I do and how I do it.

PERPETUAL SATISFACTION

"If you'll hold on to me for dear life," says GOD...
"I'll...give you a long drink of salvation!"
PSALM 91:14, 16 MSG

Take stock of your life. Behold the imperfections, the bitterness, the broken dreams. Your hands show the stains of every evil deed and missed opportunity to do the right thing. Inside clangs a hard heartbeat like a pickax against stone.

Insensitivity, mistrust, and selfishness leave you famished, thirsty, with nothing to share, and no one to accept your gift.

You fixate on your own worst efforts. You promise better behavior. You choose to punish yourself. You insist that even if you get it right this time, you'll never be acceptable to God.

God helped the psalmist understand that personal effort is no substitute for grasping the coattails of His perfection. Working harder to please God won't change a parched soul to one perpetually satisfied.

To be transformed is to hold on to God for dear life—not because you are whipped and without choice, but because this is the only choice that responds to God's love, redemption, and salvation. This is a choice that restores a broken man. This is rescue—drink deep.

Dear God, I'm tired of knowing I can never do enough good before
I fail again. I'm tired of the inner thirst that longs for satisfaction
I've never experienced. I want to cling to You because nothing
else has power to change me. Help me long. Help me cling.

LIMITLESS

Joseph of Arimathea asked Pilate for the body of Jesus. . . .
He was accompanied by Nicodemus, the man who
earlier had visited Jesus at night.
JOHN 19:38–39 NIV

J esus invested in the lives of common men who became disciples. He reprimanded the religious leaders for following a mental checklist while resisting heart transformation. Their commitment to God was reduced to a sad game of *show and tell*. They considered themselves elite and concluded they should advertise their distinction.

Before Jesus was crucified His disciples deserted Him. *After* He died there were two religious leaders who surprisingly stood for Jesus even though His own disciples had abandoned Him.

Joseph of Arimathea was the only one to offer a tomb for Jesus' burial. Nicodemus was a Pharisee who saw Jesus as someone who had divine solutions when his religious order offered a collective shrug.

Even nice, decent, and *good choice* people need Jesus. It's easy to think the self-righteous are beyond God's love. You might think they are annoying in their willingness to make you feel small in your faith. Joseph and Nicodemus prove that Jesus even came for the *holier-than-thou*.

His ability to transform is limitless.

Dear God, prevent me from making judgments about those I think
are outside Your willingness to redeem, including the self-righteous.
May I remember Your love has no limits. You reach those who know
they need rescue and those that stubbornly post a NO HELP
REQUIRED sign. Help me share this news with both.

ANSWERED PRAYER

"May the LORD our GOD be with us as he was with our ancestors;
may he never leave us or abandon us. May he give us the desire
to do his will in everything and to obey all the commands."
1 KINGS 8:57–58 NLT

E arth's wisest king wanted assurance that God would never leave or abandon, and he wanted God to give the people a desire to obey.

Today you can trust that God is always with you (Hebrews 13:5) and believe that the desire to follow is inspired by God's Spirit (John 14:17). Solomon's prayer became a foundation for transformation.

You can't move mountains, turn hard hearts soft, or rescue yourself from even one sinful choice. Then again, what you can't do, God has already done. Before you thought to ask for help, He offered.

First Corinthians 10:13 MSG says, "God will never let you down; he'll never let you be pushed past your limit; he'll always be there to help you come through it."

You can't go where God is not (Romans 8:38–39). When your heart is shattered, He's close (Psalm 34:18). When you need to get out of the storm, He's your refuge (Psalm 46:1).

Dear God, I'm grateful You choose to stay with me and allow Your
Spirit to teach, guide, and help me do what You ask. Help me
never be too preoccupied to walk with You.

LIFTED. MAJESTIC.

The Lord reigns, He is clothed with majesty; the Lord is robed,
He has girded Himself with strength and power; the world also
is established, that it cannot be moved. Your throne is
established from of old; You are from everlasting.

PSALM 93:1–2 AMPC

Bernard J. Cigrand taught in Waubeka, Wisconsin. In 1885, Mr. Cigrand asked his students to commemorate the birth of the American Flag. *They did.*

Cigrand was an advocate for a Flag Day celebration for three decades and wrote more than two thousand articles promoting the concept. In 1916, President Woodrow Wilson made the first presidential Flag Day declaration. Cigrand's persistence was rewarded even though he passed away years before Congress made their declaration.

This celebration has meaning for many. It's natural, patriotic, and commemorative.

Maybe you have a desire to establish a *God day* in your personal list of celebrations. It could be the day you were convinced to believe, or it could be a *daily* celebration. Psalm 118:24 (ESV) says, "This is the day that the LORD has made; let us rejoice and be glad in it."

You don't have to limit your recognition of God to a single day each year. He possesses awesome attributes, so you might determine the celebration never needs to end.

Dear God, thank You for this country, Your patience, and my new
life. There is much to celebrate today. Help me include
You in each moment of rejoicing.

PURPOSE DELAYED

"Simon, son of John, do you love me more than these?"
John 21:15 esv

Simon Peter was perhaps the most impulsive disciple. Knee-jerk reactions were common. Acting before he thought? A first response. Peter promised more than he could deliver, said he was more faithful than was possible, and pledged to never leave. *He failed.*

Maybe you identify with Peter. Maybe you're tired of making promises you can't keep.

There's good news. Jesus didn't give up on Peter. He won't give up on you. After Peter's laundry list of failures, Jesus wanted to know if Peter (Simon) loved Him more than the things that distracted him. When Peter affirmed his love, Jesus gave him a glimpse of his future, saying, "Feed my sheep" (John 21:17 esv).

Peter was a sinner, faithless when difficulty came, denied Jesus, and yet was the man God used to build His church (Matthew 16:18).

The sum total of your sin means two things will happen. First, God will need to deal with your sin. Second, He still has purpose for your life.

Without dealing with your sin, you delay the discovery of purpose.

Don't dismiss your sin as unimportant. It's hard to move to new life when you refuse to turn your back on the old life, on the life that's always left you with regrets.

Dear God, help me understand the impact of my sin. Help me turn away, follow You, discover purpose, and celebrate the gift of new life.

THE STRESS OF DOUBTING

When doubts filled my mind, your comfort
gave me renewed hope and cheer.
PSALM 94:19 NLT

Belief and doubt seem to coexist in any state of transition. When you move to a new town, accept a new job, or buy new home, you can believe it's a good decision, but might occasionally doubt you made the right choice.

It's never God's design to leave His family in doubt. You'll notice the psalmist admitted misgivings, but God sent reassurance that brought about hope and encouragement. That's the transition point between doubt and belief. God will send personal reminders that there is no reason to doubt the One who knew you before you were born. *No doubt.*

Jesus told His disciple Thomas to stop doubting. He told a man who asked Him to heal his son that there should be no doubt what He could do. That man replied with raw honesty, "I believe. Help me with my doubts!" (Mark 9:24 MSG).

You will not be commended for doubting God, but you may unintentionally be putting yourself in line for a divine reminder of God's faithfulness.

God's kindness resolves the tension between a life without Jesus Christ and one that answers Jesus' call to "Follow me" (Matthew 8:22).

Dear God, thank You for giving me so many reasons to believe—and no
reasons to doubt. When I find myself doubting, may that stress find
relief in the assurance of hope and the comfort of encouragement.

THE INVITATION

Today, if you hear his voice, do not harden your hearts.
PSALM 95:7–8 ESV

Every day, every hour, every minute, the *God of all* is extending an invitation to new life. Men may say they never received the invitation, deny the invitation is real, or refuse the invitation. Despite their rejection, God's invitation stands.

Second Corinthians 6:2 (NLT) says, "The 'right time' is now. Today is the day of salvation." Because it's the right time, because salvation is available in this moment, take a moment to review today's verse. Again, it says, "If you hear his voice, do not harden your hearts."

If you thought God would call to you in a bold way, that His voice was like the sound of thunder, or that you could demand that God provide a sign, you should remember that God's voice is described as a whisper (1 Kings 19:12).

You may not always understand what God is saying. Lean in, get quiet, and focus. Once you hear His message, make obedience your first response.

To harden your heart is to resist God's will and insist you know more than God. This is a bit like an army private arguing with a five-star general. You don't know as much as you think. God knows more than you give Him credit for.

Dear God, I don't need to argue with You, resist Your instructions, or assume I'm wiser than You. Help me refuse arrogance and accept Your invitation to new life.

SPIRITUAL DROUGHT

Elijah the Tishbite, of the inhabitants of Gilead, said to Ahab,
"As the LORD GOD of Israel lives, before whom I stand, there shall
not be dew nor rain these years, except at my word."

1 KINGS 17:1 NKJV

King Ahab walked away from God. He was selfish and offered free samples of pure evil. Ahab was a man whose choices to defy God exceeded any king before him. He provoked God and followed the non-god Baal.

If Ahab's heart was dry and barren, maybe he would see his error if the land itself was dry and barren. The prophet Elijah was sent by God to tell Ahab that the rains would indeed stop, and it wouldn't rain again until Elijah said so. This was a very personal lesson in how bankrupt and hollow Ahab's ideas were.

Like Ahab, you may need to go through personal and spiritual drought to get to the place where you will admit your rebellion and ask God for help.

He offers living water. *Are you thirsty?* His Word offers aged meat. *Are you hungry?* His kindness introduces salvation. *Are you in need of rescue?*

Dear God, I'd like to say my choices are perfect, but they're not.
Help me avoid a self-imposed drought that keeps me from
Your refreshing love, grace, and forgiveness. May I see You
as the One who never gives me reason to walk away.

JESUS: TRANSFORMED

"God raised [Jesus] from the dead, freeing him from the agony of death, because it was impossible for death to keep its hold on him."

ACTS 2:24 NIV

In the beginning, Jesus was with God the Father (John 1:1). He was the Creator of all (Colossians 1:16). He is God's Son (Matthew 3:17). When the *Always Was* stepped into this world, He did so as the promised one, world changer, and life rearranger. He brought kindness, shared wisdom and friendship.

Mostly, Jesus came to bring life (John 1:4), light (John 8:12), and love (1 John 4:19). He offered acceptance, forgiveness, and restoration. He was praised and then rejected. In that rejection, the Creator was sentenced to death *by His creation*.

The sacrifice of His life provided the only sin payment God would accept. Jesus took care of your greatest need.

The last breath of God's Son transformed the relationship you can have with God. On day three, "God released him from the horrors of death and raised him back to life, for death could not keep him in its grip" (Acts 2:24 NLT).

Jesus: transformed to be your Savior.

Dear God, why is it so easy to minimize the incredible change that comes through rescue? Why can I begin with gratitude and eventually feel as if You owe me? Help me keep Your sacrifice in perspective. May new thinking instill gratitude where complacency once lived.

BETTER ANSWERS

*Peter said, "I don't have a nickel to my name, but what I do have,
I give you: In the name of Jesus Christ of Nazareth, walk!" He grabbed
him by the right hand and pulled him up. In an instant his feet and
ankles became firm. He jumped to his feet and walked.*

ACTS 3:6–8 MSG

The man wanted money. Maybe he was hungry. He was injured and couldn't walk. In his experience, a few coins were all he could expect from the *generosity of the compassionate*.

The apostle Peter knew the man was looking for a handout, but Peter offered something surprising. The apostle essentially said, "I don't have two nickels to rub together. I've got something better." Peter didn't ignore the man or make light of his condition. He offered an answer to prayer.

Weak legs were made strong. One step followed another. This unexpected encounter was like welcoming a new season of living. He welcomed a future bolder than his dreams.

God may not give you exactly what you pray for. You might get a purpose and plan when you asked for something as common as money, strength for a task when you thought your best days were over, or equipping for your next great assignment.

*Dear God, help me accept an answer to my prayer that is bigger
than my request. Help me understand that the way You
answer brings me in contact with Your purpose for me.*

WISDOM SEEKER

*Jehoshaphat said, Is there not another prophet
of the Lord here whom we may ask?*
1 KINGS 22:7 AMPC

King Jehoshaphat followed God. He worked to eliminate idol worship in Judah. Israel's king, Ahab, wasn't interested in following God. Ahab asked Jehoshaphat to help him reclaim land from a foreign nation. Jehoshaphat offered to help, but also wanted to know what God said.

False prophets told Ahab that God would give him the land. Jehoshaphat asked for a second opinion. That opinion was a true prophet's dire warnings about Ahab's plan.

Jehoshaphat should have listened. The land was not reclaimed. King Ahab was killed.

If you're a dad, you'll find yourself in need of wisdom. You can turn to your friends and see if their *second opinion* adds clarity, but it's the wisdom of God that totally transforms your ability to make a good choice.

Ahab didn't care what God thought. Jehoshaphat was talked into going against the wisdom of God. You get to consider a better choice. Psalm 119:105 (MSG) says, "By your words I can see where I'm going; they throw a beam of light on my dark path."

Opinion polls, peer pressure, and a misplaced sense of obligation can never make up for a dad's willingness to boldly follow God.

*Dear God, shine a spotlight on my next step. May I be wise
enough to step within the brilliant gleam of Your leading.*

MR. ENCOURAGEMENT

Joses, who was also named Barnabas by the apostles (which is translated Son of Encouragement), a Levite of the country of Cyprus, having land, sold it, and brought the money and laid it at the apostles' feet.

ACTS 4:36–37 NKJV

Before naming Saul (Paul), Luke introduces Barnabas. He was the man God used to befriend the future apostle. We call him by his nickname and remember him as Paul's foremost missionary companion.

Barnabas is first named because he sold some land and gave the money to the apostles in order to meet needs within the Christian community. Later, he stood with Paul when he turned into a new man passionate about the life-changing Gospel of Jesus Christ.

People struggled to trust a man who had Christians killed and imprisoned. Barnabas stepped up and walked with Paul to places where God could use them to share His love across the Roman empire.

Maybe you had a champion when you began your journey with Jesus. Maybe you are a champion for others. Maybe both.

God uses human encouragement to help you continue new steps in your spiritual journey. You might be tempted to give up without it. Someone else might take steps forward because you shared it.

Dear God, I wouldn't be where I am today if someone hadn't shared what they knew about You. Show me how I can encourage someone who may be in the same place I was.

ALL GOOD

"You will see neither wind nor rain, says the LORD, but this valley will be filled with water. You will have plenty for yourselves and your cattle and other animals. But this is only a simple thing for the LORD, for he will make you victorious over the army of Moab!"

2 KINGS 3:17–18 NLT

The people of Moab owed Israel a large tribute of sheep and wool. When a new king was named in Israel, Moab decided it didn't need to continue the payment.

Israel's soldiers marched seven days through the desert. They became weakened by thirst. In their hour of need, God promised plenty of water in the valley outside Edom. The next morning God delivered not just water but also a stunning victory to Judah and Israel.

God can take the worst situations and transform them into events that demonstrate His power, serve His purposes, and rescue His people.

You've probably read, "We know that in all things God works for the good of those who love him, who have been called according to his purpose" (Romans 8:28 NIV). The Bible is filled with stories of how God took circumstances, people, and choices, turning them into something that brings praise to the lips of those who witness God's good plan.

Dear God, help me remember You aren't just the God who made things perfect and watched us destroy them. You are the God that can take any circumstance and make it part of Your good story.

WHAT YOU BELIEVE

The LORD is good; his steadfast love endures forever,
and his faithfulness to all generations.

PSALM 100:5 ESV

If what you believe leads to change in your thinking, can it also lead to change in the way you act? Consider this. If you believe that looking out for your own interests is your highest priority, it will change the way you think about other people—because no one will be more important in your thinking than you. When you think you are the most important, then it changes how you act toward others—because their needs will not provide any real motivation for you to help.

If you believe God is good, His love never fails, and He has never once given up the title of *Faithful and True*, then it changes how you think about God. It also changes how you think about yourself. God's commands will have more meaning than your personal ambition. Other people will become more important than your handcrafted bucket list.

Belief always transforms thinking. Thinking always determines actions. Actions always speak the truth about what you believe.

Dear God, I want to believe the right things so my thinking matches
Your truth. May my actions prove that—more than just accepting
an idea to consider—I have invited Your truth to actually change who
I am. May my mind and heart agree that Your goodness, love,
and faithfulness offer the change I've always needed.

THE VIEW FROM HERE

[Naaman] went down and dipped himself in the Jordan seven times,
as the man of God had told him, and his flesh was restored
and became clean like that of a young boy.
2 KINGS 5:14 NIV

The king of Israel received a note from the king of Aram: "I am sending my servant Naaman to you so that you may cure him of his leprosy" (2 Kings 5:6 NIV). What did the king know about healing? Nothing!

Leprosy was a skin disease. Anyone with the disease was considered unclean. The king had an obligation he could not fulfill and an unclean man walking unchallenged in the streets.

The prophet Elisha heard about Naaman and invited him to drop by. Through God's power, Elisha told Naaman how he could be healed: submerge in the Jordan River seven times and the leprosy will vanish. *It did.*

God's grace was offered to someone who was a foreigner. This story is a wide-open window overlooking a level playing field. Jesus came to pay the sin price for all humanity. *His love?* No restrictions. *His forgiveness?* Available to all who confess.

This long-distance view of grace reveals a rescue plan that includes you. Forgiveness comes standard.

Dear God, sometimes I think the Old Testament is irrelevant to me
today. Thanks for healing Naaman so I could see that everyone
on earth has reason to trust Your love and grace.

HELP!

*God, listen! Listen to my prayer, listen to the pain in my cries.
Don't turn your back on me just when I need you so
desperately. Pay attention! This is a cry for help!*
Psalm 102:1–2 msg

L ife bolts from the starting blocks when you finally recognize change is needed. Then again, as long as you're comfortable where you are, there's little interest in looking for, adopting, or initiating change.

Repentance recognizes you've been running the wrong race and insists you turn around and switch tracks.

The psalmist wasn't saying, "Hey God, if You're not too busy, could You give me some advice?" He wasn't even implying that he would try to avoid asking for help by working harder. The psalmist said, "This is a cry for help!" If you want to try to figure things out on your own, God will let you. Expect less than ideal results.

The psalmist sends out a distress call. When God steps in, desperation becomes hope, crying turns to joy, and pain is treated with mercy.

When you don't know what to do, step back and invite God's solution. Transformation is not a *do-it-yourself* project. Accept God's help.

*Dear God, I am guilty of taking control of my own desperate moments.
Somehow I have convinced myself that You appreciate my efforts.
When I insist on doing things my way, though, I fail to include You
in the solution. Because I will need help, remind me to ask.*

THE WAY GOD ANSWERS

He will listen to the prayers of the destitute.
He will not reject their pleas.
PSALM 102:17 NLT

To be destitute means to be penniless, bankrupt, and without support. The psalmist is clear that the prayers of those in need are prayers that God hears. You can be certain God hears all prayers, but the emphasis here is that the prayers of the destitute are important to Him.

If you are becoming a new creation, if God is changing your thinking, and if you are serious about paying attention to the things God is passionate about, then you may be used by God to help transform the circumstances of the bankrupt.

You've read enough in this book to see that God changes people, circumstances, and lives. You're wrong to look at a need and assume someone else will take care of it (James 2:16). Why spend time becoming a new creation if you insist on acting like an old one?

One of the best reasons to help others is that more than once in your life you needed help—and God sent it—often through a willing person.

Dear God, may I never withhold Your love when it's within my power to share it. May I never accept Your grace and refuse to reflect it. May I never receive forgiveness and then refuse to forgive others. May I always be pleased to be Your answer to the prayer of someone in need.

BROUGHT TOGETHER

Many who were paralyzed or lame were healed.
So there was much joy in that city.
ACTS 8:7–8 ESV

Jesus performed many miracles. These stories populate the Gospels of Matthew, Mark, Luke, and John. When Jesus returned to heaven, and God's Spirit came to live among men, the miracles didn't stop.

The apostle Philip took advantage of each *God opportunity*. People were healed, questions answered, and demons fled as Philip moved through the Samaritan crowd.

The people of Samaria were not used to outside help. The people of Israel usually didn't associate with them. Most people in Samaria had Jewish relatives, yet they were shunned because a parent or grandparent wasn't an Israelite.

A story like this is important because of the healing of Samaritans, but also because these *left-out people* were suddenly brought together in Jesus Christ—regardless of name, ancestry, and skin tone.

The rescue plan of God is not a test run, a limited time offer, or available only on a first-come-first-served basis.

Do not withhold God's rescue plan from people God never rejected. It's good news for you and it will be for them.

Dear God, help me be so focused on Your message that I remember it's priceless to all people in all nations. I want to be so overpowered by the completeness of Your rescue plan that I believe there's no one who falls outside Your circle of love.

LEARN AND SHARE

Joash began to rule over Judah in the seventh year of King Jehu's reign in Israel. He reigned in Jerusalem forty years. . . . All his life Joash did what was pleasing in the LORD's sight because Jehoiada the priest instructed him.

2 KINGS 12:1–2 NLT

A disciple is one who wants to learn. The person teaching is one who chooses to pass on what they know. The disciple needs help and the teacher offers help. From a strictly human standpoint, the primary winner in this scenario is the disciple.

Take King Joash for instance. He is remembered as a good king, but the Bible credits the one who helped the young king learn to follow God and obey His commands. Jehoiada the priest made a long-term investment in the king's life.

He wasn't the only one to make such an investment. Moses invested in the life of Joshua. Elijah invested in the life of Elisha. Jesus invested three action-packed years into the lives of His disciples. Barnabas invested in the life of Paul.

Many men will say that when someone helped them in their spiritual journey, it led to significant change. Such relationships can accelerate growth and keep God at the forefront of personal decision-making.

Who has invested in your life? With whom will you invest time, talent, and treasure?

Dear God, I need to remember that You created mankind for relationship. Help me know when to share and when to learn.

COMPASSION

As a father shows compassion to his children,
so the LORD shows compassion to those who fear him.
PSALM 103:13 ESV

Compassion was once considered a personal weakness. It was the enemy of self-sufficiency. It meant mercy, grace, and love were extended to people who needed to learn a lesson. It seemed to offer a free pass to individuals who made yet another wrong choice.

Then you were handed your first child in the hospital, and all you could think about was the love you felt for that child. You went out of your way to demonstrate how much they meant to you. Compassion for your child changed you—and that same compassion will change them.

Love identifies who you are (John 13:35) and how you came to be this way (John 3:16). You respond to love. All humans do. Maybe that's why God makes a big deal about it.

Compassion comes from God. You're never more like God than when you share it. Love means your child will give your message another listen.

God's love instills trust, and somehow feels like the home you've always wanted.

Dear God, let me recognize Your compassion so I can share it with my children. May I take Your compassion and pass it on to those who think this gift is the stuff of fairy tales, fables, and folklore. May Your love transform me so compassion for others becomes as natural as breathing.

WORTHLESS TO WORTHY

*They followed worthless idols and
themselves became worthless.*
2 KINGS 17:15 NIV

When people today look for meaning in anything but God, they follow the same pattern as the kings and people of ancient Israel—a pattern that leads inevitably to a meaningless and degrading existence.

Second Kings 17 shows how people who had seen God's great miracles soon traded relationship with Him for idolatry.

The book of Acts describes how Saul (later Paul) became a follower of Jesus. The scales fell off and he began to see his particular brand of religion for what it was—worship of a system instead of a Savior. As Saul left it behind, he "grew more and more powerful and baffled the Jews living in Damascus by proving that Jesus is the Messiah" (9:22 NIV).

If a religious system, or money or success, or anything else is promising the meaning you long to experience, then heed the lessons of God's Old Testament people and His New Testament apostle.

The psalmist sums up the "worth more" life well when he writes: "But from everlasting to everlasting the LORD's love is with those who fear him, and his righteousness with their children's children—with those who keep his covenant and remember to obey his precepts" (Psalm 103:17–18 NIV).

*Lord, show me the worthlessness of the idols
in my life and tear them down.*

WHEN GOD APPRECIATES MEN

There was no one like him among all the kings of Judah, either before him or after him. He held fast to the LORD and did not stop following him; he kept the commands the LORD had given Moses. And the LORD was with him; he was successful in whatever he undertook.

2 KINGS 18:5–7 NIV

When 2 Kings says "there was no one" like Hezekiah among all the kings of Judah, it does so for a specific reason: "He held fast to the LORD and did not stop following him" (18:6).

When Acts 10 explains how an angel visited a centurion, the writer uses the angel's words to specify the reason: "Your prayers and gifts to the poor have come up as a memorial offering before God" (Acts 10:4 NIV).

When men "hold fast to the LORD" and don't stop following Him, they are rewarded with the appreciation of God the way Hezekiah and Cornelius were.

When you hold fast to the Lord and continue following Him, you experience the appreciation of God as well. Sometimes this shows up in recognition and success. Always it shows up in a deeper relationship with the One "clothed with splendor and majesty" (Psalm 104:1 NIV).

Lord, it amazes me that You, my Creator, would appreciate Your own creation so much. I'm so glad You desire to bless me when I hold fast to and follow You. Help me experience the majesty of Your appreciation!

GOD IN THE DETAILS

" 'I have heard your prayer and seen your tears; I will heal you.' "
2 KINGS 20:5 NIV

How do you know the difference between God's intervention and random chance, between God's providence and mere coincidence? In one form or the other, this is one of the first questions asked by new believers. Some never stop pondering it. So how do you know the difference?

Several times in 2 Kings 19 and 20, the details in God's intervention are so specific, there is no doubt God stepped into both Hezekiah's and Isaiah's lives.

In Acts 10, Peter and Cornelius both experienced the precision of God's involvement in new revelation and in physical healing. The Lord's presence was obviously in the details.

In Psalm 104, God wraps and makes and sets and brings. His involvement in the workings of this world disavows chance. He likes to be asked specific requests and loves to answer them in detail.

When you pray, do you pray with God's precision in mind? Do you ask attaching details? When you do, it's easier to know that the good that comes your way actually comes from Him—not coincidence or chance.

As seen above, God told Hezekiah, "I have heard your prayers and I have seen your tears; I will heal you." He hears your specific prayers and responds to them. You can find Him in the details.

Lord, teach me to pray in detail so that I can find You in them.

THE DEPENDENCE IN INDEPENDENCE DAY

*"You were sorry and humbled yourself before the LORD. . . You tore
your clothing in despair and wept before me in repentance.
And I have indeed heard you, says the LORD."*

2 KINGS 22:19–20 NLT

After battling British forces, the early colonists celebrated the fact
that their *dependence* on one another made *independence* from the
British monarchy possible.

The value of dependence in securing independence also appears in
the histories of the kings of Judah and the Christian church.

After several evil and oppressive kings who had been slaves to foreign
gods, Josiah came to the throne. He read the scriptures, humbled himself,
and wept in God's presence over the condition of his people. His overt
dependence on the writings of Moses and the prophets freed the kingdom
of Judah from personal and national oppression (2 Kings 22).

In Acts 11, the people's dependence on God's revelation to Peter
freed Gentiles from centuries of spiritual exclusion. They praised God,
saying, "So then, even to Gentiles God has granted repentance that leads
to life" (Acts 11:18 NIV).

The psalmist emphasized the importance of dependence on God
when he wrote, "All creatures look to you" (104:27 NIV).

Do you live by a personal declaration of dependence on God?

*Lord, today help me understand that dependence on You
is the only way to secure true and lasting independence.*

MEN WHO MATTERED

Neither before nor after Josiah was there a king like him who turned to the LORD as he did—with all his heart and with all his soul and with all his strength.

2 KINGS 23:25 NIV

After the painful stories of numerous kings who woke up each morning thinking only about how to please themselves, Josiah stepped up to the throne.

His passion for doing the right thing honored God so distinctly that the people around him began to change their morning thoughts from self-love to the love of God and neighbor. He was a man who mattered to the people of God.

Similar commitments stood out in the life of the disciple Barnabas. He was called "a good man, full of the Holy Spirit and faith" (Acts 11:24 NIV). The result of his actions, like Josiah's, changed the commitments of his colleagues and neighbors, so that "a great number of people were brought to the Lord." He was a man who mattered to the church.

Josiah's and Barnabas's commitments to change self-love to love for God and neighbor echoes in a psalm they both probably sang: "I will sing praise to the LORD all my life; I will sing praise to my God as long as I live" (Psalm 104:33 NIV).

Lord, may I wake tomorrow morning determined to love You first and foremost.

BLINDED BY THE LIGHT

Remember the wonders he has done,
his miracles, and the judgments he pronounced.
PSALM 105:5 NIV

God created human beings with dispositions that benefit from remembering His judgments. This is one of the reasons He has the psalmist instruct His people to remember not only the miracles but also "the judgments he pronounced" (Psalm 105:5 NIV). How does remembering these negative events help?

In the Old Testament, human judgments often followed patterns designed to warn an audience. When the king of Babylon punishes Israel, the text says, "They killed the sons of Zedekiah before his eyes. Then they put out his eyes" (2 Kings 25:7 NIV). The king's goal was to have people remember the blinding as a warning. Remembering consequences can improve behavior.

Paul rebuked a sorcerer named Elymas: "Will you never stop perverting the right ways of the Lord? Now the hand of the Lord is against you. You are going to be blind for a time" (Acts 13:10–11 NIV). The temporary blinding led to the proconsul's conversion, because it authenticated the words of the disciples. Remembering results can strengthen faith.

Like human judgments, God's judgments fulfill a purpose. Remembering them improves the human condition—changing personal dispositions, reinforcing trust, and reenergizing commitments.

What judgments of God mentioned in the Bible might help you refocus your sight today?

Lord, help me remember one of Your judgments today
so that my dispositions might better reflect Yours.

DESCENDANTS AND DESTINIES

He remembers his covenant forever,
the promise he made, for a thousand generations.
PSALM 105:8 NIV

Have you ever wondered about the value of studying the genealogies in the Bible? If so, today's readings provide meaningful answers.

In Psalm 105, the poet uses the lineage of Abraham, Isaac, and Jacob to rehearse how God keeps His promises and to remind His children that they have not been forgotten. The detail in the list of names encouraged the original recipients of the psalm and, by extension, later readers like you who can take comfort from their encouragement.

First Chronicles also uses genealogy to show God's promise-keeping character, but in addition it shows His interest in individuals, not just nations. The detailed way God kept His promises and showed His compassion to the individuals and families in the Old Testament is the same way He will keep His promises and show His compassion to you and yours.

Paul's sermon in Acts 13 traces the lineage of Jesus from Israel's ancestors through their stay in Egypt, their inheritance of the promised land, and their transition from having judges to kings (Acts 13:14–34). Paul's historical development reminds readers that God's promise of a Messiah was fulfilled in detail—detail that continues to impact every man's destiny.

Will you look for God in the details of your routines today?

Lord, thank You for the way Your attention to detail reminds
me of Your ultimate control and compassion.

THE HONORABLE YOU

*There was a man named Jabez who was more
honorable than any of his brothers.*

1 CHRONICLES 4:9 NLT

The genealogies say little about the individuals listed, but 1 Chronicles singles out a man named Jabez because he was honorable.

What makes a man worthy of the kind of notation that Jabez received?

Sometimes it is easier to answer this question by reading through the Bible's history books and looking at those who lacked honor. For instance, today's reading in 1 Chronicles singles Reuben out because he gave in to sexual indulgence (5:1).

Acts records that many Jewish leaders were jealous of the disciples and slandered Paul as he attempted to explain Jesus (13:45). Later, the writer adds that as Paul and Barnabas ministered healing in Iconium, some of the Jews intentionally poisoned the minds of the crowds (14:2).

Self-indulgence, jealousy, and septic speech dishonor a man, while self-control, promoting another's success, and nurturing words honor him.

What do people write in their mental histories about you at work, at home, and at your church?

Psalm 105 reveals how the Lord tested Joseph's character while he was unaware (105:19). This is how God tests—in the secret and hidden hours.

Will you be honored for your self-control, your constant promotion of another man's success, and the healing in your words?

*Lord, help me work harder at controlling myself, at celebrating
another man's success, and at supporting others with my words.*

TRUSTING MERE MORTALS

[God] answered their prayer, because they trusted in him.
1 CHRONICLES 5:20 NLT

What is it like to be called a god? Paul and Barnabas knew. After they performed a miracle at Lystra, the crowds began to worship them, saying they were Zeus and Hermes in human form. Stunned, Paul and Barnabas tore their clothes and reminded the worshippers, "We are merely human beings—just like you!" (Acts 14:15 NLT). Did they react this passionately because they knew personal disaster comes to those who place their trust in humanity?

To help the audience understand the importance of trusting God over human beings, Paul adds, "In the past he [God] permitted all the nations to go their own ways, but he never left them without evidence of himself and his goodness" (14:16–17 NLT). Even today it is easier for people to "go their own ways," to trust humans, rather than the One they cannot see.

Even in the most anxiety-producing moments, you can show your trust in God by calling out to Him—like the struggling armies of Israel (1 Chronicles 5:20).

Psalm 105 includes a retelling of the effort God extended in Egypt to remind His people that a meaning-filled life comes through trusting Him over humans.

What about you? Will you trust God's wisdom over the insights of men?

Lord, show me how to find my life's deepest meaning through trusting Your Word instead of the human insights I hear every day.

YOUR MISSION

He brought out his people with rejoicing,
his chosen ones with shouts of joy.
PSALM 105:43 NIV

How dull the movies would be if every agent had the same mission—and how predictable the outcomes! There is something inspiring in a variety of nearly impossible tasks.

The same is true for the mission given to each individual in real life. No two assignments are identical. Your assignment, should you choose to accept it, is vital.

The Bible presents multiple examples of this. First Chronicles says some were "in charge of the house of God" (9:11 NIV). Others were "responsible for ministering in the house of God" (9:13 NIV). Each family accepted their mission, and some fulfilled their mission over multiple generations.

In the book of Acts, Paul and Barnabas were appointed (15:2) to go talk with the other apostles about whether new believers needed to follow Old Testament requirements. They accepted their mission.

What's more, the psalmist says that at the end of the mission to leave Egypt, the Lord "brought out his people with rejoicing, his chosen ones with shouts of joy" (Psalm 105:43 NIV).

The result of accepting a mission and carrying it out is the happiness and fulfillment that only God can give. After all, those who accept a mission learn almost immediately that only God makes the mission possible.

Lord, please take the ordinary routines of my every day
and use them to do the impossible in me and through me!

BECAUSE OF WHO HE IS

Yet he saved them for his name's sake,
to make his mighty power known.
PSALM 106:8 NIV

God reverses human mistakes. It's part of who He is.

Have you ever found yourself struggling with the results of your sin or someone else's, despairing of any hope of a meaningful future? If so, you're not alone.

The children of Israel felt this way when they labored as slaves in Egypt. They struggled every day as a result of their sin in making other things priorities over against spending time with God (Psalm 106:6). But, because of His character (His "name"), God reversed the situation and gave them the promised land. He can do the same for you.

When Paul and Barnabas strongly disagreed about their ministry and ended their friendship (Acts 15), God, because of who He is, reversed the situation and brought them together again (1 Corinthians 9). He restores relationships because of His name.

When King Saul died because he "did not inquire of the LORD," God "turned the kingdom over to David" (1 Chronicles 10:14 NIV) and reversed the situation for the nation of Israel.

Because of who He is, and because His love for you is everlasting, God can fix your failures.

Lord, help me learn to say with the psalm writer, "Praise the LORD. Give thanks to the LORD, for he is good; his love endures forever" (106:1).

UNDERSTANDING THE TIMES

*[They were] men who understood the times
and knew what Israel should do.*
1 Chronicles 12:32 niv

Some men fit into their cultures and mechanically follow their routines, while others learn to understand the times in which they live.

Among the thousands of fighting men who followed the Lord and David, a few "understood the times." These men from Issachar were singled out because they saw their work as anything but routine.

Understanding the times led Paul and his companions to find a place of prayer where they were able to share the Gospel with listeners who were potentially more receptive. They knew the wisdom of sharing Jesus with people who were already meeting to pray (Acts 16:13).

Both groups of men, the men from Issachar and Paul and his companions, studied the best course to take. They redeemed their routines. They thought outside the popular ideas boxed in the sound bites and mediated meanings of their cultures.

Do you understand the times? Or do the times define you just as they defined those in Israel who forgot God? (Psalm 106:13, 21). Reading the scripture passages tied to each day's devotional makes all the difference.

*Lord, help me be less influenced by my culture and
more like the men who understand the times.*

WHAT SAY YOU?

They rebelled against the Spirit of God,
and rash words came from Moses' lips.

PSALM 106:33 NIV

What do you say when friends don't respond the way you think they should?

As noted above, "rash words came from Moses' lips" when God's chosen people wouldn't stop complaining.

What do you say when God doesn't respond the way you think He should?

David became angry when he thought God responded inappropriately. David had caused the death of a friend by not moving the ark of the Lord in the prescribed way, but he blamed God for His supposedly unfair response (1 Chronicles 13:11;15:13). Later, after David made things right, God's astonishingly patient love allowed David to lead the celebration that welcomed the ark home.

By contrast, after being imprisoned for telling people about Jesus, Paul and Silas sang God's praises. They accepted the fact that the Lord alone sees how His seemingly inappropriate actions fit into the bigger picture. Their astonishingly patient love led to the jailer and his entire family becoming believers.

Like Moses, David, Paul, and Silas, you may endure difficult relationships, unfair treatment, social persecution, abuse at work, and even prison and torture (Acts 16:22). None of these experiences will seem appropriate or God-planned.

Will you wait for the inevitable miracle? If so, what will you say?

Lord, help me believe so deeply in Your character that what
I say in response to Your actions worships You!

THE BIG AND LITTLE

*Then he gave a loaf of bread, a cake of dates and a cake
of raisins to each Israelite man and woman.*
1 Chronicles 16:3 niv

Some people notice the little things. Their days are full of blessing people and God—by doing small things that matter.

After returning the ark of the covenant, David gave gifts. First "a loaf of bread" to meet daily needs. Then "a cake of dates and a cake of raisins" so even the poor could celebrate with festive foods. Some people think about the little things that make a big difference.

Later, David said to Nathan the prophet, "Here I am, living in a house of cedar, while the ark of the covenant of the Lord is under a tent" (17:1 niv). He realized he had done more for himself than he had done for God. Some people notice the bigger things.

In a city called Berea, a group of Jews spent every day examining the scriptures to "see if what Paul said was true." They are singled out as possessing "more noble character" (Acts 17:11 niv).

Character is what a gracious God offers to those without it. This includes those who have "wasted away in their sin" (Psalm 106:43 niv). His character supplied their daily needs (air, sunshine, rain, food, and clothes) and sent His only Son to die for their sins.

Character shows in the little and big.

Lord, help me meet a need for someone today.

REPURPOSING

Save us, LORD our God, and gather us from the nations, that we may give thanks to your holy name and glory in your praise.

PSALM 106:47 NIV

When Paul talked with philosophers in Athens, he pointed out the irony in their thinking about idols: "Since we are God's offspring, we should not think that the divine being is like gold or silver or stone—an image made by human design and skill" (Acts 17:29 NIV).

Paul knew that humans tend to recreate God in their image, so he repurposed their idols to better connect the good news with that particular city's cultural bent.

When King David captured articles of gold and silver fashioned into idols, he repurposed them. He dedicated them "to the LORD, as he had done with the silver and gold" he had received from "all these nations" (1 Chronicles 18:11 NIV).

Like the psalmist, the kings of Israel, and the apostles, Jesus' followers dedicate whatever this world might offer them—wealth, success, notoriety—to the purposes of God.

Are there things in your life that take priority alongside your fellowship with the Father and other believers? If so, you can dedicate most of those things to God and repurpose them so they become ways of sharing Jesus Christ with your culture.

Lord, help me repurpose the idols the world tempts me with so that I can use all things for Your purposes.

NO SALE PRICES HERE

But King David replied to Araunah, "No, I insist on paying the full price.
I will not. . .sacrifice a burnt offering that costs me nothing."
1 CHRONICLES 21:24 NIV

Human cultures tend to champion frugality as a costume for selfishness. Few people are willing to pay the price that repentance exacts.

When David's disobedience hurt the people around him, he attempted to purchase a threshing floor to sacrifice a burnt offering. When the owner offered it freely, David surprised him by saying he would not offer a sacrifice that cost him nothing. David knew the harm he had brought on others exacted a heavy price.

When you have wronged someone, do you try to get by with sacrificing as little time as necessary? With saving as much money in the transaction as possible? Or, like David, do you recognize the deeply personal nature of your offense and pay the full price?

Serving each other requires sacrifices of time, effort, and money. When Paul served in Corinth, he made tents with Aquila and Priscilla, even though he could have required the Corinthians to pay his way. His was not a cheap faith (Acts 18:2–3).

Sacrifice was personal for David and Paul—and for Jesus.

Lord, help me remember that Your sacrifice is my inspiration.

WITH HIM

Let them give thanks to the LORD for his unfailing
love and his wonderful deeds for mankind.
PSALM 107:15 NIV

H ave you ever felt the job you're doing doesn't matter?

Here are some of the jobs assigned in Old Testament times: "Twenty-four thousand are to be in charge of the work of the temple... Four thousand are to be gatekeepers." At times even the military commanders had to stop leading their troops to help choose workers "for the ministry of prophesying, accompanied by harps, lyres and cymbals" (1 Chronicles 23:4–5 and 25:1). Although these routines certainly had moments of meaning, there had to have been days when repairing building damage, scrubbing bowls, listening to complaining employees, and practicing musical instruments seemed patronizing and pointless.

In New Testament times, some invited popular leaders like Paul and Apollos to their homes (Acts 18:26), while others spent long months accompanying Paul to discussions in the lecture hall of Tyrannus (19:9–10). How did these individuals make such moments meaningful?

Perhaps they spent the unrewarded and unrecognized hours remembering the One who brought them out of darkness. Maybe they learned to spend less time comparing and more time giving "thanks to the LORD for his unfailing love and his wonderful deeds for mankind" (Psalm 107:15).

Happiness comes in knowing you are working *with Him.*

Lord, help me thank You for Your love and work so that I can see
my routines as an important part of Your redemptive plan.

THE MARVELOUS UNIVERSE

[They were] capable men.
1 CHRONICLES 26:7 NLT

The popular Marvel Universe dims before yours.

The Bible records numerous stories of the *marvelous* works God did in and through the "capable men" described in 1 Chronicles 26:7, 9, and 30–32. Unlike fictional Marvel heroes, these real men made a lasting difference through the power of God at work in them.

The apostles were similar men. Luke tells us, "God gave Paul the power to perform unusual [*marvelous*] miracles" (Acts 19:11 NLT). Thankfully, the power of God shows up today in many additional miracles such as witnessing, counseling, mentoring, business transactions, and parenting. In other words, the same marvelous power now works in and through you.

Then again, power can create problems too.

For example, as Paul's fame spread, others tried to mimic his power. In one instance, a demon interrupted their attempts, saying, "I know Jesus, and I know Paul, but who are you?" (Acts 19:15 NLT). That's a scary conversation!

Pride will always diminish the marvel in what God is doing in you and through you.

You can combat this, and enjoy the power of God, by giving thanks each day for "his wonderful [marvelous] deeds for mankind" (Psalm 107:21 NIV).

*Lord, help me evaluate my pride so that I can marvel
at the universe in which You've placed me.*

ALWAYS ON HIS MIND

*"The LORD searches every heart and understands every desire
and every thought. If you seek him, he will be found by you."*
1 CHRONICLES 28:9 NIV

What kind of driver are you? The reality is, no one wants to sit idling behind distracted drivers whose phone conversations and text messages cause them to miss green lights. Once they start moving, their distracted driving can be dangerous.

That's true for your faith too.

First Chronicles makes it clear God searches every thought and motive of every man. Only Jesus' perfect thoughts and motives, given at the cross to humanity, provide true fellowship with God. Only when believers examine their thoughts and motives impartially can they reroute distractions and avoid the crashes that shadow unengaged minds.

Unengaged minds create thoughtless reactions to current events, political topics, social movements, and ministries. Luke says that a riot rocked a major city and the masses gathered, yet "most of the people did not even know why they were there" (Acts 19:32 NIV).

It's tempting to follow downhill ruts in a thoughtless, aftermarket approach to life. Then again, the repair costs can be demoralizing.

A focused mind helps you grow closer to the One who loved you first, and who turns "the desert into pools of water and the parched ground into flowing springs" (Psalm 107:35 NIV). *That* road trip is worth all the mental effort it requires.

*Lord, help me engage my mind so my thoughts
and motives will intentionally honor You.*

IT'S ALL IN THE ASK

God said to Solomon, "Because your greatest desire is to
help your people, and you did not ask for wealth, riches,
fame. . . . I will also give you wealth, riches, and fame."

2 CHRONICLES 1:11–12 NLT

What you ask for often determines what you live for.

King Solomon asked God for wisdom and knowledge so he could do the work God had given him.

Similarly, Acts 20 records Paul's wise ask. Even though he knew jail and suffering were ahead, Paul asked the church leaders in Ephesus to take care of God's people in their city. That was far more important to Paul than any possible monetary gift.

Solomon and Paul wouldn't fit well in the contemporary workplace or fashionable church. Their requests were not for the wealth, riches, and fame so popular then and now. Instead, they asked for things that would make their work for God prosper.

Do you find yourself asking God for help loving your coworkers, reaching out to your neighbors, and assisting widows, orphans, or latchkey kids?

The psalmist wrote, "Those who are wise will take all this to heart; they will see in our history the faithful love of the LORD" (Psalm 107:43 NLT).

Do you see the Lord's faithful love working in you and through you?

So much of the meaning in life, after all, is in the ask.

Lord, help me ask for the things that matter most.

CENTER STAGE

All the priests who were present had purified themselves,
whether or not they were on duty that day.
2 CHRONICLES 5:11 NLT

Christians from media-saturated cultures find pretense easy. It's part of the social fabric.

It's why polite people smile and reply, "Fine," when asked how their day has been.

But pretense can create bipolar believers—men who are unaware they have become actors on a Christian stage. Scott Wesley Brown wrote a song about this titled "Pray for Me." In it, he admits it's "often easy to wear the servant's mask" while actively resisting doing what servants do best. This happens when Christians smile center stage yet don't prepare for life in the slow lane.

The scripture quoted above says the priests purified themselves so they would be ready to serve God any day of the week.

Paul said, "I have done the Lord's work humbly and with many tears" (Acts 20:18–19 NLT). Like the temple priests, his wasn't an "on" and "off" workweek. Whether he was manufacturing tents or preaching and teaching, he started each day ready.

Similarly, David sang, "I will wake the dawn with my song" (Psalm 108:2 NLT). He too started each day prepared to serve God wholeheartedly. Continuing to read a devotional book like this can help you do the same.

Lord, help me prepare to serve You, whether I'm onstage or off today.

THE BIG IF

*" 'If your descendants guard their behavior and faithfully follow my Law
as you have done, one of them will always sit on the throne of Israel.' "*

2 CHRONICLES 6:16 NLT

Eight times in today's first Bible reading you will come across the word *if.*
God says it in the verse quoted above. Then Solomon prays the
other seven "ifs" as requests.

"If" populates the scriptures. Yes, even the most godly man faces
positive and negative consequences for his actions.

Paul thought and prayed about the consequences of remaining faithful
to the Lord. He told to those who pressed him to steer a different course:
"You are breaking my heart! I am ready not only to be jailed at Jerusalem
but even to die for the sake of the Lord Jesus" (Acts 21:13 NLT).

David thought about such things as well. He wrote concerning his
enemies, "I love them, but they try to destroy me with accusations even
as I am praying for them!" (Psalm 109:4 NLT).

What *if* David had chosen to stop loving and praying for his enemies?

What *if* Paul had chosen to agree with those who wanted him to stop
moving ahead?

What *if* Solomon had chosen to use the new temple to promote his
own agenda?

Life is an accumulation of all the results of how you handle life's "ifs."

*Lord, I promise to guard my behaviors today
so that I can experience Your good in each "if."*

THE DIVINE ASSIST

But you, Sovereign LORD, help me for your name's sake;
out of the goodness of your love, deliver me.
PSALM 109:21 NIV

Some of the most watched sports videos are clips of basketball and soccer assists.

There is something inspiring in watching skilled athletes unselfishly set up others in order to achieve their team's goal. This is all the more true in the mysterious workings of the Holy Spirit, although His assists are more difficult to film and observe. For the uninitiated, it's easy to miss the Spirit's MVP moments.

Scripture records many assists in vivid detail.

The wisdom assist given to Solomon when the queen of Sheba came to test him with the most pressing unanswered questions of her day. "And Solomon answered all her questions. There was nothing hidden from Solomon that he could not explain to her" (2 Chronicles 9:2 ESV).

The divinely choreographed governmental protection that assisted Paul when the crowds in Jerusalem tried to kill him (Acts 21:15–32).

The history-based cry of the psalmist when he prayed, "But you, Sovereign LORD, help me for your name's sake" (Psalm 109:21 NIV).

Watching a divine assist is more compelling than a dozen of the best sports clips—and much more faith-promoting. Learning to see His assists keeps life fascinating!

Lord, help me spend more time today
replaying Your assists in my life.

WHO DO YOU HEAR?

*But he abandoned the counsel that the old men gave him,
and took counsel with the young men who had grown
up with him and stood before him.*

2 CHRONICLES 10:8 ESV

E very man chooses whom he listens to.

King Rehoboam asked for counsel from the old men who served his father, but then chose to follow the counsel of "the young men who had grown up with him." Within days, this mistake cost him most of his kingdom. It also cost him a great deal of respect and admiration.

Paul followed the counsel of Ananias, "a devout man according to the law, well spoken of by all the Jews" (Acts 22:12 ESV). As a result, he became a significant change agent in the history of the church and lived a life full of travel, danger, miracles, and intrigue.

David begins Psalm 110 with the words, "The LORD says." When David listened to God, he became a man "after his [God's] own heart" (1 Samuel 13:14 NIV). When he didn't, he ruined the lives of the people he was supposed to serve.

The decisions of Rehoboam, Paul, and David remind readers that it's usually best to follow the advice of older "well spoken of" men. Ultimately, though, your best advice comes from what "the LORD says."

*Lord, help me carefully examine the best human
advice and always follow Yours.*

SLAPPED IN THE FACE?

The high priest. . .ordered those standing near
Paul to strike him on the mouth.

ACTS 23:2 NIV

No one likes to be treated unfairly.

Whether you've been falsely accused at work, misjudged by neighbors, or wrongly criticized at church, you do not walk that road alone.

King Asa traveled there. When the Spirit of God came on Azariah son of Oded, he went out to meet Asa and said, " 'The LORD is with you when you are with him. If you seek him, he will be found by you. . . . Be strong and do not give up, for your work will be rewarded' " (2 Chronicles 15:2, 7 NIV). Asa faced criticism from those who wanted to continue in their sin, but God honored him.

Paul walked that path. At trial, he was falsely accused and then struck by angry hands (Acts 23:1–2). Although Paul had to confess the error in his initial response, he allowed God to use the situation and God honored him for it (Acts 23:3–11). Whether you are wronged at work, in your community, or in your church, remember God alone will judge the nations (Psalm 110:6). The same God who watched over Asa and Paul watches over you.

Lord, strengthen me in difficult times. Help me always
remember that You honor those who honor You.

SCHEMING

"For the eyes of the LORD range throughout the earth to strengthen those whose hearts are fully committed to him."

2 CHRONICLES 16:9 NIV

Even good people change.

A king who usually depended on the Lord, Asa later used his own clever schemes to undermine the work of an adversary. Although his plan appeared to work, the prophet Hanani confronted Asa about his failure to depend on God. Instead of agreeing with Hanani and apologizing, Asa became so enraged "that he put him in prison" and "brutally oppressed some of the people." Later, when afflicted with a disease in his feet, Asa "did not seek help from the LORD, but only from the physicians" (2 Chronicles 16:10, 12 NIV).

What caused the drastic changes?

Maybe it wasn't a midlife crisis, low blood sugar, or a deficit from his childhood. Maybe all that changed was that he became more *committed* to human resources than to God.

Could this happen to you?

Paul also used clever schemes to bend the will of his adversaries. The difference is that God encouraged most of those attempts and, whenever Paul erred in judgment, he apologized (Acts 23:5).

The "fully committed" man goes to God for help first, because God's plans are trustworthy and "established for ever and ever" (Psalm 111:7–8 NIV).

Lord, help me to ask You for advice and then to follow Your lead rather than my own resources.

TAKE COURAGE

"Take courage as you fulfill your duties, and may
the LORD be with those who do what is right."
2 CHRONICLES 19:11 NLT

A ll work that involves people requires courage.

Jehoshaphat's work involved hundreds of thousands of people—and it took courage every day. So, when he blessed the workers in Judah, his blessing included the appeal to "take courage." He knew that the recent jobs he had assigned required assessing motives and handing out decisions. He also knew courage's bravery and resolve were necessary for completing these tasks (2 Chronicles 18–19).

Paul's actions also required courage. When he waited two years in jail for the authorities to finish trying his case (Acts 24:27), he had the courage to think through the wisest approach he could take to make things right. Bravery and resolve led him to employ a specific Roman law in his defense. He eventually appealed to Caesar (Acts 24:1–25:12).

The psalmist's lyrics inspire courage when he writes, "Even in darkness light dawns for the upright, for those who are gracious and compassionate and righteous" (Psalm 112:4 NIV).

Like Jehoshaphat, will you pray for courage for yourself and others? Like Paul, will you muster the courage needed to face the darkness?

Lord, give me the courage to walk out of the darkness
and into the light that "dawns for the upright."

APPRECIATION BECOMES YOU

From the rising of the sun to the place where it sets,
the name of the LORD is to be praised.

PSALM 113:3 NIV

Sometimes you become the good you appreciate in someone else.

This is especially true in praising God. When you appreciate His goodness, when it invades your mind and exits your body in praise, something supernatural happens. The more time you spend praising God deep within your soul, the more attached you become to Him.

When Jehoshaphat faced the terror of approaching armies, he "appointed men to sing to the LORD and to praise him for the splendor of his holiness as they went out at the head of the army" (2 Chronicles 20:21). When they reached the battlefield, their enemies were already dead. So, "all the men of Judah and Jerusalem returned joyfully. . . They entered Jerusalem and went to the temple of the LORD with harps and lyres and trumpets" (20:27–28 NIV).

Unlike his heir who never praised God and who "passed away to no one's regret" (21:20 NIV), Jehoshaphat appreciated God and was praised.

Paul praised God from prison and ended up sharing Jesus with the Roman emperor (Acts 25:27).

Appreciating God changes you so much that others eventually can't help but notice.

Lord, help me remember that no matter where
I am today, Your name is to be praised.

COACHES

They became his advisers, to his undoing.

2 CHRONICLES 22:4 NIV

In every sport, coaches make a difference.

Poor coaches focus on their fame or fortune. Good coaches focus on helping their players and team improve.

Smart players play for good coaches.

Have you assessed the "coaches" in your life recently?

When Ahaziah inherited the throne at age twenty-two, he didn't dismiss the coaches his unsuccessful dad assembled around him. Instead, those same individuals "became his advisers, to his undoing." He reigned for only a year because he followed their miserable advice.

During a court proceeding in Acts, Paul told King Agrippa how he had spent years following bad advice: "On the *authority of the chief priests* I put many of the Lord's people in prison, and when they were put to death, I cast my vote against them" (Acts 26:10 NIV). It wasn't until Jesus intervened that Paul began to evaluate what he and the people around him were actually saying and doing.

What about the people around you? Are they the kinds of coaches who put your improvement first? Or are they more concerned about their reputations and the results of their leadership?

Thank them if they're working to secure your best future. Then again, examine their advice carefully if they are not.

Lord, thank You for letting me play on Your team. Please help me find Your wisdom in the coaches I spend time with today.

MISTAKES

"The LORD can give you much more than that."
2 CHRONICLES 25:9 NIV

Have you ever made a poor decision and then found your pride made it difficult to back out?

Maybe you purchased a car you couldn't afford or approved a bad business decision. Instead of losing your shirt on the car or losing face over your decision, did you try to make it work?

Amaziah spent a lot of money on a poor decision. When a messenger from God confronted him, he replied, "But what about the hundred talents I paid?" (2 Chronicles 25:9 NIV). Can you hear his thoughts? *Surely God doesn't want me to waste the money I already spent or appear unqualified in front of my people?* The messenger's response refocused Amaziah's pride: "The LORD can give you much more."

In other words, there's no reason to worry about how a mistake will be perceived if you believe in God. After all, He honors those who own their mistakes and who do the right thing whatever the personal cost.

The book of Acts records how, as Paul owned his mistakes, rulers respected him. Prior to traveling as a prisoner to Rome, his captor, "in kindness to Paul, allowed him to go to his friends" (Acts 27:3 NIV). That's not how captors treated prisoners in the ancient world, but it is how they treated the apostle who trusted the God who gives "more."

Lord, help me be more comfortable with owning
my mistakes so that I can watch You be You.

POWER PROBLEMS

As long as he sought the LORD, God gave him success.
2 CHRONICLES 26:5 NIV

Have you watched people struggle with power?

Promotions sometimes weaken friendships because people struggle with how to respond to authority and the power attached to it.

At sixteen years of age, King Uzziah did well with power. He sought the Lord and listened to the prophet Zechariah. As a result, he was one of the few good kings in Jerusalem. But, as is often the case, "after Uzziah became powerful, his pride led to his downfall" (26:16 NIV). It was like power and pride flipped a switch and one day Uzziah strutted into the temple thinking he could do whatever he pleased (26:19).

Power tempts all people, but only some are able to resist its dangers.

When Paul didn't die after being bitten by a poisonous snake, the people said he was a god (Acts 28:6). Yet afterward Paul didn't act like a god. He chose to stay a prisoner in order to talk to more people about Jesus, and he continued to serve the churches. Paul handled power well because he sought God first and foremost.

Both Uzziah and Paul knew the positive power perspectives in the lyrics of the psalmist. Uzziah forgot them, but Paul never did. "He will bless those who fear the LORD—small and great alike" (Psalm 115:13 NIV).

Lord, help me carefully examine how I handle
power and authority today.

REMOVE THE FILTH

"Hear me, Levites! Now consecrate yourselves, and consecrate the house of the LORD, the God of your fathers, and carry out the filth from the Holy Place."

2 CHRONICLES 29:5 ESV

After a sixteen-year-reign by his father, Hezekiah radically changed the direction of Judah. Ahaz was exceedingly wicked, including burning some of his sons as offerings to his horrific false gods (2 Chronicles 28:2–3). In his very first month as king, Hezekiah cleansed the Lord's temple (2 Chronicles 29:3–19) and restored biblical worship there (29:20–36).

It's never too late to change direction. In his first few weeks as king, Hezekiah acted decisively on the Lord's behalf and everything changed for many years. You can enact that same type of change in your own family, no matter your upbringing.

Think about your spiritual lineage. Did your grandfather or father walk in spiritual darkness, making decisions that displeased the Lord?

Become a Hezekiah in your family.

Consecrate yourself and your household, remove any filth, and enter into a time of rejoicing because of the Lord's subsequent provisions—much as Hezekiah and the people experienced in 2 Chronicles 29:36.

Lord, give me the faith and the courage to act on Your behalf. Where my family has gathered filth, and maybe even cherished it, I will remove it and restore true worship and praise to You, for Your glory, honor, and praise.

THE LAND OF THE LIVING

For you have delivered my soul from death, my eyes from tears, my feet from stumbling; I will walk before the LORD in the land of the living.
PSALM 116:8–9 ESV

As the presumed author of Psalm 116, David may have been thinking about his many trials, including Saul's attempts on his life, or perhaps his own son rebelling against him. In any case, David eventually experienced deliverance and comfort from the Lord, and that led to him walking before the Lord "in the land of the living."

That little phrase is important.

Bible commentator Matthew Henry points out that the land of the living is "is a land of mercy, which we ought to be thankful for; it is a land of opportunity, which we should improve." He goes on to note that the promised land is called the "land of the living" in Ezekiel 26:20; it's a place where the Lord promised to set beauty.

You've been delivered from sin and death. You may have even been delivered from your enemies. So what does walking in the land of the living look like for you? Are you walking in freedom or stuck in bondage? Is the other side of your transformation beautiful, or is it messy and ugly?

You've been transformed by the Gospel. Walk in the newness of life.

Lord, I haven't always chosen to walk in Your mercy and grace, but I want to change that. Empower me to make a better choice today.

A SLIPPERY SLOPE

*God gave them over to a base and condemned mind to do things
not proper or decent but loathsome, until they were filled
(permeated and saturated) with every kind of unrighteousness.*

ROMANS 1:28–29 AMPC

God made Himself known to humankind. Because they didn't honor and glorify Him, or even give Him thanks (Romans 1:21), He gave them over to their baser desires. Romans contains a long list of such sins, including unnatural sexual relations, greed, malice, envy, jealousy, strife, deceit, gossip, and treachery (1:26–29).

This is what the life of the unregenerate person looks like. But if you aren't careful, your life can look like this too, since sin is a slippery slope. One glance can lead to flirting. A seemingly harmless conversation over lunch with a colleague can lead to gossip or spread strife. You are called to a different life—one that offers life and truth.

Run back through that list of sins this morning and determine which sins you are guilty of. Confess your guilt to God. The next time you catch yourself leaning in the direction of one of those sins, call on the Lord for the Holy Spirit to enable you to resist.

*Lord, I see myself in several of the sins listed in Romans 1.
I repent, knowing they do not honor or glorify You.
Empower me from on high to live a life that
truly reflects Your character.*

A DIFFERENT MAN

*Now when [Manasseh] was in affliction, he implored the LORD his God,
and humbled himself greatly before the God of his fathers, and prayed
to Him; and He received his entreaty, heard his supplication,
and brought him back to Jerusalem into his kingdom.*

2 CHRONICLES 33:12–13 NKJV

King Manasseh rebuilt the high places Hezekiah had broken down.
What's more, he raised up altars for the Baals, made various horrible
idols, practiced witchcraft, and more. But everything changed when
he was hauled into Assyrian captivity. There he cried out to the Lord
for forgiveness. The Lord heard him and did something completely
unexpected—He reestablished Manasseh's kingdom.

Manasseh was a different man when he returned to Jerusalem. He
removed the idols, repaired the altar, and reinstituted sacrificial peace
offerings. His response to forgiveness was amazing. He began to walk
with the Lord and his behavior completely changed.

Your past probably doesn't include witchcraft or idolatry, but you
can easily recall behavior that was displeasing to the Lord. How has your
life looked different since the Lord heard your initial cry for forgiveness?
What have you removed from your life?

If the Spirit has prompted reminders of current behaviors that need
to be changed, repent and walk with the Lord anew.

*Lord, whenever I see such a clear difference in a person in the
scripture, it reminds me that I'm not always as quick to show
evidence of the transformed life. Forgive me, Lord.*

RENEWED PASSION

*Open to me the gates of righteousness, that I may enter
through them and give thanks to the LORD.*
PSALM 118:19 ESV

Part of today's Bible reading comes from 2 Chronicles 34, which goes into detail about Hilkiah, the priest, who found the lost Book of the Law. He passed it along to the king's secretary, who read it to the king, which caused much grief. King Josiah tore his clothes over the realization at how far his country had strayed from God. Grief then led to great reforms.

In Psalm 118:18, the psalmist said he had been disciplined severely by the Lord. Like Josiah, he took action immediately after encountering the Lord's rebuke. The change was so complete that the psalmist couldn't wait to enter the temple and thank the Lord.

Does either of these scenarios resemble your immediate response after the Lord has spoken to you? Do you long to worship Him, recognizing that His mercy is greater than your sin? If not, then your view of God's mercy is too small. Jesus paid it all for your sins so you could be free to worship and obey the Lord, free from guilt and shame.

If sin is currently weighing you down, repent and worship the God who loves you intimately.

*Lord, make me a Josiah in my family and in my workplace.
Give me a renewed passion for Your Word and for
worship. And may it lead to great reforms.*

COUNTED AS RIGHTEOUS

[Abraham] staggered not at the promise of God through unbelief;
but was strong in faith, giving glory to God; And being fully persuaded
that, what he had promised, he was able also to perform.

ROMANS 4:20–21 KJV

A braham fully believed that God would make his name great, and that all the families of the earth would be blessed through him, just as God promised in Genesis 12:1–3. As a result, it was "counted unto him for righteousness" (Romans 4:3 KJV). But, the scripture says those words were not written for his sake alone, but that you too would be counted as righteous when you believe in the God who raised Jesus from the dead.

What does that mean for you today?

Consider the object of your faith. Are you placing your faith in your ability to keep the law? In your acts of obedience? In your church attendance or Bible reading? Or is it in the God who raised Jesus from the dead? His promise to you is eternal life.

Do not stagger at God's promise through unbelief in the wrong thing. He is faithful, even though you are not.

Father, You are a covenant-keeping God, faithful to the end.
Conversely, I am a sinner who often strays from my promises to
You. But I never want to stray from my faith in Your gift of eternal life.

GLORYING IN TRIBULATION

And not only that, but we also glory in tribulations,
knowing that tribulation produces perseverance;
and perseverance, character; and character, hope.
ROMANS 5:3–4 NKJV

The man who has been justified by faith has peace with God through the Lord Jesus Christ (Romans 5:1). Not only does he glory in the hope found in Christ, but also in tribulation. That sets him far apart from the person who hasn't been justified by faith and is devastated when tribulation comes.

Consider your last tribulation. Maybe it was an illness, or a job loss, or an injury. Maybe it was something more severe, like losing your home or a family member. After undergoing a period of mourning your loss, whatever it was, how did you respond? Did you see the spiritual benefit in it?

Not that God wants you to find happiness as a result of your loss, but He does want your loss to transform and shape your character. And ultimately, He wants to give you eternal hope through temporal pain. Lean on Jesus Christ and show the world what the power of the Gospel looks like.

Trust Him to use your deepest heartache for the advancement of His kingdom in you.

Lord, like everyone else, I have experienced tribulation. And I haven't always done so gracefully. Give me a kingdom perspective so I can be more like Christ, radiating eternal hope to those around me.

HOW GOES THE BATTLE?

Wherewithal shall a young man cleanse his way?
by taking heed thereto according to thy word.
Psalm 119:9 kjv

The author of Psalm 119 is unknown, but whoever wrote it knew something about how difficult it is to stay clean in an impure world. In Charles Spurgeon's commentary, he describes young men as being "full of hot passions." Note that "passions" is plural. And John Wesley seems to agree that the call for the Christian here is to "purge himself from all filthiness of flesh and spirit."

If you are a little older, you know that this battle to remain pure isn't unique to the young. The flesh cries out for money, power, status, and sex. "But the fruit of the Spirit is love, joy, peace, forbearance, kindness, goodness, faithfulness, gentleness and self-control" (Galatians 5:22–23 niv).

Apart from a regular diet of God's Word, you have no chance of withstanding the fiery darts of Satan. So, Christian, how goes the battle? If you find yourself losing the battle to the flesh, ask yourself if you're spending enough time in the Word of God, and then choose to dive in deeper.

Lord, I confess that I often try to fight spiritual battles in my
own strength, rather than relying on Your Spirit to guide me as
I consume Your Word. Forgive me, Lord, and reignite my
passion for the Bible, so that I may represent You well.

ALREADY CLEANSED

*On the fourteenth day of the first month, the returned exiles
kept the Passover. For the priests and the Levites had
purified themselves together; all of them were clean.*

EZRA 6:19–20 ESV

As the exiles returned from Babylon, they were vigilant to reestablish their religious practices prescribed in the old covenant. To their credit, the priests were faithful to purify themselves, which could have taken anywhere from one to six days depending on the types of purification rituals they had to perform.

It's easy to begin a new religious routine, isn't it? You hear a sermon one Sunday, or you read something in a book that fires you up, so you promise to be more routine with your daily quiet time. But during that first or second day, you confess your sin and the Lord speaks to you about making amends with somebody, or some other sin, and the next day it feels more difficult to approach the Lord with zeal.

The beauty of the Christian life is that Jesus Christ has made you clean. The Lord will continue to call you to a life of purity, but you never have to worry about Him viewing you as unclean. You've been transformed by the blood of Christ.

*Lord, sometimes I count on my works to see myself as clean in Your
sight. In reality, my purity was secured on the cross. Thank You!*

NO CONDEMNATION

Likewise the Spirit also helps in our weaknesses. For we do not know what we should pray for as we ought, but the Spirit Himself makes intercession for us with groanings which cannot be uttered.

ROMANS 8:26 NKJV

In today's reading of Romans 8, you are told that those who live according to the Spirit have set their minds to the things of the Spirit (8:5). You won't do so perfectly, but doing so at all means the Spirit is at work in you.

What happens when you feel so spiritually weak that you aren't even able to pray as you ought? Two truths spring to life from today's passage. First, the Spirit Himself prays for you in such instances (Romans 8:26). And second, there is no condemnation to those who are in Christ Jesus (Romans 8:1).

This isn't an admonition to go easier on yourself when you are straying spiritually. Instead, it's an encouragement to trust in and rejoice that God isn't finished with you. What's more, if you are experiencing His guidance, direction, and correction, take heart.

God will be faithful to complete the work He started in you.

Lord, I confess to being prideful when I'm checking all the spiritual boxes, and I'm also quick to give up hope when I'm not doing so. Thank You for reminding me that the Spirit is both interceding for and transforming me.

TESTIFYING BEFORE KINGS

I will speak of Your testimonies also before kings and will not be put to shame. For I will delight myself in Your commandments, which I love.
PSALM 119:46–47 AMPC

The author of this psalm was fully prepared to testify for the Lord in front of kings without feeling shame. He did so because he delighted himself in God's commandments, which he loved. He didn't live a perfect life. In fact, he had several great failings. But he found his way again by delighting in and holding fast to truth, and it empowered him to act accordingly.

Are you experiencing spiritual defeat, unable to get past your failures? Maybe you feel like Satan has picked you out and placed you on the shelf, rendering you useless for the kingdom. Or maybe you've just allowed yourself to become so busy that you've neglected the Word and therefore haven't witnessed to anybody for months or years.

If any of these are true, immerse yourself in the Word, delight in it, and you'll find spiritual power from on high. That power will give you the courage you need to stand for truth in this wicked and perverse generation.

Lord, I don't know why I continually falter when life becomes difficult. I earnestly desire to witness for You. Yet I allow the cares of this world to choke the spiritual life out of me. Forgive me, Lord. Renew and restore me.

A CHANGE OF DIRECTION

For I could wish that I myself were accursed and cut off from Christ
for the sake of my brothers, my kinsmen according to the flesh.

ROMANS 9:3 ESV

I n today's verse, Paul expresses his heart's desire for his countrymen, the Jewish people. His willingness to sacrifice his own salvation is the ultimate indicator of his transformation. He was transformed from a man who violently persecuted Christians to a man who would give up eternity if others were saved. Bible commentator Matthew Henry noted this about Paul's desire: "Love is apt to be thus bold, and venturous, and self-denying."

As passionate as Paul was for his people, ultimately he became an apostle to the Gentile world, again showing evidence of the transformed life. He was more concerned about God's will than his own.

How about you? Do you share Paul's passion for a certain people group? Have you shared that with God? Would you give up that desire if He placed you in different circumstances among a different people group?

Do you want what God wants? If your honest answer is "not yet," offer up your desires to Him, knowing His ways and plans are perfect.

Lord, I earnestly desire to see people who share my background
converted to Jesus Christ. Give me opportunities to share the
Gospel with them. If Your will is different, I will receive it,
knowing Your ways are much higher than mine ever could be.

LET YOUR LIGHT SHINE

Those who fear you shall see me and rejoice,
because I have hoped in your word.
PSALM 119:74 ESV

Have you ever met someone for the first time and sensed that he might be a Christian? Maybe that person expressed a deep love for others or used a certain phrase that led you to believe he was in the family of God. Such instances are always refreshing and often lead to a deeper conversation and connection than would have otherwise occurred.

If you've ever had a window seat on a red-eye flight and happened to look down toward the ground, you saw lights spread out across the landscape even though you were 30,000 feet in the air. Maybe it gave you pause, wondering what life was like for those particular people. Similarly, the Christian carries a light within him wherever he goes—into his home, his workplace, and the community. His light burns brighter and is easier to see when he's spent ample time in the Word.

So, Christian, how bright is your light? Do other Christians see it? Do non-Christians inquire about it? If not, plug into the life-giving source of the scriptures and recharge.

Lord, may the words of Jesus Christ from Matthew 5:16 (ESV) be true of me today: "Let your light shine before others, so that they may see your good works and give glory to your Father who is in heaven."

HOW LONG, LORD?

How many are the days of Your servant [which he must endure]?
When will You judge those who pursue and persecute me?
PSALM 119:84 AMPC

The author of Psalm 119 suffered from persecution for his steadfast conviction to live by the Word of God (119:85, 87). Eventually, he wondered how much longer he could bear it before tasting death. Notice that he didn't take matters into his own hands. Instead, he asked God to act against those who were after him.

The new believer pants for truth. He devours the Bible and is willing to do whatever it says. But when he faces persecution, or sometimes just pushback, he becomes disillusioned, wondering why others aren't interested in God's precepts. As he matures in the faith, he sees the culture's distaste for the Word as the norm and he seeks to proclaim the truth more faithfully.

Have you pulled back from sharing the truth, knowing the message you're sharing is unpopular? Don't lose heart. Your mission is to spread the message of the kingdom while leaving the results to the Father.

Lord, I confess to being a people pleaser more than a truth proclaimer. I know that sharing the truth in love is a scriptural mandate. Yet when I do so, few people seem to listen. Stiffen my backbone, Lord, that I may press on in faithfulness to You.

SIX-HOUR WORSHIP SERVICES

They remained standing in place for three hours while the Book of the Law of the LORD their God was read aloud to them. Then for three more hours they confessed their sins and worshiped the LORD their God.

NEHEMIAH 9:3 NLT

After Israel rebuilt the temple and walls, Ezra read from the Book of the Law for seven successive days. It was followed by a solemn assembly (Nehemiah 8:18). A few weeks later, they assembled again to confess their sins and fast (9:1–2). Then, for the next six hours, they heard from God's Word, confessed more sin, and worshipped the Lord.

Because they were starting anew, they took their sin seriously.

How does this practice compare or contrast to your attitude about worship? Do you check your watch throughout the service, thinking about what you're going to do afterward, or are you fully engaged? Do you zone out sometimes as the Word is read from the pulpit, or is it having its way with you? Do you offer short cursory prayers of repentance, or do you ask God to search your heart to reveal the evil that lies within, and then respond accordingly?

If your heart hasn't been fully present during worship, you can change that this weekend.

Lord, I realize that my lack of focus during worship reveals that my heart is sometimes cold toward You. Forgive me, Lord. Reignite my passion for You.

GOING ALL IN

Therefore, I urge you, brothers and sisters, in view of God's mercy,
to offer your bodies as a living sacrifice, holy and pleasing
to God—this is your true and proper worship.
ROMANS 12:1 NIV

In today's key verse, Paul calls believers to offer their bodies as a living sacrifice—as a true and proper act of worship. This is a reference to the old covenant sacrificial system.

Albert Barnes goes into more detail in his commentary: "In the case of an animal, it was slain, and the blood offered; in the case of any other offering, as the first-fruits, etc., it was set apart to the service of God; and he who offered it released all claim on it, and submitted it to God, to be disposed of at his will."

Likewise, you are to release your claim on your life and offer it to God to be disposed of at His will. Consider your eating habits, your work, or how you handle money or spend your leisure time. Have you offered these up to the Lord to do with as He pleases? If not, this is the scriptural call on your life today.

Lord, in today's key verse, Paul is calling me to go all in with You. This is
a radical, countercultural way to live, but how can I do anything else?
Indeed, how—given the sacrifice You've made for me?

LONGING FOR SALVATION

*Mine eyes fail for thy salvation, and for the
word of thy righteousness.*
PSALM 119:123 KJV

The author of this psalm had been looking for salvation for so long that his eyes were beginning to fail him. In other words, the more he aged, the more excited he got about the fulfillment of his salvation in heaven.

As Christians age, their attention often turns toward heaven. Many express an interest in going sooner rather than later. It's not because they have lost hope here on earth, but because their eyes, ears, nose, hands, legs, and memories are failing. They long for renewal and the hope of heaven. Traditionally, younger Christians too have lived with the hope of heaven in mind.

How about you? What do you spend the most time thinking about? What are your eyes fixed on? Finances? Security? Finding love? Your job? Your wife? Your children? Scripture has much to say about all these topics, but they should never be the central focus for the believer. You are indeed a sojourner just passing through this world. You are called to love God and love others while you are here. And never lose sight of the eternal.

Allow the eternal to fill you with great joy today.

*Lord, the cares and concerns of this world are often my main
focus. Reorient my thoughts, fixing them on eternity.*

PUT ON JESUS CHRIST

But put on the Lord Jesus Christ, and make no provision
for the flesh, to gratify its desires.
Romans 13:14 esv

I n today's passage, the apostle Paul provides a one-two punch for living the victorious Christian life. First, he doesn't tell the Christian to stand strong in his own strength, but rather to put on the Lord Jesus Christ. That means to take on His ways and to take on His views. Second, the Christian is to make no provision for the flesh. The Greek word for "provision" here means "forethought."

Are you minding your spirit, making it a priority to put on Jesus Christ every day? If you aren't doing so daily, hourly even, you stand little chance of winning the battle against the flesh. According to Romans 13:13, the sins of the flesh include drunkenness, sexual immorality, sensuality, quarreling, and jealousy.

What specific steps are you taking to smash provisions for the flesh? Do you need to unsubscribe to a certain cable channel? Attend meetings to help you stay sober? Talk to somebody about your jealous streak? Start an anger management recovery program?

You know your areas of weakness. Paul calls you to go on the offensive and take decisive action against them.

Lord, I have many weaknesses and all too often I try to stand
against them in my own power. Remind me every morning
about the importance of putting on Jesus Christ.

BEARING WITH FAILINGS

We who are strong have an obligation to bear with the
failings of the weak, and not to please ourselves.

ROMANS 15:1 ESV

The call in today's verse is for the strong Christian—the man who is deeply rooted in Gospel truth—to bear with the failings of his weaker brother. Such failings, according to Bible commentator John Gill, "are not subversive of the fundamental doctrines of the Gospel." In other words, these believers take strong stands on secondary issues rather than the core of orthodoxy.

Examine your current relationships with weaker brothers. How well are you bearing with their misunderstandings on secondary and tertiary issues? Are you quick to try to correct them, feeling good about the fact that you are the stronger brother? This is the very thing Paul forbids here. It's an indicator that you may not be as strong as you think.

If you find yourself in this boat, recall your early days as a Christian. You may have been a bit zealous over secondary issues, even with the unconverted. Then consider the ways in which a stronger brother gently listened to and guided you in such matters.

Become that brother. Care more about the weaker brother's sanctification—which is a process, not an event—than you care about being right.

Lord, I'm not always quick to bear with the failings of my weaker
brothers. I'd rather be known for my love for them rather
than as someone who always offers correction.

SPEAK UP

"If you keep quiet at a time like this, deliverance and relief for the Jews will arise from some other place, but you and your relatives will die. Who knows if perhaps you were made queen for just such a time as this?"

E sther faced possible death if she approached King Xerxes about Haman, the king's most powerful official. Haman planned to destroy all the Jews throughout the empire. But Esther's relative, Mordecai, challenged her, saying she may have been made queen for this very reason—to give voice to those who would otherwise perish. You know the rest of the story. She spoke up and saved her people.

Esther is a model for the Christian to place more value on the lives of the innocent than on himself. Today, believers are the loudest voices for the unborn, who sometimes face violent deaths before they escape the womb. Have you added your own voice for their cause, knowing you may be shouted down by opposing forces? Do you speak up for people who are bullied or shamed?

Who knows if perhaps you were placed in the position you hold for such a time as this?

Lord, I'm often weary from fighting for good causes, but I know that You value life and are calling me to sacrifice my current status and reputation to speak for those who cannot. Embolden me to do so.

PRONE TO WANDER

I have strayed like a lost sheep. Seek your servant,
for I have not forgotten your commands.
Psalm 119:176 niv

For most of this psalm, the author expresses his faith in God and His Word. Still, he's compelled to end with a confession. As much as he believes, it isn't enough to keep him on track spiritually. He still needs God's guiding and sustaining hand.

The human heart is prone to wander, even postconversion. Surely, you've felt it. Sometimes it starts with one sin and quickly progresses. Other times, it starts with hardship. Either way, before long, you're further away from the Lord than you ever intended to be. This is why sheep need shepherds who are willing to do whatever it takes to keep their sheep in the fold.

When is the last time you prayed a prayer like the one in today's key verse? Ask the Lord to seek for you, even if and maybe especially if you recognize you are in the pigpen. In the power of the Spirit, rise up and run straight toward the Father.

Praise God, He is always at the ready to run back to us.

Lord, today's verse cut me to the quick. Indeed, my heart is prone
to wander. It's not because I don't love You or Your Word. It's because
my heart is tainted with sin. Forgive me, Father. Seek me.
I'm listening for Your voice.

HONORING OUR SISTERS

*I commend to you our sister Phoebe, a servant of the church
at Cenchreae, that you may welcome her in the
Lord in a way worthy of the saints.*
ROMANS 16:1–2 ESV

Several commentators believe Phoebe was the bearer of this epistle from Paul to Rome. She'd proven herself as a trustworthy servant. The word is used to describe a deacon or deaconess. She is believed to have spent ample time ministering to female converts in the church at Cenchreae and may have even opened her home there for Christians to gather. She now needs to travel to Rome where Paul wants the church to welcome her with open arms as a sister in Jesus Christ.

Surely you know sisters in Christ who are worthy of such high praise for their Christian work. Their work is often done behind the scenes or in homes across the city. As was the case in Paul's day, your sisters in the faith are responsible for so much of the ministry that occurs in the local church. They often out-serve the men.

What can you or your church do to express appreciation for them? How can you show everyone that they are noticed?

Lord, thank You for the many sisters in Christ who have worked tirelessly and without acknowledgment in my local fellowship. Make me a Paul as I seek to express my thanks for everything they have done.

HOLD EVERYTHING LOOSELY

"Naked I came from my mother's womb, and naked shall I return.
The LORD gave, and the LORD has taken away;
blessed be the name of the LORD."

JOB 1:21 ESV

I magine losing all your children and all your property today. Would the first words out of your mouth be anywhere near as God-honoring as Job's words quoted above?

In his book *Living above the Level of Mediocrity*, Chuck Swindoll recalls a conversation he had with the late Corrie ten Boom. She said, "Chuck, I've learned that we must hold everything loosely, because when I grip it tightly, it hurts when the Father pries my fingers loose and takes it from me!" This was a woman who lost family members in Nazi concentration camps, including her beloved sister Betsie. She knew something about great loss and yet, like Job, she honored God by maintaining a loose hold on everything in this life.

This is what the transformed life looks like. It doesn't deny heartache, nor does it fail to mourn when the situation warrants it. But it also sees life through the lens of the kingdom and is willing to accept whatever happens because God is in control. Sometimes He gives, and sometimes He takes away.

The child of God blesses Him either way.

Lord, the heartache I've experienced has blinded me at times
from seeing life through the lens of the kingdom.
You are in control. Blessed be Your name.

REPLACE THE VOICES

Now we have received not the spirit of the world, but the Spirit who is from God, that we might understand the things freely given us by God.
1 CORINTHIANS 2:12 ESV

Ancient Greece placed a high value on worldly wisdom and philosophy. That's what makes Paul's statement in today's verse stand out. Then as now, if a Christian wanted to understand the things of God, he couldn't rely on what the world around him offered. Instead, he needed to rely on the Holy Spirit.

Today, you probably aren't tempted to look up to and emulate Greek philosophers, but you might be drawn in by self-help motivational speakers whose advice often subtly elevates the flesh or personal desires over the biblical principle of sacrifice and dying to oneself.

Which voices are you allowing to speak to you on a daily basis? Examine the list of authors, podcasters, radio and TV hosts, websites, and magazines you enjoy on a regular basis. Are they consistent with scriptural teachings? Or are they appealing to your fleshly desires?

After rooting out several, quickly replace them with godly voices who will help you understand and rely on the Holy Spirit. You don't necessarily need special training.

Quiet your heart, open the Word, and the Spirit will speak to you.

Lord, the world is a noisy place. So many people claim to have answers to my problems. May I trust Your Spirit alone to guide me.

GIVING YOUR LIFE AWAY

*It is useless for you to work so hard from early morning
until late at night, anxiously working for food to eat;
for God gives rest to his loved ones.*
PSALM 127:2 NLT

Bible commentator Adam Clarke believes the psalmist in today's verse is alluding to the daily and nightly watches Nehemiah instituted. He instituted them due to people's fatigue from working too many hours a day. In any case, this passage expresses God's desire to give plenty of rest to His loved ones.

What is your work-life balance these days? If you are in management or run your own business, you might feel like you have to burn the candle at both ends. The Bible, however, calls the transformed saint to live differently. Maybe you need to take a different position within your company, or maybe you need to change companies.

How might your family benefit if you were to do so? Would you be able to attend more soccer games, dance recitals, and school events? Would you be able to take the lead around the dinner table and facilitate a discussion over a verse of scripture?

Everyone gives his life away for something. Some do so for financial security. Others do so for folly. And still others do so for spiritual riches. Choose the latter. It will far outlast any financial riches you might accumulate.

*Lord, my family is my priority, but I confess that I don't always
live like that. Lead me as I endeavor to make changes.*

A PROPER RESPONSE

When reviled, we bless; when persecuted, we endure;
when slandered, we entreat. We have become, and are
still, like the scum of the world, the refuse of all things.
1 CORINTHIANS 4:12–13 ESV

The apostles became models for the early church in a culture that didn't want to hear the grace-centered Gospel that they were heralding. As a result, they were reviled, persecuted, and slandered. In Christlike fashion, they responded with blessing, endurance, and entreatment.

In Luke 23:34 (ESV), Jesus uttered these words about the ones who hung Him on the cross: "Father, forgive them, for they know not what they do."

You too live in a culture that is growing more and more hostile toward the Gospel and those who proclaim it. What is your first instinct when someone mocks your faith or slanders you for what you believe? Is it one of self-defense? Or is it love for people who don't know any better?

In reality, their hearts are riddled by sin. They are unable to turn the other cheek, but you have been called to do just that. The next time you face hostility for your faith, endure it, even going so far as to wish the other person well. It might just soften his heart.

Lord, in our highly polarized culture, I often try to out-argue people who don't agree with Christianity. Infuse me instead with love for my enemies.

HEARTFELT TRUST

I wait for the LORD, my soul doth wait, and in his word do I hope.
PSALM 130:5 KJV

In his commentary, Charles Spurgeon offers this simple explanation of what it means to wait for the Lord: " 'Waiting for the Lord' is patiently bearing our affliction, whatever it may be, and confidently looking forward to deliverance from it in God's good time. The expression, 'my soul doth wait,' is stronger than 'I wait'; it implies heart-felt trust and confidence."

When affliction comes, how quick are you to take action rather than simply waiting on the Lord while bearing your affliction patiently? Perhaps you do so because your soul isn't waiting on the Lord. Perhaps you lack heartfelt trust and confidence in His deliverance or in Him providing you with the grace to endure.

Take some time today and write down what it would look like for your soul to wait on God in your current situation. Pray about it before you do. Maybe you can pray during one of your break times. Or maybe you can jot down today's key verse and meditate on it throughout your workday.

Also, consider your countenance. Will others be able to tell when you are afflicted or will they see someone who has something they do not?

Lord, I want to exhibit heartfelt trust and confidence in You in the midst of affliction. May it be so today as I set about to glorify You.

MY REDEEMER LIVES

"For I know that my Redeemer lives, and at the last he will stand upon the earth. And after my skin has been thus destroyed, yet in my flesh I shall see God."

JOB 19:25–26 ESV

J ob's three friends, Eliphaz, Bildad, and Zophar, did far more damage than good by repeatedly insisting that his great losses were due to sin. Imagine sitting around with a small group of close friends after losing your family only to have them make such accusations. It would be enough to cause a person to lose hope—that is, unless his hope is in a great Redeemer, like Job's was.

What you believe deep down in your heart is revealed during the most tumultuous times of your life. What have difficult times revealed about your faith? Have you clung to Jesus Christ, believing that He has conquered sin and death? Do your hardships cause you to long for the day when you will see God? Or have your experiences rattled your faith, causing you to doubt God and doubt eternity?

Job didn't have the benefit of knowing Jesus Christ personally. He knew only that God was inherently a redeemer. You, however, have a personal relationship with the King of kings and Lord of lords. Trust Him anew today.

Lord, at times the burdens of this world feel too heavy to carry.
But You have promised to give me rest both now
and in eternity. Thank You!

YOUR BODY IS HERS

The wife does not have authority over her own body but yields
it to her husband. In the same way, the husband does not have
authority over his own body but yields it to his wife.

1 CORINTHIANS 7:4 NIV

In an age of individualism, the notion of not having authority over one's own body in the context of the marriage bed seems rather foreign. Sex is not supposed to be withheld, except for an agreed-upon season, so the two of you can devote yourselves to prayer (1 Corinthians 7:5).

Maybe you've pointed out today's verse to your wife at some point in the past when she has been less than willing to have sexual relations with you. But have you considered the ramifications of not having authority over your own body? It means more than simply being willing to have sexual relations with your wife when she desires to do so. It also means your body belongs solely to her, not to any acts that commentators used to call self-pollution. Have you kept yourself pure for her in every way?

Yes, your wife may have some issues to work through. You can't do that for her. But as a man who has been transformed by the Gospel, you can be pure for her. Do so without fail.

Father, I'm often quick to point to my wife's responsibility
in this text and slow to assume my own. Forgive me.

DWELLING TOGETHER IN UNITY

Behold, how good and how pleasant it is
for brethren to dwell together in unity!
PSALM 133:1 KJV

In the broad sense of the word (which seems to be the context in today's verse), men find it difficult to live together in unity. They backbite and have their own interests at heart to the point of disunity. Consider Abraham and Lot or the more extreme case of Joseph and his brothers. Then again, when unity prevails, it is wonderful and pleasant.

The word *dwell* in today's verse means to sit down, abide, and continue. If the world is supposed to take notice of people dwelling together in unity ("Behold!"), shouldn't Christians be the model for such behavior?

What are you doing to dwell in unity with fellow believers? Are you breaking bread with them regularly? Are you present in their lives during good times and bad? Are you prayerfully working through the implications of the Gospel together? If not, then this is the call.

Start this week by reaching out to a brother in Christ and asking him if he'd like to begin meeting regularly. If that doesn't work out, then keep your eyes open at church for men who might be willing to do so.

Father, I know how important it is to live out my faith in community,
but I'm not always quick to take action. Help me do so this week.

A TIME TO SOW

Your name, O LORD, endures forever,
Your fame, O LORD, throughout all generations.
PSALM 135:13 NKJV

The unknown author of this psalm praises God for His goodness, His sovereignty, His control over the weather, and His justice. When you consider the Father's absolute power and majesty, it's difficult to do anything other than praise Him.

As a member of the family of God, you have different priorities than you did prior to conversion. You went from caring mostly about your immediate wants and needs to caring about praising the Lord for redeeming you, and then obeying Him. As political leaders rise and fall, and as culture shifts from one set of "truths" to another, you think more about God's enduring name throughout all generations. As such, the salvation of the next generation is always on your mind.

What are you doing to sow into the generation behind you? Are you discipling hungry new believers? Are you teaching them in some capacity? Are you engaging in conversation with them? They can grasp and then run with the baton of faith only if you hand it to them. But handing it to them is just the first step.

You need to train them to run for the long haul.

Lord, often, my thoughts are not on training the next generation.
Change my heart, oh God. Give me opportunities to speak to
the generations behind me about Your enduring name.

WHAT IS YOUR PORTION FROM GOD?

"What would be my portion from God above and my heritage from the Almighty on high? Is not calamity for the unrighteous, and disaster for the workers of iniquity? Does not he see my ways and number all my steps?"

JOB 31:2–4 ESV

God's awareness of your actions can mean both good news for the righteous and a sobering wake-up call to those living disobediently. God is aware of the steps you take in holiness or in service of your own ego, and you will bear the fruit of your decisions and see consequences before God. The challenge? Sometimes it appears that the wicked are blessed and the holy are cursed. That illusion may appear to be the case for now, but what is built on the rock of obedience will surely stand the test of time.

The life of faith trusts that God will reward people for what they have done, and so you must look to the long term as you consider the impact of your actions. Today's temporal benefit may lead to tomorrow's curse. Whatever you can gain today by living disobediently, you cannot outrun the justice of God. The good news is that you also can't outrun God's mercy and forgiveness.

As you set out to right your wrongs, God will surely bless you, even if you don't see that blessing today.

Lord, help me love Your teachings and follow Your ways, even if obedience means greater challenges today.

RUN THE RACE TO WIN IT

Don't you realize that in a race everyone runs, but only one person gets the prize? So run to win! All athletes are disciplined in their training. They do it to win a prize that will fade away, but we do it for an eternal prize.

1 Corinthians 9:24–25 nlt

By God's grace you have been saved and adopted into His family. There isn't anything you can do to merit God's mercy or to earn God's love. Having said all of that, Paul makes it abundantly clear that you can lose your grasp of God's presence, become distracted, or pursue something other than God's will. Jesus' parable of the seeds and the four types of soil say as much.

The solution to receiving God's grace and mercy is the discipline of an athlete, a commitment to training that aims for an eternal reward that will never fade away. While the disciplines of prayer, silence, study, or meditation may all appear difficult at first and challenging to incorporate into your day, they can grow easier over time.

Much like an athlete growing in strength and endurance, your ability to focus on God and to set aside time for God can grow and improve over time.

Jesus, give me the gifts of patience and endurance as I seek You today so that I will not grow weary but will grow in Your grace.

DO THE SKIES REMIND YOU OF GOD?

*Out of the north comes golden splendor; God is clothed with awesome
majesty. The Almighty—we cannot find him; he is great in power;
justice and abundant righteousness he will not violate. Therefore men
fear him; he does not regard any who are wise in their own conceit.*

JOB 37:22–24 ESV

The simple acts of observing and appreciating the majesty and power
of nature can work wonders for your faith and add a healthy dose of
realism to your self-assessment. Those who think of God as smaller and
less powerful—while imagining they are in control and worthy of greater
honor and praise—will struggle with insecurity and fear about the future.

The proper response to God's power, which surpasses the grasp of
the human mind, is a reason for respectful worship and awe, fearing that
God could do away with anyone who violates His commands. You stand
alone on God's mercy and hope that all people will come to a saving
knowledge of Him.

Your own wisdom and accomplishments don't stack up well against
God's. The best thing you can do today is to step outside for a moment,
admire the brilliance of the sun in the sky, and recall that this is only a
small demonstration of God's infinite and eternal power.

*Lord, may I see Your power and mercy with clarity
so that I never think too highly of myself.*

CALL OUT TO GOD IN FAITH

Though I walk in the midst of trouble, you preserve my life. You stretch out your hand against the anger of my foes; with your right hand you save me. The Lord will vindicate me; your love, Lord, endures forever—do not abandon the works of your hands.

PSALM 138:7–8 NIV

When going through difficult times or seasons of suffering, it's understandable to feel abandoned by God and alone in your distress. These are common themes in the Psalms, and the fear of abandonment is to be expected when living by faith. However, each trial and difficulty is also an opportunity to reach out to God and to ask the Lord to draw near. God may not spare His people from trouble, but that doesn't mean they are abandoned.

Today may be the day to call out, "Lord, do not abandon me!" There's always pressure to appear that you have your act together and your faith is strong, but an honest prayer may be the most hopeful step you can take today.

Acknowledging the fear of abandonment asserts that God is real, present, and able to help, even if your faith is struggling. Such a prayer based on the Psalms can be a step in your restoration.

Lord, I do not know what tomorrow will bring, but I trust that You are present today and that You will care for me in days to come.

ENJOY WHAT GOD GIVES YOU

*He has made everything beautiful in its time. Also, he has put eternity
into man's heart, yet so that he cannot find out what God has done from
the beginning to the end. I perceived that there is nothing better for
them than to be joyful and to do good as long as they live.*
ECCLESIASTES 3:11–12 ESV

God's cure for the restlessness of religion and the resentments of consumer society is to patiently wait for God's work and to enjoy what you have. Rather than worrying about what will come next and whether you can control it, God's blessing to you is the beauty of His work in your life. If you trust God to work in you, then the outcome God brings about will be a source of rest and comfort. Religious striving can sometimes interfere with the slow, deep work of God in His people.

If patience and endurance are called for when it comes to waiting on God's redemption in your life, then enjoyment is equally important for the challenges of consumer society. Gratitude fights against the disruption of advertisements and comparisons to others, enabling you to be fully present among the people and places in your life.

God intends for you to enjoy your family, friends, and community.

*Lord, help me see the blessings You have granted to me,
and teach me contentment as I enjoy them today.*

ALL IN LOVE OR NOTHING

If I had the gift of prophecy, and if I understood all of God's secret plans and possessed all knowledge, and if I had such faith that I could move mountains, but didn't love others, I would be nothing.

1 CORINTHIANS 13:2 NLT

The spectacular gifts, talents, and actions of God's people can have a way of overshadowing the far more mundane moments of love and mercy shown to others. However, when it comes to the tally that means the most to God, a small act done with pure love is far more important than the great act done for personal gain or other mixed motives. While those able to impress can draw a crowd, those shaped by God's love and committed to sharing that love are those who impress God.

Do you have insecurities about your talents and accomplishments? Do you struggle with the comparison trap? Paul's words are good news for you today. The most important thing you can do today in God's eyes is to love someone, even in the smallest act. Perhaps doing many small acts in great love is the kind of training ground you need.

Before you try out a great act of service to others, it's preferable to learn what it is to ground your service in love. Then, when you are established in God's love, you will be prepared to serve others in ways that are meaningful and lasting.

Jesus, help me experience the Father's love for me and Your loving sacrifice for all so that I follow Your example of loving service.

GOD'S SEARCH AND RESCUE MISSION

Search me, God, and know my heart; test me and know my
anxious thoughts. See if there is any offensive way in
me, and lead me in the way everlasting.
PSALM 139:23–24 NIV

As you celebrate Labor Day, today's key verse may offer a helpful opportunity to bring your anxieties or concerns about work, finances, or your future to God. God is present in your work and can bring blessings through your work. However, work can also be a source of stress and fragmentation. Ask God to reveal what is in your heart as you contemplate work or the work of others, and seek God's direction in the way of redemption and life.

How does it strike you to ask God to "search" you? Do you want God rooting around in your life and examining your heart? Do you welcome a test from God or the unearthing of your anxious thoughts? Perhaps such revelations would be disruptive or discouraging for you.

Nevertheless, there is no other path to healing. God must search your heart and uncover anything that is wounded or offensive so that He can bring healing and transformation. While the searching part of the mission can be difficult, the rescue will always make it worthwhile.

Father, I trust that You desire my healing and redemption from
sin. May Your light uncover any darkness in my life.
May I see Your path to everlasting life.

BETTER TO BE WISE THAN POWERFUL

But I say that wisdom is better than might, though the poor man's wisdom is despised and his words are not heard. The words of the wise heard in quiet are better than the shouting of a ruler among fools.

Ecclesiastes 9:16–17 esv

How far can strength and superior numbers carry someone? When superior wisdom comes along, strength and power may meet its match.

You may face the temptation to grow in strength, influence, power, or wealth for the sake of security. Powerful allies can be viewed as indispensable. Conventional wisdom surely would push you in this direction.

However, the wisdom that God gives can become a greater resource than the strength and influence of men. Although God's wisdom is overlooked and even scorned at times, it is surely more effective and life-giving, providing benefit to many others besides yourself. It is a gift from God that's freely given—provided that you ask for it and trust God to guide your steps.

There will always be people who shout and demand to be noticed, but you have the ready help of God standing by to support you. When others shout and claim to be in charge, you can rest in the quiet confidence and wisdom that God grants.

Lord, help me trust in Your wisdom and guidance so that I will not be dismayed or misled by those who lead with force and intimidation.

CONSIDER THE WORDS OF OTHERS

*And what value was there in fighting wild beasts—those people
of Ephesus—if there will be no resurrection from the dead? And if there
is no resurrection, "Let's feast and drink, for tomorrow we
die!" Don't be fooled by those who say such things,
for "bad company corrupts good character."*

1 CORINTHIANS 15:32–33 NLT

If the words of others reveal what is in their hearts, then those who call into question the central belief in the resurrection reveal their denial of God's power.

Although you may believe that you can win over people who deny something vitally important like the resurrection, remain cautious. Denying the resurrection means they will make choices and live in such a way that underestimates or dismisses the power and presence of God. Their decisions can have a corrupting influence on your own life and the kinds of choices you make.

The company you keep is essential for the health of your faith. This is why Jesus began His ministry with a small community of disciples. What's more, this is why fellowship and gathering have been so important throughout the history of the church.

The people who can affirm your faith, and who can support you in the highs and lows of life, will ensure that your faith is stable and able to stand the trials that will surely come.

*Jesus, lead me to people of faith who can
affirm and support my hope in You.*

BEWARE THE DANGEROUS DELIGHTS OF EVIL

Do not let my heart be drawn to what is evil so that I take part
in wicked deeds along with those who are evildoers; do not let me
eat their delicacies. Let a righteous man strike me—that is
a kindness; let him rebuke me—that is oil on my head.

PSALM 141:4–5 NIV

The writer of this psalm offers a warning. Those committed to acts of evil will be appealing, and the fruits of their work against God will appear to be delicacies. At first, then, the choice to follow the ways of God and the ways of evil won't be easy, or even black and white. There will be many things to desire about the path away from God. It may appear wiser, more pleasurable, and more rewarding in the end.

How can you be assured that you can stay near to God and away from the deceits of evil? The tactic in this psalm is the kindness of a rebuke from a righteous friend. Do you have people around you who can tell you the truth? Place yourself in the company of righteous friends, family, mentors, and leaders who are invested in your spiritual health.

In what kind of spirit do you receive their rebukes? Do you view each as a blessing or even a commissioning to live in holiness before God?

Lord, help me see the blessing in a righteous rebuke so
I can turn away from evil and pursue Your goodness.

WORSHIP AND JUSTICE ARE JOINED TOGETHER

"Your new moons and your appointed feasts my soul hates. . . . Wash yourselves; make yourselves clean; remove the evil of your deeds from before my eyes; cease to do evil, learn to do good; seek justice, correct oppression; bring justice to the fatherless, plead the widow's cause."
ISAIAH 1:14, 16–17 ESV

What should you do before you approach God for worship? According to Isaiah, sin isn't the only barrier between people and God. Actively supporting or ignoring injustice and oppression are serious matters in the eyes of God. In fact, injustice and suffering offend God to the point that He cannot tolerate the worship of such wayward people.

This is a process. Leaving sin behind may require some intentional time spent relearning what it looks like to live in faithful obedience. Turning away from sin or confronting injustice will take time and effort. Isaiah suggests that you can begin to look for the most vulnerable in your community, from the fatherless to the impoverished to the widows struggling to support themselves. While you may not have the resources on your own to help someone, you may be able to assist a relief group or church in their God-ordained work.

If you have a sense that God is distant or far removed during worship, this attention to justice and mercy may offer a helpful place to begin.

Lord, help me see the needs around me and give me wisdom to respond in ways that are helpful and restorative for others.

HOW GOD RESPONDS TO SUFFERING

Even when we are weighed down with troubles, it is for your comfort and salvation! For when we ourselves are comforted, we will certainly comfort you. Then you can patiently endure the same things we suffer. We are confident that as you share in our sufferings, you will also share in the comfort God gives us.
2 CORINTHIANS 1:6–7 NLT

Suffering may be inevitable, but if you trust in God, you will never suffer without God's compassion and support. As Paul faced the trials and difficulties of his ministry, he found that he could reach out to God for the support that no one else could provide. This deep intimacy with God made it possible for him to continue in his ministry and offered him a deeper sense of security in the salvation of God. He could look at the comfort provided by God as a confirmation that God was with him.

As you receive God's comfort for your suffering and difficulties, you will also have a gift that you can offer generously to others, sharing the comfort of God with them. Perhaps you'll gain an insight or a sense of perspective that will prove especially useful for others.

God takes no delight in your suffering, but God will bear your burdens with you and support you. Such gifts can be duplicated and shared readily.

Jesus, help me recall You are present and able to help me endure trials and suffering, and grant me the generosity to share Your comfort with others.

CALL ON GOD FOR STABILITY

*Rescue me from my enemies, LORD, for I hide myself in
you. Teach me to do your will, for you are my God;
may your good Spirit lead me on level ground.*

PSALM 143:9–10 NIV

Where do you turn when life becomes disrupted and uncertain? If going into hiding sounds like a good plan, the Psalms agree, to a point. Seasons of instability and fear are opportunities to discover where you place your hope, and the Psalms encourage you to hide yourself in God alone, placing all your hope in God's provision.

There are plenty of opportunities to hedge your bets. The life of faith is full of detours and missteps, and you will surely need God's grace on plenty of occasions.

If you hope to be transformed by the Lord, then you will need God's instruction and guidance. You've been given the Spirit of God, and you can ask boldly for the wisdom and change of heart that will enable you to live differently.

As life throws obstacles and unexpected twists in your way, the Spirit of God can lead you to the security of level ground. That will allow you to stand firm in the presence of God with confidence and peace.

*Lord, I depend on You alone to defend me. May I hear Your Spirit
with clarity today so that I can find the stability You provide.*

WAITING FOR GOD'S RESTORATION

The people who walked in darkness have seen a great light; those who dwelt in a land of deep darkness, on them has light shone. You have multiplied the nation; you have increased its joy; they rejoice before you as with joy at the harvest, as they are glad when they divide the spoil.

ISAIAH 9:2–3 ESV

A season of loss, darkness, or doubt can be exhausting, especially if you don't have any hope for the future. You may not know what will change things or how God could show up again. You may not have guarantees of the timing or the details. You can only wait, often without the answers and resolution you crave.

As the people of Israel waited for the Lord to return and to restore them, they had no idea how Jesus would reveal God's kingdom among them. Some were ready for the Lord's return, while many others were not.

As you wait on God and seek the Lord's direction, perhaps it may help to consider that the best you can do during this season is to remember. Remember that you can't predict the details, but you can rest assured that the Lord will come.

At the right time, the Lord will provide joy and His transforming presence.

Lord, help me wait with patience and expectation for Your return and restoration.

GOD PROMISES JUSTICE TO THE WORLD

And the Spirit of the LORD shall rest upon him, the Spirit of wisdom and understanding, the Spirit of counsel and might, the Spirit of knowledge and the fear of the LORD. And his delight shall be in the fear of the LORD. He shall not judge by what his eyes see, or decide disputes by what his ears hear.

ISAIAH 11:2–3 ESV

What happens when the Spirit of the Lord comes down?
According to Isaiah, the Messiah will reveal things as they truly are and begin to reveal the desires of God. The Messiah will bring about justice and equity for others, and judge with fairness and impartiality. He will reveal God's desire for His people to live in holy reverence of Him. He will also address the systems and laws that can harm others.

You are living in the tension between what God desires for this world and what this world is apart from God's wisdom, understanding, and justice. The world is not run according to the fear of God. It's more likely that people want to get away with what they can for as long as they can.

The wisdom and knowledge of God that the Messiah brings is fully aware of God's power and justice. Such fear of God recognizes that you will reap what you sow soon enough, so it is best to live obediently and to delight in God's commands.

Lord, help me see the wisdom and joy of Your ways so that I will receive the reward of the righteous.

WHERE DO YOU SEEK HELP?

Blessed are those whose help is the God of Jacob, whose hope is in the LORD their God. He is the Maker of heaven and earth, the sea, and everything in them—he remains faithful forever. He upholds the cause of the oppressed and gives food to the hungry.

PSALM 146:5–7 NIV

Where do you turn in times of need? Have you ever been in a situation that felt completely beyond your resources and capacity?

These are the times when those who lack relational, material, or financial resources turn to God. Those who suffer from hunger, oppression, or injustice can call out to God for help, and God will be attentive to their cries.

If you have experienced privations, consider how you can extend your trust in God more completely. If you are in a season of security, consider asking God how you can answer that prayer for someone else. Perhaps your generosity could become the provision of God in someone else's life.

Whether you join God in cries of desperation, or you join God in helping others during their times of crisis, you will find yourself linked with God's deepest desires for people and transformed by the joy of this partnership with God.

Father, I trust that You can provide for the needs of those who cry out to You. May I rest in You and remain generous and aware for the sake of those around me.

YOU ARE A NEW PERSON IN CHRIST

So we have stopped evaluating others from a human point of view.
At one time we thought of Christ merely from a human point of
view. How differently we know him now! This means that
anyone who belongs to Christ has become a new
person. The old life is gone; a new life has begun!
2 CORINTHIANS 5:16–17 NLT

How does it change your perspective after reading that you are a new person in Jesus Christ? Perhaps you feel encouraged by being transformed. Then again, you may be wondering why holy living and obedience to the teachings of scripture are such a struggle.

What should God's people do when the old life remains persistent and powerful? One place to begin may be your perspective. Are you seeing Jesus for less than He truly is? Or are you seeing Him as the risen Son of God who conquered death and offers God's life to all?

Correcting your perspective won't change everything overnight, but if you can see Jesus as He truly is and then accept the fantastic possibility that you belong to Him, you can take steps forward. You can move away from guilt, discouragement, and alienation.

You can rest assured that Jesus Christ will transform you through His union with you.

Jesus, help me see Your divine power with clarity.
May I accept Your gracious union with my life today.

WHY DO YOU SERVE GOD?

We serve God whether people honor us or despise us, whether they slander us or praise us. We are honest, but they call us impostors. . . . Our hearts ache, but we always have joy. We are poor, but we give spiritual riches to others. We own nothing, and yet we have everything.

2 CORINTHIANS 6:8, 10 NLT

Paul didn't serve God for the honor and praise of men. He didn't expect to have a life free from pain and suffering. He certainly didn't own many possessions or boast of riches as a way of supposedly confirming God's blessing in his life.

Some people expect to be highly regarded and respected for following Jesus, for advocating for God's justice on earth, or for holding others accountable. Those who have such hopes will surely be disappointed sooner rather than later.

You have so much to gain by serving God, but that gain will hardly look like the praise and esteem of the masses, let alone significant wealth and prosperity. The gain that no man can touch in your life is the joy of God and the comfort of His presence.

Whether you are wealthy or poor, healthy or sick, you can share this joy with others freely without reservation or limit.

Jesus, help me seek You and Your spiritual riches so that I will never let the disregard of others pull me away from my calling to share You with others.

GOD'S PROMISE TO REMOVE SORROW FROM THE EARTH

*He will swallow up death forever; and the Lord GOD will wipe away
tears from all faces, and the reproach of his people he will
take away from all the earth, for the LORD has spoken.*

ISAIAH 25:8 ESV

Sorrow and death are a reality on earth, at least for now. Looking into the future, Isaiah offers you the assurance that God desires to eradicate every reason for tears and the looming threats of death. The damage of words and accusations will be relegated to the past.

Of course, such promises don't seem to do a whole lot to help with your trials today. The promise of God removing death doesn't change the lot of those who are breathing their final breaths today, and the promise of no more tears in the future doesn't remove the sorrow and laments of those suffering the pain of loss today. The hope offered here is in the future, and yet it does reveal something of God's character. God does not want death and sadness to be the norm in this world.

The hope of God today is that death does not have the final word, even if sickness, sorrow, and loss are realities to face now. God knows that all is not well, and He has come alongside you to bear your burdens with you.

*Lord, may I experience Your comfort and presence
when I bear the weight of sorrow and pain.*

THE LORD DELIGHTS IN HIS PEOPLE

Let them praise his name with dancing and make music to him
with timbrel and harp. For the LORD takes delight in his people;
he crowns the humble with victory. Let his faithful people
rejoice in this honor and sing for joy on their beds.

PSALM 149:3–5 NIV

What kind of mind-set do you bring to worship? Do you wonder if God is present? Do you worry what God thinks of you? It's possible that you may believe God could take you or leave you.

If you come to God in humility, and if you acknowledge your need for His mercy, then you have nothing to fear. More importantly, you can rest assured that God takes delight in you. He desires for you to be confident in His support and to come into His presence with songs of praise. God does not want His people to be gloomy. Rather, His presence can bring great rejoicing to those who live according to His teachings.

Today is the day to rejoice in the Lord and His presence. Music and singing belong in worship, and you are invited to participate in it. When you return home, you can continue to sing to the Lord, even carrying these songs to your bed at night.

Lord, may Your songs of praise and joy be on my lips this week
so that I can fully delight in Your mercy and goodness.

GIVE GENEROUSLY IN FAITH

Remember this—a farmer who plants only a few seeds will get a
small crop. But the one who plants generously will get a generous
crop. You must each decide in your heart how much to give.
And don't give reluctantly or in response to pressure.
"For God loves a person who gives cheerfully."
2 CORINTHIANS 9:6–7 NLT

Sharing your financial and material resources is an opportunity to see God work in others and to learn how God can meet your most basic material needs.

Passages like this have been used as a proof text for prosperity preachers, assuming that cheerful givers will receive "generous crops" of vast financial wealth. This is hardly the case, since Paul himself is open about lacking finances at times and having to make and sell tents to pay his own way.

Rather, this is an assurance that joining in God's generosity for others creates opportunities for God's abundant blessings, which will take many forms, to be spread among those in God's family.

While Paul does assure cheerful givers that God will provide for their needs, this is not an assurance of riches and prosperity for those who give generously. This is an opportunity to join in God's generosity, to see others become blessed, and to entrust your future into God's care and provision.

Giving can be a joyful, faith-filled action.

Jesus, help me give generously to those in need,
and may I trust my basic needs to Your loving care.

HOW TO USE AUTHORITY

I may seem to be boasting too much about the authority given to us by the Lord. But our authority builds you up; it doesn't tear you down. So I will not be ashamed of using my authority.

2 CORINTHIANS 10:8 NLT

How can you use your authority well, avoiding the trap of abusing it for self-aggrandizement while also avoiding the error of neglecting the influence you have?

The fine line that Paul set out is a vision for authority that builds up others. This is the kind of authority to be talked about, to be regarded highly, and to be used frequently in Christian community. This kind of authority may result in someone being held in high esteem by a group, but such esteem is hardly its primary aim.

What kind of influence do you have right now? Are there ways you can more actively support others, build them up with encouragement, or prepare them for the work God has set before them? Christian authority gives away influence, spreads out the authority of God, and empowers others to grow to their full potential in Christ.

Whether or not you see yourself as a leader, you have authority and influence to share for the benefit of God's people.

Jesus, help me share my influence and authority well for the building up of others, and may I remember my place as Your child, never thinking too much of myself.

GOD IS MERCIFUL BUT HONORS YOUR CHOICES

"For the waywardness of the simple will kill them, and the complacency of fools will destroy them; but whoever listens to me will live in safety and be at ease, without fear of harm."

PROVERBS 1:32–33 NIV

God's wisdom is readily available to you. Do you gladly ask God for it? You would expect everyone to jump at this opportunity to take advantage of God's mercy and provision in their lives, but so often obstacles get in the way. From distractions that divert that attention, to misplaced confidence in one's wisdom, to feelings of unworthiness before God, it's easy to miss out on God's wisdom.

There are severe consequences for complacency and waywardness. God honors the choices of His people even if His mercy and grace are abundant for all who turn from their paths to follow Him.

Proverbs frequently offers you the choice between two paths—one that leads to life and one that heads to destruction. Life can appear more complex than that, with various options and plenty of gray areas.

There is something simple about recognizing your need for God's wisdom, and trusting that God's wisdom can help you in ways far beyond your own abilities.

Lord, grant me the grace and wisdom to listen to You and to live my life according to Your direction.

WEAKNESS BECOMES STRENGTH IN GOD

Three different times I begged the Lord to take it away. Each time he
said, "My grace is all you need. My power works best in weakness."
So now I am glad to boast about my weaknesses, so that
the power of Christ can work through me.

2 CORINTHIANS 12:8–9 NLT

Any strength that you have becomes a liability compared to the strength and support that God provides. The risk is that you may make the crucial error of relying on your strength, wisdom, and experience to accomplish things. However, your own power will eventually let you down or lead you astray. God's wisdom and strength is far more reliable and enduring.

This is why Paul is so insistent on boasting of his weaknesses. Anything that reveals his need for God and his own inadequacy is a plus for him.

In what ways could you say that you are weak or struggling to follow the teachings of Jesus? Are there parts of your life that you struggle to control? These are the areas where you have an invitation from God to confess your weaknesses and to rely fully on God's power.

You can find strength in the place where you thought you were least likely to look for it.

Jesus, may I humbly confess my weaknesses and failures to You today so
that I can fully rely on You and Your power as my source of strength.

WAIT ON GOD'S STRENGTH

Have you not known? Have you not heard? The LORD is the everlasting God, the Creator of the ends of the earth. He does not faint or grow weary; his understanding is unsearchable. He gives power to the faint, and to him who has no might he increases strength.
ISAIAH 40:28–29 ESV

Waiting on God does not feel like a very productive or proactive strategy on first look. Waiting feels like being stuck and failing to step out in faith. However, waiting can be a vital act of faith that can make a difference in the big picture of life. Waiting can acknowledge that you don't know which way to go on your own and that you require God's strength and wisdom.

While you may grow weary and run out of energy, God is an inexhaustible resource. There is no weariness in God, and if you rely on God, you can tap into this power for your own life. The static act of waiting on God can lead to renewed energy and strength, giving you the resources to continue when life grows difficult. The less powerful you feel, the more "qualified" you are to receive an infusion of God's strength.

As you wait on God, consider the reputation of God. The stories of God's deliverance offer encouragement to endure seasons of struggle and difficulty.

Lord, You are more than able to give me strength when I am weak and give me direction when I am lost.

CALLED TO BENEFIT OTHERS

*"I will give you as a covenant for the people, a light for the nations,
to open the eyes that are blind, to bring out the prisoners from
the dungeon, from the prison those who sit in darkness."*

ISAIAH 42:6–7 ESV

You have been called by God and sealed with Him in a holy covenant for the benefit and blessing of others. The light of God in your life isn't just for your own guidance and direction. God is with you to guide you and to use you as a guide for others. The stakes are far greater than your own salvation. Many others will see the light of God through you and will be able to find their way forward because of His work in you.

Isaiah wrote for people who were spiritually trapped and sometimes confined by the constraints of exile in a foreign land. The "prison" here could be both literal and metaphorical, and God's concern is for both the physical and spiritual freedom of people. The liberation and transformation of God in your life are meant to be passed on to others.

What kinds of prisons do you see around you? Are there ways you can live as a light to people who are bound, whether physically or spiritually?

Jesus, help me generously share Your light with others so that they can discover the transforming power of Your light in their lives.

HOW DOES GENEROSITY CHANGE YOU?

Honor the LORD with your wealth, with the firstfruits of all your
crops; then your barns will be filled to overflowing,
and your vats will brim over with new wine.
PROVERBS 3:9–10 NIV

Generously giving your best to God recognizes that accumulating wealth, building your own reputation, or fabricating your own network of security are mirages set to pass away.

In fact, it would be a severe tragedy to hold back from giving your wealth to God. That puts you in danger of relying too much on money or possessions. Jesus frequently warned that being rich puts people in danger of hell, in part because wealth can become a de facto deity, a source of false comfort, security, and provision.

If you want to have hope that you will manage your money well, then you need to learn to give it away. Generosity teaches you that God provides for your needs, and so you can afford to make a space for worship in your life and make donations to those in need.

Only when you've learned to give money away reliably does God consider you prepared to handle greater amounts of money. God doesn't prioritize your comfort, but He does want to ensure that you are secure in Him alone.

Lord, help me avoid the trap of wealth so that I can
live in the prosperity of Your presence.

GOD WILL WIN

"Turn to me and be saved, all the ends of the earth! For I am God, and there is no other. By myself I have sworn; from my mouth has gone out in righteousness a word that shall not return: 'To me every knee shall bow, every tongue shall swear allegiance.'"
ISAIAH 45:22–23 ESV

God will not share His worship with anyone or anything else in this world. Even those who are confident and powerful today will have to bow down and worship God. The challenges and threats of today cannot stand before the power of God and the assured day of reckoning. This is true even if it appears that God is on the losing end of so many causes and conflicts.

How does the image of all people and authorities bowing down to God one day change your perspective today? Do you find that sometimes you've imagined God as powerless or weak? Have you imagined that your circumstances or certain people are stronger and more influential than they are?

Life may be a series of shifts and reorientations in light of the truth of God's power and presence. The choice you make today to live in obedience to God and to follow God's direction for your life will be what stands the test of time—extending even into eternity.

Lord, help me remember that You have overcome every principality and power in the world.

WEAR YOUR IDENTITY IN CHRIST

For you are all children of God through faith in Christ Jesus.
And all who have been united with Christ in baptism
have put on Christ, like putting on new clothes.
GALATIANS 3:26–27 NLT

Through your union with Jesus Christ and baptism into His family, you have received a new identity that you can never lose to anything in this world. However, while nothing can separate you from Christ, you can choose to leave that new identity behind much like someone who leaves a new set of clothes behind at home. You have been reconciled with God and have the identity of His beloved child. That is a truth you can claim today as your own. You can choose to "wear" it or you can discard it.

While there is nothing you can do to change your position in Christ, how have you left it behind at times? Have you let the distractions and priorities of life interfere with the saving power of God in your life? The opportunities for obscuring this transforming position in Christ are many. Perhaps the best step you can take to secure this truth today is to seek out someone who is joined in Christ with you.

Seeing the life of God in others may remind you of what you've also inherited in Christ.

Father, help me rest secure in my identity as Your child.

LIVE AS GOD'S CHILD, NOT HIS SLAVE

*And because we are his children, God has sent the Spirit of his Son
into our hearts, prompting us to call out, "Abba, Father."
Now you are no longer a slave but God's own child.
And since you are his child, God has made you his heir.*

GALATIANS 4:6–7 NLT

The Christian life is meant to be lived as a child of God, seeking the Spirit's confirmation of God's presence and acceptance. If you are seeking to obey God out of duty or out of fear, you have unintentionally demoted yourself from child to servant in the eyes of God.

Consider what you're hearing in your heart today. Are you hearing that you aren't good enough for God or that God is angry at you? If you don't hear the Spirit's voice calling out "Abba, Father," then you can rest assured that you aren't hearing from God.

Today is an invitation to be reoriented by the Holy Spirit. Every other priority, possession, and goal in life pales in comparison to the inheritance you have been promised in Christ as an heir in God's family.

There is an inheritance of peace and joy in God that belongs to you if you are willing to seek the Spirit's voice in your life. Gladly accept this new identity as a beloved child of God the Father today.

*Father, help me hear the truth today about
my identity as Your beloved child.*

SHEPHERD INTERVENTION

We're all like sheep who've wandered off and gotten lost.
We've all done our own thing, gone our own way. And GOD has
piled all our sins, everything we've done wrong, on him, on him.
ISAIAH 53:6 MSG

Sheep need a shepherd. They wander off without *shepherd guidance.*
They trust wolves without *shepherd intervention.* They won't drink from a stream without a *shepherd's calming.* You are a sheep.

When sheep are left by themselves they always get into trouble. This is an unflattering but accurate comparison. Sheep are horrible at trying to manage life alone.

Without God, you'll walk toward sin. It's easy, seems convenient, and is more attractive than the sheep pen. You think there won't be any fun if you follow the Shepherd, but His guidance brings life, safety, and security.

If sheep are a common sacrifice, then God sent a surprise. Jesus, the Good Shepherd, chose to let the sheep go free while He became the sacrifice for the lost and wandering. While you went your own way, Jesus paid for your rebellion.

You will come face-to-face with change when you break free from your stubborn sheep thinking and return to the Shepherd. There's protection within His care, healing for your inner wounds, and life companionship in His presence.

Dear God, help me turn around every time I wander away from Your Son.
Help me resist the urge to run. Help me find peace in Your presence.

GOD'S SPIRIT

Walk by the Spirit, and you will not gratify the desires of the flesh.
GALATIANS 5:16 NIV

Maybe you've heard it said that if you're looking for answers, just look deep within. Whoever came up with that idea was right—*if* they meant that you have God's Spirit living within you and His wisdom and guidance provide the answers you seek. However, if they meant that you could come up with the right answer on your own, they were wrong.

Left to discover your own answers apart from God places you on a path called destruction (Galatians 6:8). When you give God the space needed to direct your steps, He'll make sure you have the right directions (Proverbs 3:6). One very powerful mark of transformation is obeying God's Spirit when He says no.

It's easy to make following an option or going to great lengths to justify why following didn't make sense. Giving in to things that violate God's commands (desires of the flesh) only proves you're skipping discipleship classes with God's Spirit. Amos 3:3 (NKJV) says, "Can two walk together, unless they are agreed?"

God sent His Spirit to be your partner in purpose, companion in commission, and sidekick in support. Never buy into the lie that you're alone.

Dear God, help me acknowledge and listen to Your Spirit.
When I feel abandoned, I make big mistakes. I don't
want to go anywhere without inviting Your Spirit.

TURN FROM THE TURNING

He will die for lack of discipline and instruction,
and in the greatness of his folly he will go astray and be lost.
PROVERBS 5:23 AMPC

If God instructs you through His Word, and if God's Spirit offers the spiritual discipline needed to stay on God's path and find rescue, then why be surprised when you choose to drop out of *God's Way Academy* only to discover how lost you really are.

It should raise a long series of red flags when you find yourself devolving into this negative transformation. God calls it folly. He sends out the *great spiritual signal flares* to demonstrate His willingness to rescue. He wants you to know that, when you fail to make *God-informed choices*, you are lured away and won't find your way back—without help.

If this is a search and rescue mission, then God is calling out your name. He knows where you are, but you will need to turn His direction (Matthew 11:28), fix your spiritual eyes on Him (Hebrews 12:1–3), and return to Him to find rest (Matthew 11:28–30).

Dear God, I am literally lost without You. I'm not sure why it's so hard
to admit I can't do everything on my own, but I live with people who
find themselves wandering away from time to time. Lead me back,
welcome me home, teach my heart to keep moving Your direction.

NO CONSOLATION PRIZE

*In him you also, when you heard the word of truth, the gospel
of your salvation, and believed in him, were sealed with the
promised Holy Spirit, who is the guarantee of our inheritance
until we acquire possession of it, to the praise of his glory.*

EPHESIANS 1:13–14 ESV

Game shows offer a consolation prize if contestants don't win. This gift is offered when there is a failed attempt at winning the game.

God doesn't offer consolation prizes. If you choose God, you get it all, and if you don't, you get nothing. When you believe Jesus is the only way, and accept God's rescue, you will be saved. The benefits? You can expect grace (access to God when you did nothing to earn His interest), mercy (not being punished for something you deserve), forgiveness, and the companionship of God's Spirit.

You also gain eternal life with God and a face-to-face relationship with Him in heaven. This inheritance is guaranteed but, just like an earthy inheritance, you will need to wait. When you get all of God, is there any conceivable consolation prize that would make life worth living without Him?

*Dear God, when I believe and accept everything that's true about Your
Son, my today is changed. Because You forgive, my yesterday is changed.
Because You offer eternity with You, my tomorrow is changed.
You offer change because You don't want to leave me the way
You found me. Thanks for caring about my every day.*

WHAT GOD LOVES

Here are six things GOD hates,
and one more that he loathes with a passion.
PROVERBS 6:16 MSG

God offered a list indicating life change is delayed by personal choice. This list touches on areas of the Christian life that may be keeping you from *new-life living*.

Perhaps God hates the actions in Proverbs 6 because they're all choices that cripple relationship. There's a rejection of God's best in favor of personal choice. Proverbs 6:17–19 (MSG) offers the list: "Eyes that are arrogant, a tongue that lies, hands that murder the innocent, a heart that hatches evil plots, feet that race down a wicked track, a mouth that lies under oath, a troublemaker in the family."

Arrogance won't show love because it believes no one is worthy. Lies are told to protect self but keep you from honorable living. Murder removes the value of God's creation but destroys one of God's master creations. Plotting evil refuses to look out for the interests of others. Racing to wickedness means you are intentionally moving away from God. Lying under oath means you have predetermined to refuse to speak truth. Being a troublemaker causes family members to battle each other.

Dear God, I want to be someone who shows others what Your love looks
like. I can't do that when I act on any of the things in Your Proverbs
6 list. Help me reject what You hate and share what You love.

FAITHFUL PROMISE

*"I will create new heavens and a new earth. The former things
will not be remembered, nor will they come to mind."*

ISAIAH 65:17 NIV

The people of Israel advanced through life with baggage from their past. Sins against God, their family, and neighbors could be listed long past anyone's interest in hearing about their *God dishonor*. There was one, however, who was very interested in hearing their personal list of treachery. The one with the listening ear was God. When the people were willing to own their sin, He was willing to embrace their interest in changing.

Today's verse might seem like something you'd read in the New Testament. You can find something similar in 2 Peter 3:13. The *God promise* of new heavens and a new earth was an indication that at some point God would transform the status quo. The *transformed* would gain access to something new and perfect. In this place, the past is forgotten, the present is perfection, and the future is without sin.

Even in the Old Testament, God was clear that He could transform lives *and* futures. He even indicates that His love will mean an intentional forgetting of your past rebellion.

*Dear God, I can't forget the sins others have committed against me—
but You can. I can't imagine a place without sin—but You are creating
one. I can only imagine things getting worse—but You made
a better promise. I'm so glad that You're faithful.*

THE ANTIDOTE

Throw off your old sinful nature and your former way of life,
which is corrupted by lust and deception. Instead, let the Spirit
renew your thoughts and attitudes. Put on your new
nature, created to be like God—truly righteous and holy.
EPHESIANS 4:22–24 NLT

God did not say, "Take off your favorite sin garment, fold it, and store it away for now. You might need it again." His idea was to radically throw a former way of life as far away as possible. He had no intention of seeing you return to sin and pick up where you left off. Instead, He said this old life was corrupted by deception and selfish desire.

God's antidote is a new nature complete with new thinking and new actions. More importantly, He did not want you to teach yourself about this new life. He gave you His Spirit and that Spirit can help breathe new ways of thinking into your mind, new attitudes in your actions, and new hope into your soul.

God has given you a new nature. *Wear it proudly.* You represent the King of all kings. *His character looks good on you.*

Dear God, why is it so easy for me to keep pieces of my past so close?
They tempt me to turn from Your new life and return to the very
things I was happy to escape. I don't want to wear
new-life clothes and speak old-life words.

FAILING GOD'S TEST

"My people are foolish, they have not known Me. They are silly children, and they have no understanding. They are wise to do evil, but to do good they have no knowledge."

Jeremiah 4:22 nkjv

You might think you're the only person who's ever wrestled with sin. You have an adversary who is happy to let you think it's just you, but the apostle Paul lamented that he didn't seem to be able to get things right (Romans 7:19–25).

God called the people of Israel foolish, silly, and without understanding. They knew the right answer but chose what caused them to fail God's test over and over—and over again.

It was as if God was saying, "I've tried so many times to help my people understand who I am, but they only understand evil."

Had the people received a master's degree in *wickedness*? They understood sin and knew how to apply it to their lives and relationships.

Sin is common, so you never need to think you have ever been the only one to face it, let alone found it easier to give in than make the right choice.

Don't resist *new-life living*. Cooperate with God, listen to His Spirit, and walk in newness of life.

Dear God, I have been foolish. I have been defiant. I have made the wrong choices. Help me walk away from my advanced degree in sin and change my major to new-life wisdom.

HEY, DAD

Fathers, do not irritate and provoke your children to anger [do not exasperate them to resentment], but rear them [tenderly] in the training and discipline and the counsel and admonition of the Lord.
EPHESIANS 6:4 AMPC

The way a father nurtures his children is another indicator of *new-life living*. Your parenting decisions may require a change in perspective.

What if God had said, "I do not provoke you to anger, My child. I never seek to exasperate you. I want to train you and I will do that through My perfect correction, consultation, and clarity"?

This changes one's perspective. It deals with how God treats you and not how you treat your children. Yet, by framing it this way, you might be able to appreciate the fact that God is not asking you to do something He has not already done for you. He doesn't want you to be harder on your children than He is with you. Don't miss the fact that, when it seems your child is difficult, the same can be said of you from your *Father's perspective*.

Train, rear, and counsel your children tenderly. Always read God's training manual.

Dear God, make my heart soft toward my child. I don't need to rule with an iron fist when You certainly haven't done that with me. Let me model Your character so Your character seems natural to my child.

NO TRADE

"Take my instruction instead of silver, and knowledge rather
than choice gold, for wisdom is better than jewels,
and all that you may desire cannot compare with her."
PROVERBS 8:10–11 ESV

If you had a choice between God's instructions for life, or a few bars of silver, which would you take? If you could learn more about the One who created you and how to have a friendship with Him, or a box of gold, which would seem more enticing? If you had a choice between making quality decisions based on God's wisdom, or some hand-cut diamonds, what's your choice?

You probably sided with the *God choices* because, after all, it's expected, right? The truth is, sometimes you will seek to trade God's instruction, direction, and wisdom for something worth much less. It's okay to admit that. However, if you think this trade is worthwhile, God clears it up when He said, "All that you may desire cannot compare."

When you struggle, be honest with God. Anything you accept in trade for the mind of God is worse than trading a brand-new luxury car for a plastic toy from a dollar store. There will never be a fair trade for God's wisdom. Never an equal trade. Never a *better than* trade. Never.

Dear God, may I never seek to trade Your wisdom. There is nothing
as valuable and nothing as life changing as knowing
Your heart and being Your student. Teach me.

STAND

Stand united, singular in vision, contending for people's trust in the Message, the good news, not flinching or dodging in the slightest before the opposition. Your courage and unity will show them what they're up against: defeat for them, victory for you—and both because of God.
PHILIPPIANS 1:27–28 MSG

One of the greatest indications of *new-life living* is a strong identity in following Jesus. You care more about what God *wants* than what people *think*. You will stand with Him and His people before you would ever think about boycotting God.

Transformation sometimes means doing something unnatural. It may not seem normal to identify yourself with a group that works toward a common goal that benefits someone who isn't even a part of the group. It's unnatural to identify with a group that will experience promised opposition.

The end of this point of transformation includes a message to those who try to stop you. In the end your obedience means "defeat for them, victory for you—and both because of God" (Philippians 1:28 MSG). When God brings new life, it impacts much more than your life.

Dear God, I often think of new life as something that applies to me because I chose to follow You. It's also something attractive to others because they see Your new life written in the living book of my life. Help me join with Your family in being courageous and unified in sharing new-life living.

ACTION REBOOT

This is what the LORD says: "Don't let the wise boast in their wisdom,
or the powerful boast in their power, or the rich boast in their riches.
But those who wish to boast should boast in this alone: that they
truly know me and understand that I am the LORD who demonstrates
unfailing love and who brings justice and righteousness
to the earth, and that I delight in these things."
JEREMIAH 9:23–24 NLT

Christopher Columbus is known for a lot of things, but exploring just one of his passions would be a good way to celebrate this day. Columbus is known for searching for a quicker way to reach the world with the message of the Gospel. His voyage was designed, in part, to see if this new route would make that possible.

What you can take away on this holiday is that your most impressive wisdom, power, and riches offer no reason to boast. The only thing you can really boast about is being friends with the God whose love brings justice and righteousness into the world. This is true no matter the year of discovery.

Transformation changes motives, resets thinking, and reboots your actions. It all begins with obedience—agreeing to do the next thing God asks.

Dear God, I want Your great adventure for me. I want to
follow You because Your plan is better than mine.
I want others to hear me boast, "It's all You, God!"

THE WAY OF INSIGHT

"Leave your simple ways, and live, and walk in the way of insight."
PROVERBS 9:6 ESV

Wade out into deeper water, move past the starting line, and remove the barriers that define your comfort zone.

Putting off participation in a *God plan* might make sense to you. If you could just have a little more time to adjust to the idea of doing something bigger than your current spiritual skill set. You want God to be patient with procrastination. Things are moving too fast.

There are things you need to do because God wants you to do them. But as long as you say, "I'll get around to it," then you're comfortable in your deferred promise. After all, you can continue to push that deferment as often as convenience suggests it's a sensible option.

God says, "Go!" and you throw up a stop sign and expect God to bless you for disobedience. You can come to believe that because God offers grace, obedience is completely optional.

New-life living is tied to your willingness to follow. The sweat equity of obedience is not because work is essential to rescue, but because trusting God's directions is needed in order to draw closer to the *direction giver*.

When God gives insight, don't hesitate. Do something with what you're learning.

*Dear God, give me a heart that wants what You want.
Give me eyes that see the needs You see. Give me feet
that take Your message because You said, "Go!"*

NO ROOM

*Don't fret or worry. Instead of worrying, pray. Let petitions and praises
shape your worries into prayers, letting God know your concerns.
Before you know it, a sense of God's wholeness, everything coming
together for good, will come and settle you down. It's wonderful what
happens when Christ displaces worry at the center of your life.*

PHILIPPIANS 4:6–7 MSG

Fear is humanity's standard default. Whenever bad things happen, fear
gets called up to the majors. If you find yourself fearful, it's common,
and you're normal. *God doesn't want you to be normal.*

He wants to transform what keeps you up at night into a willingness
to let Him take care of things. Imagine getting a new appliance. Plug it
in, but it doesn't work. Do you automatically think, *Great, all I have is a
paperweight!* Maybe you pick up your phone and call the appliance store.
Prayer is a little bit like that. It's the call you make when concerns, anxiety,
and fear show up uninvited and suggest life doesn't work.

Fear doesn't stay in the same place where faith is found. If your prayer
demonstrates faith, then fear has to leave. It has no choice because you
can't be concerned about the future and absolutely believe God has it
taken care of at the same time.

*Dear God, send fear on a one-way trip away from my soul. Remind me
that You are worth trusting and that, when I do, I have nothing to fear.*

HEART REPLACEMENT

The heart is deceitful above all things and beyond cure.
Who can understand it?

JEREMIAH 17:9 NIV

You want to do the right thing. You know it's a good idea. You plan to stick to your decision. Then? *You don't.*

It's not that you don't love God. *You do.* It's not that you don't have good intentions. *You try.* It's not that you don't experience disappointment. *It keeps you company.*

New-life living is understanding that when all you do is rely on your own efforts, you'll fail more often than succeed. The reason is simple—your heart can't be trusted. You can't understand why it does what it does. But you *can* let God change it.

Your inner deception will have to deal with God's truth. Your tendency to manipulate will have to adjust to God's plan. Your desire for self-preservation will need to make room for God's mercy and love. Then He'll want you to give His love to others—and He will always make sure you have enough.

You will need to become a man after God's own heart. God wants to replace your deceptive heart with His own.

Dear God, I don't think I would even need Jeremiah 17:9 to tell me I have a deceptive heart. I've witnessed it more times than I want to admit. Give me Your heart, eyes, and mind so I can examine life, circumstances, and others from Your perspective. This is the change I need.

COMING CHANGE

*The mouth of the righteous is a fountain of life, but the mouth
of the wicked conceals violence. Hatred stirs up strife,
but love covers all offenses.*
PROVERBS 10:11–12 ESV

These verses and those surrounding them represent a battle between the changed and the unchanged, the new and the old, the transformed and the status quo.

The *changed* offer life-giving words. The *unchanged* speak words that incite riots. The *new* chooses love that results in reconciliation. The *old* feels like a bad family reunion. The *transformed* seeks peace. The *status quo* enjoys a good brawl.

You have your own internal war. There are moments when you're all about peace, reconciliation, and kind words. There are also moments when you want to speak your mind without caring how it affects those who hear your voice.

New-life living isn't the result of a magic wand. Instead, it's a process. God's forgiveness is the result of acknowledging you blew it. His transformation is the result of continuing to admit your mistakes and then obeying God's blueprint for living.

You won't get where you need to go on your own. If change is a process, then let God direct the progress. Cooperate with Him. Let the old become new, and the status quo undergo transformation, and then *become* the promised change.

*Dear God, let me welcome Your plans for me with open arms. Let me
welcome them like a trusted friend. Let me keep them as close as family.*

ENGAGED FOR LIFE

And set your minds and keep them set on what is above (the higher things), not on the things that are on the earth. For [as far as this world is concerned] you have died, and your [new, real] life is hidden with Christ in God.
COLOSSIANS 3:2–3 AMPC

When you engage in *new-life living*, expect to be misunderstood. Your thinking and decision-making will change. To your friends, and maybe your family, you will no longer seem like the person they've always known.

As long as your *friends list* includes people who don't follow Jesus, you can expect them to think the old you has died and the man they once knew doesn't exist anymore. *They're right.* You've put *old-life living* to death and it's normal when old friends don't understand.

First Corinthians 2:14 (NLT) says, "But people who aren't spiritual can't receive these truths from God's Spirit. It all sounds foolish to them and they can't understand it, for only those who are spiritual can understand what the Spirit means."

The good news in this *old-life funeral* is that the new life you live acts as a megaphone to those who see the difference—and now want to know more about the change that can make them new.

Dear God, help me remember what I learn from You isn't always understood by people I care about. Give me the right words. Give them something to think about.

SPOKEN WORDS

The lips of the righteous know what is acceptable,
but the mouth of the wicked what is perverse.
PROVERBS 10:32 NKJV

Transformation alters the way you speak. Rude comments begin to fade. Kind words? Newly spoken by a tongue ill-used to forming the sounds of decency. Where it was once easy to speak profane words, those same words begin to sound unnatural and leave you feeling oddly uncomfortable. Bitter stories are countered with reminders of God's forgiveness. You might even surprise yourself.

Does this mean you will never slip and say something you regret? *No.* Words leading to remorse will also be spoken. They land on the floor of conversation like dead men's bones. You may discover that your word choices will change because they no longer fit with *new-life living*.

Spiritual speech patterns help identify you as someone who represents Jesus, the *Change Maker*. Your new language isn't a matter for pride. It's one more identifying mark that Jesus is changing more than your eternal destination.

You can use your words to be critical, dishonest, or hateful. Much different words convince others that you love Jesus and that His love has real power to change lives.

Dear God, sometimes I think my words don't really matter.
Sometimes I think I can separate my life with You and the life
I live among other humans. You never did. May my
mouth reflect the change You're making in me.

NO SOCIAL CLUB

Use your heads as you live and work among outsiders. Don't miss a trick. Make the most of every opportunity. Be gracious in your speech. The goal is to bring out the best in others in a conversation, not put them down, not cut them out.

COLOSSIANS 4:5–6 MSG

God did not invite you to *new-life living* to engage in a spiritual social club that is exclusive and unwelcoming. He did not ask you to change just so you no longer need to associate with those who haven't chosen to follow Him.

The trouble with this thinking is that we're told in scripture that "we're Christ's representatives. God uses us to persuade men and women to drop their differences and enter into God's work of making things right between them" (2 Corinthians 5:20 MSG).

A representative is someone who shares what he knows about the one he represents. You can't do that if you refuse to tell others how they can be friends with God.

There is an old song that asks children whether they should hide what they know about Jesus (their light) under a bushel. The answer is a universal *no!* Nothing has changed. It's still a perfect answer.

Dear God, help me find an enthusiasm for sharing the best news I've ever heard with people who thought it was a rumor. If You can change me, then help me connect with people who need an introduction to real change.

TRADING MY SIN

*Whoever is steadfast in righteousness will live,
but he who pursues evil will die.*
PROVERBS 11:19 ESV

I f you ever needed a practical reason to trade your sin for forgiveness, turn your back on your past for *new-life living*, and discover trust where suspicion used to live, then there is good news just waiting to be read.

Choose new life and really live (Ephesians 4:22–24). Follow the path leading away from God and instead experience death (Romans 6:23). It would probably help to understand that when God speaks about life, He's speaking about eternity after your body dies. When God describes life for the Christian, it is being with Him for eternity. When He describes death, it is a place where you are separated from Him forever.

In practical terms, accepting God's rescue plan means *never* being separated from Him. An even greater reason to invite change is that you discover in the present what it's like to be a child of God. You gain His wisdom, discover His plan, experience His love, receive His forgiveness, and find a deep well of grace. And it's all yours.

There's no reason to wait (again, see Ephesians 4:22–24). There's no other answer (John 14:6). Tomorrow is never promised (James 4:14).

Dear God, a decision for You gives my present power because my future is taken care of. Why should I keep silent about this wonderful gift of life?

GRATITUDE. JOY. DISCIPLESHIP.

How we thank God for you! Because of you we have great joy as we enter God's presence. Night and day we pray earnestly for you, asking God to let us see you again to fill the gaps in your faith.

1 THESSALONIANS 3:9–10 NLT

God wants those who sin to turn away from their failings and follow Him (2 Peter 3:9). Angels rejoice when they do (Luke 15:10). The apostle Paul made life change a big deal (see verse above).

Paul was grateful. He expressed joy over good news. He wanted to do everything he could to help new believers in their faith journey.

Sometimes discipleship is viewed as an optional advanced course. After all, most people who seek God are told that they can come to Jesus just as they are. The value of going beyond a weekend worship service is something the individual often feels they could take a pass on.

Paul felt that if discipleship was a big deal to Jesus, it should be for him and to any who've experienced life change.

Discover gratitude and joy by learning more and living out the lessons.

Dear God, help me see the value in discovery. The more I get to know You, the more I want to know. The more I trust, the more I see You as trustworthy. Maybe someone needs to hear me say that. Give me the courage.

THE DAWN OF JOY

"Young women will dance and be happy, young men and old men
will join in. I'll convert their weeping into laughter,
lavishing comfort, invading their grief with joy."
JEREMIAH 31:13 MSG

The people of Israel were in trouble. Their sin, and unwillingness to turn from it, resulted in a *national time-out*. They needed to think about what the good God had done and their unwillingness to acknowledge His instructions. They enjoyed His blessings but turned their back on the *blessing giver*.

The prophet Jeremiah shared God's message about a future transformation. The people would first enter a time of sorrow. Their lives would be defined by trouble. However, when sin was removed as their *go-to* response, then God would restore their lost joy.

A great companion verse is Psalm 30:5 (MSG), "The nights of crying your eyes out give way to days of laughter."

Grief is something you have experienced at some point in your life. It is a season of sorrow and trouble, but it doesn't need to last forever. If it requires a turning from moral failure, *do it.* If it requires learning from God's Spirit, *listen.* If it requires leaving bitterness behind, *don't look back.* Joy may be on the way.

Dear God, sorrow comes because of decisions I make, but it can also
come from life circumstances I would not have chosen. Help me
see through the darkness to the dawn of Your joy.

BRING ON THE PEACE

Be at peace among yourselves.

1 THESSALONIANS 5:13 NKJV

*B*e at peace among yourselves. Five words that represent *new-life living.* Five words that assign responsibility to those who read them. Five words that helped define the early church.

John 14:27 (NKJV) helps define this peace. Jesus said, "Peace I leave with you, My peace I give to you; not as the world gives do I give to you."

God's peace isn't always the absence of conflict, but it's brought to light by how you respond to conflict. Troubling circumstances don't have to boss you around and tell you what to do. Choose your response wisely. It's the visible fruit of personal transformation.

When your life isn't defined by peace, it could be that God is working to transform your response. You could have trust issues with the God who offers peace—peace you can't begin to understand (Philippians 4:5–7).

First Timothy 5:13 describes four things that leave you without peace. First, being idle. Second, spreading gossip. Third, being a busybody. Fourth, saying things you shouldn't.

A lack of peace leaves you restless. You compensate by doing and saying things that leave footprints of disharmony. God's peace is equal parts knowing what to avoid and knowing God can be trusted.

Dear God, bring new-life answers to old internal battles.
Help me avoid things that push peace away. Help me
stay close to You as You change me.

CONVERSATION STARTER

*"Call to me and I will answer you and tell you great
and unsearchable things you do not know."*

JEREMIAH 33:3 NIV

Jeremiah was human, so he could never boast perfection. Then again, he represented people who steadfastly resisted transformation. Still, God had an offer to make.

Call to Me. When God said this, the people stubbornly refused to allow Him to lead. They may not have denied His existence, but all they could see was what they had to give up if they came back to God.

I will answer you. God would not be silent. He would not display a cold shoulder. He would not treat them the way they treated Him.

I will tell you great and unsearchable things. God offered His people an education. The things they didn't know, He would explain.

The people refused to call. They did not listen. They would not learn. God had shown mercy, love, and patience to them, and yet it was rewarded with mockery and dismissal.

He offers the same terms to you. Call and He'll answer. Listen and His Spirit will teach. You can refuse His offer, but why? It's one of the best offers you could ever accept.

*Dear God, I've read enough to know that Your plan for new-life living
is for my benefit. You don't keep me from fun things as much
as You protect me for the best things. Help me call.
Thanks for answering. Thanks for teaching.*

GOOD MOTIVE?

As for you, brothers, do not grow weary in doing good.
2 THESSALONIANS 3:13 ESV

Many people think Christianity is a religion of people trying to do good things. Yet doing good can make you feel obligated, obligation makes you feel resentment, and resentment makes you want to stop doing good things.

That's where weariness comes in. You can get tired of feeling as if people expect you to be the *doer of good things*. Perhaps this is a part of *new-life living* that's been misunderstood. You want to help some people. Some are helped because it's the right thing to do. Maybe you've never considered an even greater motivation.

You don't work harder so God might like you. Instead, the work you do opens doors to expressing other parts of your transformed life. You can express kindness and love, but you can also express good news by helping someone who is open to learning more about Jesus. The act of helping may be less important than what others learn from your willingness to help.

Paul's encouragement to stand strong and keep helping others may have had everything to do with never missing opportunities. The opportunities are introducing others to God, and that's hard to do from your easy chair.

Dear God, make me willing to help others and share Your love.
May Your compassion run through my actions. May opportunities make
this transformed life useful. I'd love to see someone else transformed.

LOVE TRANSFORMATION

*The purpose of my instruction is that all believers would be
filled with love that comes from a pure heart, a clear conscience,
and genuine faith. But some people have missed this whole
point. They have turned away from these things and spend their
time in meaningless discussions. They want to be known as
teachers of the law of Moses, but they don't know what they are
talking about, even though they speak so confidently.*

1 TIMOTHY 1:5–7 NLT

When Christians miss the core teaching of God's love, they may speak truth, but no one wants to listen. They argue points of order. They've never missed a question in Bible trivia. But the question of relationship with God never gets an adequate answer.

New-life living *should* be filled with learning more about what God wants, but some learn Bible facts as if preparing for debate club. They want to know the right answer but have never allowed *God's love sermon* to change how they interact with others.

Change in the Christian life doesn't come from knowing Bible facts. Instead, it comes from being changed by the love that transformed your destiny from death to life, bitterness to betterness, and justice to mercy.

---

*Dear God, I want to allow Your love to change the way I treat people. Let
me not use what I learn to make people feel stupid. May what
I learn make me a friend who just happens to know You.*

COMPARE AND CONTRAST

A God-loyal life keeps you on track;
sin dumps the wicked in the ditch.
PROVERBS 13:6 MSG

A good look at before and after *new-life living* is found in Proverbs 13. Sin takes you on the Indulgence Express where you are encouraged to give in to everything you've ever wanted to experience with no regard for consequences. Then, when you're used up, washed up, and fed up, sin opens the Indulgence Express doors and rolls you into the ditch. As the express pulls away, you can hear the driver's raspy voice say: "I'll be back to see if you want another ride. Don't bother asking God for help. You're too pathetic to rescue."

It's easy to believe the lie, isn't it? You know you've made wrong choices, and those choices have kept you from asking God for help. Sin encourages more sin and has no intention of offering you a way out.

Transformation by God, however, takes you to a place that offers freedom *from* sin's grip and freedom *to* live with the best choices. It's ironic how many can't break from the abusing accuser, when freedom is the immediate gift of *trusting God*.

Dear God, accepting Your great gift is easy, but it can be one of the most difficult choices anyone can make. The change can be dramatic and not everyone will be happy with the decision. Thanks for giving me new eyes to see the beauty of Your gift.

"PUT ME IN, COACH"

Exercise daily in God—no spiritual flabbiness, please!
Workouts in the gymnasium are useful, but a disciplined life
in God is far more so, making you fit both today and forever.
1 TIMOTHY 4:7–8 MSG

M ost exercise programs focus on what you eat and how you make your body do what they think it should do. There has to be choice, commitment, and consistency. You might start with an iron will, but then collapse like aluminum.

Maybe you're a gym rat. You arrive early, stay late, do more reps than suggested. You go home with a mixture of exhaustion and euphoria.

The human body can be transformed through effort, attention, and exercise. You might even pay more attention to physical fitness than your spiritual life. Paul said exercise is a good thing, but it only benefits a *finite* body. If you paid as much attention to your spiritual fitness, it has greater value because it keeps you fit in this life and in *eternity*.

Pay attention to what you put into your mind. Spend some time doing what God asks you to do. Share *this* fitness plan with others.

Transformation with cooperation prepares you for your ultimate destination.

Dear God, I admit I don't spend enough time with You to call
it a workout. As my spiritual trainer, Your Spirit can get me into
shape. I want that. I want to be more than a spectator
in the stands. Put me in, Coach.

FAMILY ASSISTANCE

If anyone fails to provide for his relatives, and especially for those of his own family, he has disowned the faith [by failing to accompany it with fruits] and is worse than an unbeliever [who performs his obligation in these matters].

1 TIMOTHY 5:8 AMPC

Family should be the strongest form of community anyone experiences. Maybe that's why some call Christians the *family* of God.

When God created Adam and Eve, He gave each a role within their relationship that added to the fulfillment of the other person (Genesis 2:18–25). There were parents, children, grandparents, siblings, aunts, uncles, nieces, and nephews. Many times these families lived in the same geographical location. Helping family members was encouraged.

Moses said parents were to be honored (Exodus 20:12). Jesus warned the Pharisees to stop creating loopholes so they could avoid helping their parents (Mark 7:11–13).

New-life living brings you into a closer sense of care for your family (close and extended).

You are God's representative. He cares for His family. He asks you to do the same for yours.

Dear God, family is important to You. There's nothing I can do that You haven't helped me with. Help me care for my family. May they see You in my actions. Help me do the things for my family that You would do. And when I ask for help, it's an acknowledgement that You've always been my greatest resource.

TRANSFORMED AND WISE

A scoffer seeks wisdom and does not find it,
but knowledge is easy to him who understands.
PROVERBS 14:6 NKJV

God has answers, and the *transformed* discover truth from the God who promised His Spirit would teach them. There's no room for arrogance. You didn't make any discoveries without someone pointing them out. Your greatest response is gratitude that God is willing to teach. You learn from the One who actually knows it all.

Some don't honor God in their hearts or actions. They assume God's Word is wrong. They believe in the value of new and untested theories and philosophies. They're drawn to the latest ideas while making fun of the very truth that exchanges foolishness with genuine wisdom.

You once stood in a long line with the unbelieving and foolish. You weren't convinced the Bible was a trustworthy document whose author was God Himself. As you grow in faith you have discovered the Bible is the right tool to straighten out faulty thinking (2 Timothy 3:16), has answers for the future (Matthew 5:18), and will be used in eternity (Matthew 24:35).

Proverbs 3:13 (NKJV) says, "Happy is the man who finds wisdom, and the man who gains understanding." Be happy.

Dear God, Your wisdom makes my wisdom look foolish.
Keep me from thinking I know it all. Keep me reading
Your Word. Keep me learning from Your Spirit.

LEAVE A LIGHT SHINING

So never be ashamed to tell others about our Lord.
2 TIMOTHY 1:8 NLT

Should you love Halloween or loathe it? Should you celebrate it or avoid it? Should you decorate or leave your front porch dark? The following words won't try to convince you one way or the other, but what you will read is how to bring God into a day like this. *He needs to be here.*

Never be ashamed of Jesus. Never be ashamed to take Him with you to restaurants, shopping experiences, and your neighbor's house. Tell others about Jesus. Make Him a topic of discussion when the opportunity arises. Share the story of how He transformed you. It doesn't have to be strange or unnatural.

Even on a day like today, you can bring Jesus to your front door. You don't need to preach a sermon or denounce some of the reasons for the evening treat fest. Instead, you can offer creative ways to bring light. You can bring light to something children typically only recognize as a great way to amass a fortune in candy while dressing up.

If love is kind, patient, and refuses to dishonor others, then show love—*and share Jesus.*

Dear God, if love can replace fear, then help me love—not just today, but the first day of November, December, and January and all the days in between and beyond. This day is not immune from the need to show Your love to those who settle for substitutes.

STUPID DEBATES

Don't have anything to do with foolish and stupid arguments,
because you know they produce quarrels. And the Lord's
servant must not be quarrelsome but must be kind
to everyone, able to teach, not resentful.
2 TIMOTHY 2:23–24 NIV

Ever meet that know-it-all, the guy who's ready to argue and debate over anything, including topics that aren't all that important? Apparently, the church Timothy pastored had more than one of those guys, for Paul tells him to avoid "avoid foolish and stupid arguments," simply because they cause divisions and quarrels in the church.

That wasn't a good thing in Timothy's church in Ephesus, and it's not a good thing now. In fact, there are many examples of divisions in churches over matters that don't even qualify as "trivial." (One silly example: a congregation reportedly argued over whether their after-service lunch should be called a "pot blessing" instead of a "potluck.")

Nowhere in the Bible does God tell His people to avoid all controversies at all times. Several scripture passages instruct readers to contend for the faith and stand against bad teaching. Then again, God calls you to use wisdom as you determine whether a fight is worth fighting.

Father, I enjoy a good debate as much as the next guy, and I know You
want men of God to stand for Your true Gospel. Give me wisdom to
know when to speak up—and when to keep my trap closed.

THE WHOLE WORD OF GOD

All Scripture is God-breathed and is useful for teaching, rebuking,
correcting and training in righteousness, so that the servant of
God may be thoroughly equipped for every good work.
2 TIMOTHY 3:16–17 NIV

The great twentieth-century pastor and author A. W. Tozer once observed, "The Word of God well understood and religiously obeyed is the shortest route to spiritual perfection. And we must not select a few favorite passages to the exclusion of others. Nothing less than a whole Bible can make a whole Christian."

That's some well-stated truth, isn't it? And it's also a great reflection of what today's scripture verses teach about the Bible's importance and trustworthiness.

The Bible contains everything you need to know about God and about His will for your life—*everything*. Taking that a step further, today's passage tells that all scripture—meaning the *whole* Bible—is useful to the man of God who wants to be prepared to do what God has called him to do.

What do you need God to do for you today? You can turn to His written Word to find out what steps you need to take to make sure He does it for you.

Father, thank You for speaking through the people who wrote the
scriptures. Thank You for using them to help me know You better—and
to provide me all I need to be equipped to live a life that pleases You.

SPEAKING GENTLY

A gentle answer turns away wrath, but a harsh word stirs up anger.
PROVERBS 15:1 NIV

No matter how nice, amicable, and kindhearted a guy you are, you can't go through life without occasionally finding yourself in conflict with someone—your wife, your son or daughter, or a business associate or coworker.

Imperfect human beings have differing needs and desires, and sometimes that leads to personal conflict. So how can you keep those conflicts from spiraling into hotheaded arguments and divisions? Today's verse offers some very practical wisdom (the book of Proverbs has a way of doing that) for handling such situations.

When you see and hear telltale signs of anger or frustration, do your best to check your own attitude. Cool your own emotions, lower your voice, and respond to the other person with an attitude of gentleness. If you've done something to cause an angry reaction—even if done unintentionally—seek forgiveness and reconciliation, and do it quickly.

Responding to another person's anger this way will make your life easier, keep your relationships stronger, and, most importantly, glorify your heavenly Father. That's a win-win situation for everyone.

Father in heaven, Your Word tells me that one of the fruits Your Spirit should produce in me is gentleness. Work in me and make me a truly gentle person, both in my actions and in my words.

KNOW WHAT YOU BELIEVE

He must hold firmly to the trustworthy message as it has been
taught, so that he can encourage others by sound
doctrine and refute those who oppose it.

TITUS 1:9 NIV

It's probably safe to say that most Christians today aren't terribly excited when they hear the word *doctrine*—and probably less excited about knowing what it is and what it should mean to them. The word simply refers to teaching or to a system of beliefs, and that's important for all Christians.

Sound biblical doctrine is important because it is central to living the Christlike life and to explaining your faith to others. After all, you can't very well follow instructions and live by truths you don't understand, and you certainly can't explain them to others if you don't know enough about what you believe.

If you want to understand good doctrine, and that's a great goal for any believer, go straight to the source: God's Word. The Bible contains everything you need in order to come to the faith, understand the faith, and share the faith with others.

Learning good doctrine is well worth your time. Ultimately, it helps you to know and love God more deeply.

God of wisdom, You've given me Your written Word so that I can know
what I believe and why I believe it. Help me hold to sound teaching
so that I may encourage others with the message You
want me to share with others.

SEEKING COUNSEL

Without counsel, plans go awry, but in the multitude
of counselors they are established.

PROVERBS 15:22 NKJV

As Israel's third monarch, Solomon had been charged with constructing the long-awaited temple in Jerusalem. The Bible says that tens of thousands of men worked on its construction (1 Kings 5:15–16). While God had given the king detailed plans for its layout, it's probably safe to say that Solomon consulted with men who knew more about construction than he did.

Solomon was known for his wisdom, and he was probably wise enough to know that he needed some counsel from men who had the know-how needed to finish what God had assigned him to do.

It's probably right to assume that most men who have accomplished great things for God's kingdom didn't work on a small island. Instead, they humbly turned to counselors and advisers who not only saw their work with "new eyes" but also gave them wise input and instruction when needed.

What has God assigned you to do? Do you have the wisdom and humility to turn to others? Who can give you the input you need to complete a current assignment successfully?

Father, something inside me makes me an overly independent man
who wants to make his own decisions without the help of others.
Please put people in my life who can offer me solid input—and then
give me the humility to listen and act on what they tell me.

SAVED BECAUSE OF HIS MERCY

He saved us, not because of righteous things we had done,
but because of his mercy. He saved us through the
washing of rebirth and renewal by the Holy Spirit.

TITUS 3:5 NIV

You've probably heard people say that as long as they do lots of good stuff and not too much bad stuff, then they're good with God and will go to heaven when they die. All that volunteering at the soup kitchen and giving to charity has to count for something, right?

While the Bible encourages people to perform acts of kindness for others, it also teaches that no one can be saved based on things they do. Salvation, it teaches, isn't earned. Instead, it's a gift from God based solely on His marvelous, amazing mercy and grace.

Again, there is nothing anyone can do to earn God's salvation. It's a gift from a generous, loving, forgiving God. Even better, nothing in anyone's past that can disqualify that person from salvation.

Don't put down the soup ladle. Don't stop writing checks to your favorite ministry. Keep in mind that you do those things because you've been saved, not because you think they will save you. God has already taken care of that!

Precious Savior, You transformed me through the power of Your love
and Your Holy Spirit. Humble me and help me focus on the fact
that I'm not saved because of any good I've done,
but because You have shown me mercy.

AS YOU MAKE YOUR PLANS

Commit your actions to the LORD, and your plans will succeed.
PROVERBS 16:3 NLT

Have you ever drawn up what you think is a great plan—perhaps at work or for your church—only to find that the enthusiasm for it is solely yours? The harsh reality is that no matter how good you think an idea or plan is, you still need the approval of those in position to make the final decisions.

Your ultimate authority in all things is your Father in heaven, and in today's verse, Solomon offers a great bit of wisdom when it comes to planning. The best way to handle your own plans, he writes, is to start by committing what you want to do to your ultimate Boss, the One who sits on His throne in heaven.

Many seemingly great plans, even plans for what looks like a great ministry, have failed because those with the vision failed to first submit their work to God. Planning is an important part of most great or important things you do for God's kingdom. Then again, before you launch out with your plan, make sure you have the go-ahead from the ultimate decision-maker.

Father, Your written Word stresses the importance of good planning, but it also tells me I need to submit all my actions to You. Please remind me to submit what I'm thinking about doing to You for Your approval and direction.

SPEAKING WHEN NO ONE IS LISTENING

"But when I speak with you, I will open your mouth, and you shall say to them, 'Thus says the Lord God.' He who hears, let him hear; and he who refuses, let him refuse; for they are a rebellious house."

EZEKIEL 3:27 NKJV

You probably didn't read it here first, but not everyone you talk with about the Lord is going to eagerly receive what you have to say. Some may be genuinely interested, but many others will politely listen before excusing themselves from the conversation. Still others will cut you off and give you the old "talk to the hand" gesture before walking away.

You may go through times when your attempts to plant Gospel seeds yield fewer results than those of a cold-call salesman trying to peddle something few want or need. That doesn't mean you should give up. On the contrary, God calls you to continue speaking the message and then let Him do the work within people's hearts.

God calls each Christian man to tell people about Jesus. So be ready to share what Jesus Christ has done for you and what He can do for others. Always remember that your job is to speak, even when people aren't listening.

Father in heaven, it's sometimes difficult for me to speak the transforming words of Your Gospel. Help me overcome my fear of rejection and continue speaking—and then let You do the rest.

KIND WORDS

Kind words are like honey—sweet to the
soul and healthy for the body.
Proverbs 16:24 nlt

You've probably heard it said that you catch more flies with honey than vinegar. Something in human nature tends to respond better to kindness and affirming words than to criticism and browbeating.

People in all kinds of professional endeavors—from high-power business leaders to workaday construction foremen—have figured out that people who work under them tend to perform better when given verbal pats on the back for their good work.

Think the same thing might work with your wife, your children, your friends, or your coworkers? Well, if you take the wisdom of today's verse to its logical conclusion. . .yes, it would!

So if you want to see the best in the people God has put in your life (and who doesn't?), make it a point to speak words of kindness to them. Go out of your way to let them know you notice when they do well. Make it a point to tell them you appreciate them for the things they do and for who they are.

The results might pleasantly surprise you.

Father, I believe You've changed my heart and mind so that I can
be a source of encouragement to others. Whether I'm speaking
to my wife, kids, or someone at work, remind me to
speak kind words to those around me.

A HEART PROBLEM

See to it, brothers and sisters, that none of you has a sinful,
unbelieving heart that turns away from the living God. But encourage
one another daily, as long as it is called "Today," so that none
of you may be hardened by sin's deceitfulness.

HEBREWS 3:12–13 NIV

The United States Centers for Disease Control and Prevention report that heart disease is the number-one killer in US, with 25 percent of deaths attributed to heart disease. More tragic? Many of these deaths were preventable.

It's a good idea to do the things that help prevent heart disease, like eating right and getting enough exercise. But it's even more important that you prevent what the Bible calls a "hard heart."

Jesus referred to some of the symptoms of a hard heart when He asked His disciples, "Do you have eyes but fail to see, and ears but fail to hear? And don't you remember?" (Mark 8:18 NIV). Today's key verses point out the cause: sin and unbelief.

If a man is not careful, he can develop a hard heart. But it can be prevented. It's prevented by making sure you spend time in prayer and in the Word of God daily. That way you can avoid the deceitfulness of sin and live in victory.

Loving Father, today's scripture reminds me that if I'm not careful, my
sinful thoughts, attitudes, and actions can cause my heart to become
hardened. Please draw me close to You daily so I can avoid that.

A DOUBLE-EDGED SWORD

For the word of God is alive and active. Sharper than any double-edged
sword, it penetrates even to dividing soul and spirit, joints and
marrow; it judges the thoughts and attitudes of the heart.

HEBREWS 4:12 NIV

Have you ever read a passage of scripture that seemed to be speaking directly to you? Perhaps it spoke directly to your current situation. Ever feel as if God had written it as a personal note to you and you alone? If so, it's probably because you've preceded your reading with prayer, asking God to illuminate what He wants His Word to say to you that day.

The Bible is an amazing book. It's not just a big collection of great stories. It's also your comprehensive instruction manual for walking with God and living the Christian life. And when you accompany your Bible reading with prayer, God Himself speaks to you personally as you read.

In recent years, the United States Constitution has been referred to as "a living, breathing document," as if its meaning evolves to fit the needs of specific times in history. Well, God's Word is a living, breathing book. That's not because its meaning changes, but because it can speak into any situation and at any time. Ask God to speak to you again today.

Lord God, Your written Word contains everything I need to live Your
way. May I read it prayerfully and receptively again today.

SOLID FOOD

Anyone who lives on milk, being still an infant, is not acquainted with the teaching about righteousness. But solid food is for the mature, who by constant use have trained themselves to distinguish good from evil.
HEBREWS 5:13–14 NIV

I f you're a father—or if you've ever witnessed an infant growing into childhood—you know that a baby starts out consuming only milk or formula before graduating to easily digestible foods and eventually to solid food.

Today's scripture passage likens your spiritual growth as a Christian to physical growth from infanthood to adulthood. It tells those who have grown in their faith to be ready for the more "mature" things of the faith.

Think about the changes you've seen in yourself since you started walking with the Lord. Do you sense a lot of growth? Are your spirit and mind more sensitive and discerning when it comes to what pleases God and what doesn't please Him?

If the answer to both questions is yes, then you can praise God. If it's no, then humbly ask God what you need to do to start growing anew.

Heavenly Father, You've walked with me since the day You brought me into Your eternal kingdom. I want more than anything to grow in my relationship with You, but I need Your help. Give me the wisdom to know what is good for my growth as a believer.

BECAUSE HE LIVES

*But because Jesus lives forever, his priesthood lasts forever. Therefore he
is able, once and forever, to save those who come to God through
him. He lives forever to intercede with God on their behalf.*

HEBREWS 7:24–25 NLT

If you're familiar with the Old Testament system of sacrifices, you know that the priest's role was to serve as a sort of mediator. He bridged the gap between God and sinners who wanted peace and His forgiveness. In that system, people would bring their sacrifices to the priest, who would present them to God. It was an imperfect system, but one that foreshadowed what was to come.

Jesus came to be the perfect priest. He serves as the one true mediator between His perfect heavenly Father and sinful human beings. What's more, while all Old Testament priests died, Jesus lives forever and stands before the Father pleading your case.

Today, men turn to counseling, to religion, and to doing good things for others in order to find relief from their guilt and shame. Then again, nothing and no one except Jesus can give you peace with God, forgiveness of sins, and the assurance of eternal life in heaven.

Because Jesus lives, you too can live forever!

*Lord Jesus, thank You for pleading my case before God the Father.
Thank You for providing the way for me to one
day stand forgiven, cleansed, and pure.*

FOOLISH TALK

*The lips of fools bring them strife, and their mouths invite
a beating. The mouths of fools are their undoing,
and their lips are a snare to their very lives.*
PROVERBS 18:6–7 NIV

Have you ever known a guy whose mouth got him into constant trouble? He got into trouble with his friends, trouble at work, even trouble at church. Have you ever *been* that guy?

If so, today's scripture passage probably sounds a bit rough. You could easily paraphrase it to say, "Guys with big mouths often get put in their place, sometimes in painful ways."

Today's verses offer great wisdom for the man who has something of a sarcastic streak or who isn't exactly diplomatic in how he says things. The book of Proverbs includes descriptions of many kinds of fools, and one is the man who can't control his mouth. Today's passage says that a fool who says things he shouldn't can end up getting beaten, or worse.

What can you do to make sure the words *you* say don't bring you conflict and strife?

Father, I'm sometimes prone to saying things I shouldn't. I recognize that can get me in trouble with my friends, my family, and those in authority over me. Give me Your wisdom so I can speak wisely and gently instead of harshly and sarcastically.

GOD'S REAL PLEASURE

"Do you think that I like to see wicked people die?
says the Sovereign LORD. Of course not! I want them
to turn from their wicked ways and live."
EZEKIEL 18:23 NLT

It's easy sometimes to look down your nose at those you consider vile sinners. It's easy to believe they are on their way to hell and there's *nothing* they can do to change that fact. In your mind, that's justice, and God is a God of justice, right?

If you're ever tempted to think of someone as irredeemable, take a moment to reread today's verse (and while you're at it, also read 1 Peter 3:8–10). Scripture clearly teaches that a man's ability to sin will never outdo God's ability and willingness to forgive. He has saved the worst sinners in the world, and He'll continue to do so through the end of time.

Believers often sell God short in many areas, and that includes His compassion and mercy for sinners. He *wants* to save people, even those you might consider beyond His reach. Never forget that about Him, and ask Him to help you see the world with the same compassion.

Thank You, Father, for repeatedly reminding me through Your Word
that You are a merciful God who wants to forgive sin. Let me take
pleasure in what gives You pleasure. Give me a heart of
compassion for those who need Your forgiveness.

BEING A "ONE ANOTHER" BELIEVER

*And let us consider how we may spur one another on toward love
and good deeds, not giving up meeting together, as some are
in the habit of doing, but encouraging one another—
and all the more as you see the Day approaching.*
HEBREWS 10:24–25 NIV

Have you ever wondered why finding a good Bible-teaching and preaching church, and attending services there regularly, is so important? If not, try this: look up the term "one another" in the New Testament and see what it says.

Here are a few examples.

- "Be devoted to one another in love" (Romans 12:10 NIV).
- "Accept one another" (Romans 15:7 NIV).
- "Agree with one another" (1 Corinthians 1:10 NIV).
- "Serve one another humbly in love" (Galatians 5:13 NIV).

Clearly, this idea of "one another" is important to God. He wants you to make sure you fellowship with other believers. That is why He warns against neglecting meeting with other believers then, and why He warns against the very same thing today.

Yes, you can worship God on your own. You can hear His voice as you have your personal times of prayer and Bible reading. Then again, nothing can take the place of meeting with other believers in a good church.

*Lord, You didn't save me just so I could be a "Lone Ranger" Christian.
Your Word repeatedly confirms how important it is that I spend time
fellowshipping with other believers. Help me train my mind
toward being a blessing to my fellow followers of Christ.*

STANDING IN THE GAP

*"I looked for someone among them who would build up the wall
and stand before me in the gap on behalf of the land so
I would not have to destroy it, but I found no one."*

Ezekiel 22:30 niv

D o you ever look around at the state of the world today and wonder if humanity is a lost cause? Have you ever seen someone you thought was beyond the reach of God Himself?

Your very human reaction might be to give up and let things take their course. Today's verse is God's challenge to believing men who know how desperately their nation, and the rest of world around them, need God's mercy.

God loves changing hearts when one of His people chooses to "stand in the gap" on behalf of an individual, a group of people, or even a whole nation. This is what the term "intercessory prayer" means. It's praying on behalf of others, knowing that God desires to show mercy and grace, even when a situation looks hopeless.

Are you willing to stand in the gap today? Are you willing to pray, and then pray some more, for someone you know who needs God's loving touch?

*Holy Father, when I look around me and see the state of the world
today, I can't help but think that You are looking for someone
to "stand in the gap" and pray. Let me be that man!*

WHEN GOD'S INSTRUCTIONS DON'T MAKE SENSE

By faith Noah, when warned about things not yet seen, in holy fear built an ark to save his family. By his faith he condemned the world and became heir of the righteousness that is in keeping with faith.
HEBREWS 11:7 NIV

Have you ever wondered what Noah must have been thinking when God called him? After all, God called him to build a giant boat and then load thousands of animals and his family into it—because He was about to destroy the world with a cataclysmic flood.

The writer of Hebrews mentions Noah's faith and obedience. Then again, Noah was human. His senses likely told him that what God had just told him made little earthly sense.

This story in the book of Genesis is one of amazing faith on the part of one man. When you read God's instructions to Noah in Genesis 6:12–22, you find that he never questioned or tested Him. The end of this passage simply says, "Noah did everything just as God commanded him" (NIV). Because of his faith and obedience, in the face of something he could not yet see, he and his family and the animal kingdom were saved.

Heavenly Father, I know that faith means not just believing in You but also trusting You enough to listen and obey You. Please work in my heart and mind so that I obey Your commands readily.

LEARNING WISDOM

*Listen to advice and accept discipline, and at the end
you will be counted among the wise.*
PROVERBS 19:20 NIV

Guys often think that older men—the ones with the most gray hairs and lines on their faces—possess a measure of wisdom that younger men don't have. That's not a bad assumption, because older men have experienced much more life and have had much more wisdom imparted to them.

God wants every man to possess wisdom and understanding, and He uses different means to impart that wisdom. Thankfully, God will generously give wisdom to anyone who asks for it (James 1:5). That could easily be understood to mean that God supernaturally imparts wisdom and understanding so you can better understand His Word, as well as how to apply it to your daily life.

Today's verse strongly suggests that God fulfills His promise to impart wisdom through two additional avenues: instruction and discipline. In other words, God doesn't only supernaturally impart wisdom (though He does that through His Holy Spirit), but also *teaches* a man wisdom through the advice of others and through His discipline.

So ask God for wisdom, but understand that He'll use different means to give it to you.

*Lord, thank You for so generously giving me wisdom
when I ask for it. I am grateful for the instruction and
discipline You use to impart Your wisdom to me.*

ENDURING DISCIPLINE

Endure hardship as discipline; God is treating you as his children.
For what children are not disciplined by their father? If you are not
disciplined—and everyone undergoes discipline—then you are
not legitimate, not true sons and daughters at all.
HEBREWS 12:7–8 NIV

When you're going through difficulties or pain, do you ever wonder if maybe God isn't paying attention or if He doesn't care? Well, your spiritual adversary, the devil, wants you to think that way, so he tempts you with thoughts such as *I think God must hate me* or *Maybe God has forgotten about me.*

Today's verse strongly suggests that your suffering may be the surest sign that God loves you as one of His own children, for He uses hardships to discipline, train, and transform believers.

God gives His Holy Spirit, who strengthens you for your battles against sin. He also uses your most difficult life situations to help prepare you for those battles. Your part in this arrangement is to make sure you don't lose heart. Instead, submit yourself under His hand of discipline, knowing it is a sign of great things to come.

Loving Father in heaven, I confess that I don't always enjoy Your
hand of discipline on me. Yet I know that it's for my own good
and for the good of Your kingdom. It is also evidence that
I belong to You and that You love me as a son.

TO DRINK, OR NOT TO DRINK?

Wine is a mocker, strong drink is a brawler,
and whoever is led astray by it is not wise.

PROVERBS 20:1 NKJV

In today's world, when you receive an invitation to a celebration or party, it's often safe to assume that the gathering includes alcohol. While there is plenty of debate within the Christian world about whether believers should drink at all, the Bible is abundantly clear in its warnings against the overconsumption of wine and strong drink.

The apostle Paul warns, "Do not get drunk on wine, which leads to debauchery. Instead, be filled with the Spirit" (Ephesians 5:18 NIV). This is a scriptural prohibition that's accompanied by the reason for it. Then again, you probably know real-life examples of the words "which leads to debauchery," whether among friends or family members, or from your own past experiences.

It's no secret: overconsumption of alcohol leads to ruined lives, ruined families, ruined reputations, and ruined testimonies of the work of Jesus Christ in your life. Christians should seek out God's wisdom when it comes to drinking. Make sure alcohol never comes between you and the Lord. Never allow your testimony to be ruined by it.

Lord, I have seen plenty of examples of alcohol ruining lives and families.
Give me the wisdom and strength to never let alcohol affect
me or my family in a way that dishonors You.

THE KEY TO CONTENTMENT

*Let your conduct be without covetousness; be content with such
things as you have. For He Himself has said, "I will never leave
you nor forsake you." So we may boldly say: "The LORD is
my helper; I will not fear. What can man do to me?"*

HEBREWS 13:5–6 NKJV

Who hasn't looked at the possessions of those who are doing better
and felt admiration *and* pangs of jealousy over what they have?
That's one of the reasons why it's not a good idea to compare what you
have with what someone else has. Not only that, God's Word warns against
doing that, labeling it as covetousness.

Today's scripture passage strongly suggests that the key to contentment
is trusting God to care for your needs rather than trusting in your own
abilities. In that light, it echoes these words from Jesus Himself: "Look at
the birds of the air; they do not sow or reap or store away in barns, and
yet your heavenly Father feeds them. Are you not much more valuable
than they?" (Matthew 6:26 NIV).

It's all about gratitude, isn't it? That and trusting in a heavenly Father
who's looking out for you.

*Generous Father, sometimes I struggle to maintain a grateful attitude.
Help me look into my own heart and root out any covetousness
or jealousy, and then replace it with contentedness in
You and what You do for me every day.*

ACTING ON WHAT YOU KNOW

Don't just listen to God's word. You must do what it says.
Otherwise, you are only fooling yourselves.
JAMES 1:22 NLT

Someone has wisely said, "Don't fall into the trap of studying the Bible without doing what it says." That's a great paraphrase of today's scripture verse, which warns believers not just to know the truths God has provided in the Bible but to act on them as well.

Sadly however, too many Christians fail to act on what they know. The result is stunted spiritual growth and knowledge of God that is far less than what He desires in each believer.

Knowing what the Bible says to do but not doing it can be likened to knowing what it takes to be physically healthy. It takes eating right, getting plenty of exercise, and making sure you get enough sleep. If you fail to do those things, however, your body and mind won't operate at peak efficiency. . .and eventually will break down.

Today's verse tells Christian men how to get and stay healthy spiritually. Read what the Bible says—and do what it says.

Lord God, Your written Word is filled with truths to affirm, commands to obey, and examples to heed. As I spend time reading and meditating on these things, transform my mind with Your wisdom. I don't just want to know what You've said, but I want to act on it as well.

A CAUSE-EFFECT RELATIONSHIP

*What good is it, my brothers and sisters, if someone claims to have
faith but has no deeds? Can such faith save them? . . . Faith by
itself, if it is not accompanied by action, is dead.*

JAMES 2:14, 17 NIV

Think for a moment about what happens when a man takes his car in
for regular maintenance—oil changes, tire rotations, transmission
servicing, tune-ups. That man is much more likely to avoid paying for
much more expensive repairs later on. (Unfortunately, many learn this
lesson the hard way!)

That's an example of a predictable cause-effect relationship.

Today's scripture is an even better example of cause-effect, and it's
one with eternal implications.

The Bible is clear that no one is saved by his good deeds, not matter
how excellent they may be, but only through faith in Jesus Christ. It's also
clear that your faith in Christ will result in changes in how you think, how
you behave, and how you treat others.

Put another way, a living faith will always result in profound changes
within you, and those changes will always lead to good works.

How can you put your faith into action today?

*Father, show me what good works You'd like me to do today.
You've already saved and transformed me, so help make
my faith real. Make it real to me and to others through
the good I do in Your wonderful name.*

WORDS OF PRAISE, NOT SPITE

Out of the same mouth come praise and cursing.
My brothers and sisters, this should not be.
JAMES 3:10 NIV

You probably don't have to go too far back to remember the last time you talked about another person. Other people are a big part of your daily life, and talking about others is unavoidable. Where many run into trouble, however, is when they carelessly speak words that hurt another person's reputation or when they say harsh things directly to his face.

Men tend to think of speaking spiteful words as one of those "little sins." But God takes your words very seriously, and He wants you to avoid speaking negatively about others—even when what you have to say is true. That is why the apostle Paul wrote, "Do not let any unwholesome talk come out of your mouths, but only what is helpful for building others up according to their needs" (Ephesians 4:29 NIV).

So think before you speak. If the words you're thinking build up another person, speak them freely. But if they hurt that person's good name, then keep your thoughts to yourself. Instead, find something good to think and say.

Father, in and of myself, I'm prone to speaking unkind, even harsh, words to and about others. Please renew my mind daily. I want my words toward others to be uplifting and kind, not critical and spiteful.

HONEST SELF-EXAMINATION

*Lament and mourn and weep! Let your laughter be turned
to mourning and your joy to gloom. Humble yourselves
in the sight of the Lord, and He will lift you up.*
JAMES 4:9–10 NKJV

Have you ever taken your car to the mechanic for routine maintenance only to receive the news that your vehicle has a serious issue that needs to be addressed right away? No one enjoys surprise expenses. Still, it's better to spend money on things that keep you and your family safe than to put off needed automotive repairs and be sorry about it later.

That same principle can be applied to your spiritual life as well.

In today's scripture passage, James challenges his readers to engage in some deep, honest self-examination. He encourages you to pray like King David. He pleaded, "Search me, God, and know my heart. . . See if there is any offensive way in me" (Psalm 139:23–24 NIV). He says you should look at yourself with sometimes-painful honesty and appraise your thinking and actions. Make sure they are aligned with what God says He wants for His people.

Then you'll have reason for true thanksgiving.

Lord and God, help me humble myself before You and see my attitudes, thoughts, and actions as You see them. Thank You for Your promise to forgive my sin and to lift me up in Your way and in Your timing.

ACCOUNTABILITY

*Confess your sins to each other and pray for each other so that
you may be healed. The earnest prayer of a righteous person
has great power and produces wonderful results.*

James 5:16 nlt

Men don't exactly enjoy talking with others about their sin struggles. Maybe it's your independent spirit that keeps you from that kind of honest confession. Maybe it's your fear of making yourself vulnerable to others. Maybe it's your worry about being looked down on because of your real-life struggles.

As uncomfortable as confessing your sin struggles may make you feel, that is exactly what God calls you to do. Today's verse commands believers to come clean with one another so that you can pray for one another for healing and victory. There's another blessing you receive when you confess your sins that way: accountability.

Life experience says your brothers in Christ likely won't be shocked when you confess a sin you know is holding you back. In fact, when you open the lines of communication by confessing your sins, you often learn that others struggle with the very same sins. That helps you pray for one another and keep each other accountable. That, in turn, leads to victory for all.

---

*Lord Jesus, I'm not comfortable sharing my struggles and failures with
others. Humble me, and help me understand how important it is
that I make myself accountable to my brothers in the faith.*

TESTING THROUGH TRIALS

In this you greatly rejoice, though now for a little while, if need be,
you have been grieved by various trials, that the genuineness of your
faith, being much more precious than gold that perishes, though it
is tested by fire, may be found to [bring] praise, honor, and glory at
the revelation of Jesus Christ, whom having not seen you love.

1 PETER 1:6–8 NKJV

It would be the rare exception among men living in the Western world that one will have to endure anything close to the kinds of suffering and trials first-century Christians endured in the ancient Roman empire. That should stand as a further challenge to you to endure the difficulties you face with a heart of gratitude.

Nowhere in the Bible does God call men to act as though they enjoy the difficulties life throws their way. On the contrary, God allows you to bring these things to Him and ask for relief, if that is His will.

In the midst of your trials, the Lord calls you to rejoice, but not in the suffering itself. Instead, He calls you to rejoice in the good it does by confirming and refining your faith in Him.

Help me, Father, to always remember that You can use the difficulties
I face in this life to confirm the genuineness of my faith and
to strengthen me in my relationship with You.

A NEW FOCUS

As obedient children, do not conform to the evil desires you had when you lived in ignorance. But just as he who called you is holy, so be holy in all you do; for it is written: "Be holy, because I am holy."

1 PETER 1:14–16 NIV

Have you ever carefully listened to and observed a man when he becomes a father for the first time? It isn't hard to see in that man a completely new way of thinking and behaving. He's now focused on someone else, and his selfish ways are replaced with behavior that benefits the new object of his love.

When a man first begins his life of faith in Jesus Christ, the same thing happens, but on an even more profound level. Where before he was focused on his own pleasure, he now is focused on doing whatever it takes to please God and grow in his relationship with Him. His attitudes change, his words change, and his behavior changes—sometimes very quickly and sometimes over time.

This side of heaven, none will achieve sinless perfection. But when you have God's Spirit within you, your thinking changes—and you head toward holiness with great purpose.

Father in heaven, thank You for bringing me into Your eternal family. Continue daily to cleanse me of my sinful desires. May I conduct myself in a way that pleases and glorifies You.

RESPECT FOR OTHERS

*Show proper respect to everyone, love the family
of believers, fear God, honor the emperor.*

1 PETER 2:17 NIV

I t may come as a surprise, but all men (and women) feel an innate need for respect, if for no other reason than their humanity in some degree entitles them to it.

Even more surprising to many is that God calls His people to show respect for others, regardless of their beliefs or lifestyles. Still, it's not always easy to show proper respect to others, and it's especially difficult with people whose attitudes and actions show disregard for the truths revealed in God's written Word.

Even harder is showing respect for those who show you no respect in return. The actions and words of others who don't know God don't relieve you of the responsibility of treating them with respect, even when they repay it with contempt.

Respect doesn't mean giving approval or acceptance to lifestyles and actions you know God hasn't approved. And it doesn't mean respecting only those you believe have "earned it." It means simply treating those you meet, no matter how much you disagree with their views and lifestyle choices, as valued creations made in the image of God.

*Lord, let me be an example of Your amazing love and grace,
and a man who treats all people I meet with respect,
both in how I speak to them and how I treat them.*

SUFFERING UNJUSTLY

For this is a gracious thing, when, mindful of God,
one endures sorrows while suffering unjustly.
1 Peter 2:19 esv

I n today's New Testament reading, Peter addresses servants. Commentators indicate that this included people who were hired servants, or servants who were taken during war, or servants who were born in the house, and actual slaves. Whichever type of servant, the Christian was to be subject to his master, even those who treated them unjustly (1 Peter 2:18).

The Christian servant doesn't endure unjust suffering without reason. He does so to show the implications of the Gospel in his life. He does so to control his deep-seated desire to fight for justice. Ultimately, he does so to show the unjust the same sort of mercy Jesus offered on the cross. In today's key verse, Peter says an act "is a gracious thing."

How did you respond the last time you were treated unjustly in the office or another sphere of life? Did you demand justice? Demand your rights? Or did you endure suffering, knowing you are called to such a life, with the hope that your oppressor would experience the Gospel in action?

If you didn't present a Christlike attitude, resolve to do so the next time.

Lord, my automatic response to being treated unjustly is to
demand justice. Change my heart. May my desire to
represent Jesus Christ well rule my spirit instead.

REMAIN UNDEFILED

To these four young men God gave knowledge and understanding
of all kinds of literature and learning. And Daniel could
understand visions and dreams of all kinds.

DANIEL 1:17 NIV

While in Babylonian captivity, Daniel, who had been chosen for the king's service, stuck to his convictions and "resolved not to defile himself with the royal food and wine" (Daniel 1:8 NIV). Instead, he asked for nothing but vegetables and water (1:12) for himself, as well as for Hananiah, Mishael, and Azariah. His request was granted, and shortly thereafter, God gave them knowledge and understanding they hadn't had previously.

Daniel's desire to stay pure was more than admirable, and God blessed him for it. In what ways are you choosing to not defile yourself? Maybe you need to pull away from mainstream music, certain television shows or movies, or social media. Don't do it in an attempt to be completely separate from the world, but rather to remain undefiled. God may bless you for it by giving you more discernment, insight, and understanding.

As a believer, you have been called to keep a delicate yet healthy balance. Billy Graham once said, "We come in contact with the world, and yet we retain our distinctive kingdom character and refuse to let the world press us into its mold."

Lord, give me the conviction to remain undefiled in the midst
of great worldly temptation. And please give me the
wisdom to engage the world for redemptive purposes.

A GLORIOUS FUTURE

Let not your heart envy sinners, but continue in the fear of the LORD all the day. Surely there is a future, and your hope will not be cut off.
PROVERBS 23:17–18 ESV

In today's key verses, the author wants each believer to take his eyes off what is front of him—namely sinners enjoying their season of pleasure—and instead focus on the Lord and the future He promises.

How is today's Christian supposed to do this in a culture that glorifies sin and normalizes all sorts of perversions? The good news is, you aren't alone in your struggle. Christians have always needed to live counterculturally. But like them, you'll need to be intentional.

You know the types of sinners your heart envies. You don't necessarily need to disengage with them, but you can limit your interactions. Rather than gazing at what you don't have, consider what you do have.

The Lord stands at the ready to lead and guide you into paths of righteousness. Call on Him in your weakness and He will give you strength. And consider the hope you possess as a believer. You have been promised heaven, whereas the unbeliever has no hope.

*Lord, don't let my heart envy sinners. Instead, I want to fear You.
I look forward to the future You have promised, knowing it
is far more glorious than anything here on this earth.*

SAY WHAT NEEDS TO BE SAID

" 'King Nebuchadnezzar, please accept my advice. Stop sinning and do what is right. Break from your wicked past and be merciful to the poor. Perhaps then you will continue to prosper.' "

DANIEL 4:27 NLT

After having a dream that frightened him, King Nebuchadnezzar called in all the wise men of Babylon. He ordered them to tell him what his dream meant, but they weren't able to do so (Daniel 4:7). Finally, he turned to Daniel, who told the king that he would be driven from society and live in the fields with wild animals (Daniel 4:25). Yet Daniel didn't leave him without hope. If the king turned from his sinful past, Daniel said, he would prosper.

Have you ever been in crucial conversation where you had to say something difficult? Maybe you had to confront your boss, coworker, spouse, or best friend. Did you hedge your message? Or were you respectful yet completely honest?

Daniel certainly could have paid a heavy price for his honesty, but he was a man of integrity who said and did the right thing, no matter what. Are you willing to follow his example, even if you have to pay a price?

Lord, may I always be willing to say the hard thing, in love.
By doing so, I know I'll give people the opportunity
to experience Your favor.

NO GLOATING ALLOWED

Do not gloat when your enemy falls; when they stumble,
do not let your heart rejoice, or the LORD will see and
disapprove and turn his wrath away from them.
PROVERBS 24:17–18 NIV

Bible commentator John Gill make a distinction in today's verses in reference to enemies, saying: "Joy may be expressed at the fall of the public enemies of God and his people, as was by the Israelites at the destruction of Pharaoh and his host [Exodus 15:1]; and as will be by the church at the destruction of antichrist, and which they are called upon to do [Revelation 18:20]. . .but as private revenge is not to be sought."

Did somebody's name pop into your mind as you read that quote? Who are you tempted to exact private revenge against? Instead, are you willing to begin praying for him, in accordance with what Jesus said in Matthew 5:44–45 (NIV): "But I tell you, love your enemies and pray for those who persecute you, that you may be children of your Father in heaven."

The Christian is called to live differently than the world. What better way to show the world how powerful the Gospel is than by loving your enemies, even when everything in your flesh doesn't want to do so.

Lord, I want to be known as someone who loves like Jesus does.
Show me ways to love my enemies well.

MEDITATING ON THE LAW

Scoffers will come in the last days, walking according to their own lusts, and saying, "Where is the promise of His coming?"
2 PETER 3:3–4 NKJV

Christians who live with the hope of Jesus Christ's return stand out from the world. The world often considers the church to be full of simple-minded, foolish people.

According to the Got Questions website, "A scoffer is one who not only disagrees with an idea, but he also considers himself an ambassador for the opposing idea. He cannot rest until he has demonstrated the foolishness of any idea not his own."

Psalm 1:1–2 (ESV) offers the antidote: "Blessed is the man who walks not in the counsel of the wicked, nor stands in the way of sinners, nor sits in the seat of scoffers; but his delight is in the law of the LORD, and on his law he meditates day and night."

The world wants nothing to do with Jesus Christ's coming kingdom. It has been mocking believers for nearly two thousand years, not believing Jesus will ever return. What are you doing to separate yourself from those who scoff? Are you finding ways to meditate on scripture day and night? It's the only true way to stay grounded in your belief.

Lord, help me meditate on Your Word day and night. I understand that this prayer is a call to change my heart. Change it, Lord.

WALK IN THE LIGHT

*If we say we have fellowship with him while we walk
in darkness, we lie and do not practice the truth.*

1 JOHN 1:6 ESV

Walking in fellowship with God means you partake in His power, no longer living according to the dictates of your flesh. That's not to say you no longer sin. Just two verses later, John says, "If we say we have no sin, we deceive ourselves, and the truth is not in us." Instead, it means you don't accept your sin. You are unwilling to stay in sin. You are willing to fight against it by rooting it out and dragging it into the light.

Do you have a besetting sin that you have all but given up fighting because you've lost hope? If so, have you pulled away from Christian community, fearing how others might perceive your sin? The Christian life was never intended to be lived in solitude, in darkness. It was meant to be lived in light and fellowship with fellow believers.

Your church probably offers small groups. Begin attending one and resolve to be honest with the men in the group about your struggles. If your church doesn't offer small groups, find a Bible study where can live out your faith in the light with others.

*Lord, I want to walk in the light. Direct me to a group
of believers who will help me do that.*

THE HEART OF AN INTERCESSOR

*"O Lord. . .we have sinned and done wrong and acted wickedly and
rebelled, turning aside from your commandments and rules."*

DANIEL 9:4–5 ESV

After reading the prophet Jeremiah (Jeremiah 25:11 and 29:10), Daniel believed the seventy-year Babylonian exile was drawing to an end (Daniel 9:1–2). His first impulse was to intercede for God's people, confessing their sins, and saying he wasn't presenting his pleas because of their righteousness, but because of God's great mercy (9:18).

Daniel had to be in the scriptures regularly in order to understand that the seventy-year exile was indeed going to end. And then he had to be willing to intercede for God's people. Does this resemble a pattern in your own life? Are you in the scriptures routinely enough to know how you should be interceding for your nation, your city, or your family? And are you aware enough of what's going on in that you are able to confess their collective sins?

F. B. Meyer once said, "Let the first moments of the day, when the heart is fresh, be given to God. Never see the face of man until you have seen the King." Are you willing to start your day this way?

*Lord, give me the heart of an intercessor who is grounded
solidly in Your Word. I long to meet with You every
morning for communion and instruction.*

A GENTLE TONGUE

Through patience a ruler can be persuaded,
and a gentle tongue can break a bone.
PROVERBS 25:15 NIV

It's not uncommon for people to chant and shout at political leaders they disagree with, even when those leaders are just trying to enjoy a meal in a restaurant with their families. The Christian is called to a higher standard. He is to be patient with a ruler because gentleness can break through even the stoutest of hearts.

David used a soft tongue when dealing with Saul, but even he could be provoked to anger. When Nabal dealt roughly and ruthlessly with David's men, David was incensed. Then again, Nabal's wife, Abigail, acted wisely and was considerate in her conversation with David, who agreed to change his mind about killing Nabal (1 Samuel 25).

If you are a believer who attends political rallies, attends town hall meetings, or writes to your leaders, how does your behavior compare or contrast with today's key verse, especially when you don't agree with them?

Proverbs 15:1 (NIV) conveys a similar admonition: "A gentle answer turns away wrath, but a harsh word stirs up anger." Consider your reaction when someone disagrees with you. Generally speaking, aren't you more receptive to changing your mind if someone approaches you with gentleness and respect? Treating leaders the same way might just give you an opportunity to change their minds.

Lord, I'm not always quick to offer a gentle tongue,
especially when I'm passionate about a topic. Tame my tongue, Lord.

LOVE ONE ANOTHER

If we love our brothers and sisters who are believers,
it proves that we have passed from death to life.

1 JOHN 3:14 NLT

The apostle John didn't write this letter to any church in particular. Like other general epistles, it is believed to have been circulated among many diverse congregations. In this chapter, John zeroed in on the importance of loving your brothers and sisters in the faith, going so far as to say that when you do so, it is proof of your salvation.

Take an inventory of your love for fellow believers. Are you quick to show up when someone in your congregation or extended faith community is in need? Do you visit them when they are in the hospital? Do you pray for them regularly? Do you know their stories? Their passions? Their fears? Their dreams? If so, you are living the life John is heralding here. These are evidence that you have the love of Jesus Christ in you.

If you've fallen short in loving your fellow believers, do you want to do better? Your "want to" is a good place to start, and even that is evidence of a changed heart. Now is the time to act. Find a need and meet it.

Just the simplest act of love can mean so much.

Lord, I could love brothers in Christ better. Show me a specific
way to express my love for one of them this week.

RETURN TO THE LORD

"Come, let us return to the LORD. He has torn us to pieces; now he will heal us. He has injured us; now he will bandage our wounds."

Hosea 6:1 NLT

In Hosea 4 and 5, the prophet pinpoints a long list of Israel's sins, including a lack of faithfulness, a lack of kindness, a lack of knowledge of God, broken promises, murder, theft, adultery, violence, idol worship, drunkenness, prostitution, and more. Such a list of sins seems like it would be difficult to overcome. Today's key verse, however, calls God's people to do just that.

Have you committed a sin in the past, or are steeped in now, that's so heinous that you've lost hope of experiencing God's mercy and grace? The distance you feel between God and yourself is the result of the damage caused by your sin. And indeed, you will have to face the consequences for it, but God's mercy extends far beyond your worst behavior.

Jesus bore the price for your sin on the cross, settling your account with God the Father. He sees your sin as being covered in the blood of Jesus Christ. How can you continue to walk in darkness, knowing Jesus died to set you free?

Lord, I've fallen into the trap of believing that some sins are too awful to forgive, but I hear the plea of Hosea 6:1 and I repent.

JESUS IN THE FLESH

For many deceivers have gone out into the world who do not confess Jesus Christ as coming in the flesh. This is a deceiver and an antichrist.

2 JOHN 1:7 NKJV

John issued a warning for the church in today's key verse. Many deceivers, whom he calls antichrists, had gone out into the world and rejected the fact that Jesus came in the flesh. They rejected the idea of a personal God who would take on flesh and dwell among humanity. As such, they said Jesus couldn't have been truly human. And therefore, they rejected the virgin birth, which is the only way Jesus could have been born a perfect man and a perfect Savior.

As the priest of your home, your family may be subject to such false teachings at school, work, or elsewhere in the community. It is your responsibility to lead and guide your family in matters of truth. Never let them fall prey to such false teachings.

As you do, know that modern-day antichrists will take exception to your family's claims that Jesus came in the flesh. That's okay because at least they will have heard the truth, which may lead some of them out of false teaching and into the light. This would be a great passage to show them to start them on their journey.

Lord, help me prepare my family to resist modern-day antichrists by boldly proclaiming that Jesus did indeed come in the flesh.

HIS MERCY KNOWS NO LIMITS

Whoever is wise, let him understand these things; whoever is discerning, let him know them; for the ways of the LORD are right, and the upright walk in them, but transgressors stumble in them.

HOSEA 14:9 ESV

After Israel engaged in apostasy and idol worship, God the Father called for the nation to repent. If they would, He promised to heal them, to turn His anger from them, to help them blossom like vines and flourish like grain (Hosea 14:1–8). Yet only the wise understand such things, as today's key verse says.

Idol worship and apostasy (the act of rejecting your religious beliefs in favor of opposing beliefs) might seem like acts that should be beyond God's grace. Forgiving such infidelity might be beyond your ability to grasp, but God always stands at the ready to extend mercy and grace to His people—if they are willing to repent, discern His ways, and walk in them.

If God were going to pinpoint your worst sin today (maybe the one nobody else knows about), what would it be? Are you willing to repent right now and begin walking in the ways of the Lord? If so, He can't wait to welcome you back with open arms.

Lord, Your willingness to forgive and extend mercy for the worst of my sins is almost beyond my comprehension. I repent for my behavior and will embrace Your ways beginning anew today.

TRAIN HARD

*Beloved, while I was very diligent to write to you concerning
our common salvation, I found it necessary to write to you
exhorting you to contend earnestly for the faith
which was once for all delivered to the saints.*

JUDE 1:3 NKJV

The Greek word used in today's verse for "contend earnestly," according to Bible commentator Albert Barnes, is a reference to the ancient Grecian games. In other words, Jude was asking readers to put the same amount of effort into standing up for and proclaiming the Gospel as the athletes do in competing in the Grecian games.

The Olympic athlete trains his body through daily rituals. He gets up early, trains hard for several hours, eats the right foods, hydrates properly, gets ample rest, and then does the same thing every day for years on end, all in preparation for one event.

This is the type of dedication to the Gospel that Jude is calling you to demonstrate. Just as training for the Olympics doesn't allow for lackluster preparation, training to represent the Gospel well doesn't either. You may get only one shot to contend for the faith with somebody. Have you put in the training so you'll be ready?

Lord, as 1 Peter 3:15 (NKJV) says, I always want to "be ready to give a defense to everyone who asks you a reason for the hope that is in" me.

LIVE EXPECTANTLY

When I saw Him, I fell at His feet like a dead man. And He placed His right hand on me, saying, "Do not be afraid; I am the first and the last, and the living One; and I was dead, and behold, I am alive forevermore, and I have the keys of death and of Hades."

Revelation 1:17–18 nasb

When John received the Revelation of Jesus in a vision, he didn't seem to know he was meeting Jesus until He identified Himself. Many decades had passed since John had walked and talked with Jesus. Maybe it wasn't a case of failed recognition as much as it was being overwhelmed by the presence of the resurrected and glorified Lord Jesus Christ.

Have you considered how you might respond if Jesus returned during your lifetime? For the Christian who has been transformed by the Gospel, his heart sometimes yearns for nothing more deeply than to be in the presence of Jesus Christ. The troubles of this world are many, but they are nothing in the presence of Christ, the Lord and King over heaven and earth.

Do you live with the imminent return of Jesus Christ clearly in mind? If He returned an hour from now, what might He catch you doing? How might living with this in mind change how you live the second half of this month?

Lord, may I look "for the blessed hope and glorious appearing of our great God and Savior Christ Jesus" today, as Titus 2:13 (nkjv) says.

BOLD AS A LION

The wicked flee when no one is pursuing,
but the righteous are bold as a lion.
PROVERBS 28:1 NASB

What does it look like for the righteous to be bold as a lion? Abraham Ben Moses is a good example. He's a Christian apologist who was arrested in December 2017 in Indonesia and is currently serving a four-year jail term. His crime? He shared the Gospel with a Muslim taxi driver.

As of this writing, Voice of the Martyrs was ministering to his family and encouraging fellow believers to reach out to government officials and to Moses himself.

If Christianity became illegal overnight here in this country, would you continue to share your faith, knowing you too might end up in jail? That's not to say you shouldn't be wise as a serpent and as a gentle as a dove. Then again, at some point you need to speak the truth of the Gospel, and it could cost you everything.

Thankfully, if you live in the United States, you don't have to worry about such persecution—at least not yet. The most you'll have to deal with is mockery. So, Christian, how bold are you in your workplace? When you are with friends who aren't Christians yet?

Lord, I'm not as bold for the sake of the Gospel as I ought to be.
May I care less about the mockery I might receive
and more about the lost.

THE ONE WHO CONQUERS

*" 'The one who conquers will be clothed thus in white garments,
and I will never blot his name out of the book of life.' "*

REVELATION 3:5 ESV

Sardis was the first city to be converted under the apostle John's preaching in that part of the world, according to Bible commentator Matthew Henry. And it is believed to have been the first city to have left the faith. After only a few decades, the Sardis church was on life support (Revelation 3:1–2). That prompted Jesus to call for it to wake up and strengthen what little life remained—because only those who persevere have absolute assurance of eternal life.

Christian, you are called to conquer. You're called to conquer your sin, your spiritual deadness, your spiritual formality, and your incessant desire to live on your own terms. Stop valuing self over sacrifice. You will never conquer perfectly because war is messy, but as long as you wrestle, and fight, and pray, you will be considered a conqueror.

Does this describe your current spiritual condition? Or are you close to being on spiritual life support like the Sardis church? If the latter, heed Jesus Christ's warning today. Take up your spiritual weapons and prepare for battle.

You cannot win if you do not fight.

Lord, at times, my spiritual life feels closer to that of Sardis than the one Jesus calls me to in today's key verse. I pledge to begin the battle anew.

GO, PREACH THE GOSPEL

Then Amos answered and said to Amaziah, "I was no prophet, nor a prophet's son, but I was a herdsman and a dresser of sycamore figs. But the LORD took me from following the flock, and the LORD said to me, 'Go, prophesy to my people Israel.' "

AMOS 7:14–15 ESV

The false priest Amaziah grew tired of Amos's preaching against Israel. He went so far as to tell King Jeroboam that Amos was conspiring against him (Amos 7:10). In today's key verse, however, Amos said he wasn't in the line of prophets. He was minding his own business as a herdsman and farmer when the Lord told him to prophesy to His rebellious people.

The Lord often uses the weak to shame the strong (1 Corinthians 1:27). He likes to call ordinary people to do extraordinary things for the kingdom. He transforms sinners into saints, giving them a new nature and a new calling.

God probably has not called you to prophesy to the people living in Israel today, but He has called you out of darkness to proclaim light and liberty to the people living around you. Have you been obedient? You have if you have attracted an Amaziah in your life—someone who feels uncomfortable with your message. All the more reason to keep speaking God's truth.

Lord, my vocation feels pretty ordinary. I definitely don't feel like a prophet. Yet I'm willing to proclaim the Gospel today.

DON'T TRUST YOUR HEART

*He who leans on, trusts in, and is confident of his own mind
and heart is a [self-confident] fool, but he who walks in
skillful and godly Wisdom shall be delivered.*

PROVERBS 28:26 AMPC

"Follow your heart" is the most common advice you'll hear from the world. In reality, the scripture says the human heart cannot be trusted. Jeremiah 17:9 (AMPC) says, "The heart is deceitful above all things, and it is exceedingly perverse and corrupt and severely, mortally sick!" In Mark 7:21 (AMPC), Jesus says, "For from within, [that is] out of the hearts of men, come base and wicked thoughts."

Today's key verse picks up on this theme, even going so far as to call the person who leans on his heart a self-confident fool. Instead, the author calls you to walk in skillful and godly wisdom. John Wesley described a person who does so as someone who distrusts his own judgment and who seeks the advice of others, especially of God.

Commentator John Gill expanded on that and said it includes consulting and following the sacred writings of scripture. It also includes following Jesus Christ as your pattern for life and ministry. That's quite a contrast to the wisdom of the world, isn't it?

*Lord, I often allow my heart to guide me, but I can see from
the scripture that I cannot trust my heart. May I lean
on You, the scripture, for guidance.*

ADVOCATING FOR THE POOR

*The [consistently] righteous man knows and cares for the rights of
the poor, but the wicked man has no interest in such knowledge.*
PROVERBS 29:7 AMPC

According to the US Census Bureau's website, poverty is a genuine problem in America. In 2017, 39.7 million people were in poverty. That year, 9.2 percent of Americans aged sixty-five and older were below the poverty line. The Compassion International website says, "Eleven children under age 5 die every minute, and 35 mothers die during childbirth every hour" worldwide.

The righteous man knows and cares for the rights of the poor. A couple of other translations say he cares about "justice for the poor" (NIV) and "the cause of the poor" (KJV). The context of the verse is a reference to the judicial system and righteous judges. The rights of the poor are not to be trampled on, so you have a role to play in being their advocate.

You can help the poor find good representation. You can contribute to Christian legal organizations like the American Center for Law and Justice. You can write or speak to your representatives. Or you can get involved in setting up some sort of advocacy through your church.

*Lord, I've often helped the poor financially, but I haven't focused
as much attention on becoming an advocate for their rights.
Give my family direction about how we can do so.*

ROBED IN WHITE

*"These are they who have come out of the great tribulation; they have
washed their robes and made them white in the blood of the Lamb."*

REVELATION 7:14 NIV

In today's reading of Revelation 7, you get a glimpse of the end when
a great multitude from every nation, tribe, people, and language will
stand before the throne of the Lamb wearing white robes. On this first day
of winter, it's a beautiful picture of purity. One of the elders who will be
there will identify the saints as people who have endured great tribulation.

In Matthew Henry's commentary, he says, "The way to heaven lies
through many tribulations." What sort of tribulations have you endured?
Henry offers a few possible suggestions, including persecution, temptation,
a troubled spirit, spoiled goods, imprisonment, and maybe even death.
No matter how you have suffered for the kingdom's sake, know that a
day is coming when you will stand before the throne in your transformed
body and none of this will matter any longer.

That's not to say that suffering is easy, but it should give you a different
perspective. The Christian will suffer on this earth, but this won't always
be the case. Take heart.

*Lord, my troubles often weigh me down. Help me consider them
in light of eternity. I can't wait for the day when I'll stand
before You trouble-free, robed in white.*

A STRONG REFUGE

The LORD is good, a strong refuge when trouble comes.
He is close to those who trust in him.

NAHUM 1:7 NLT

Nahum had a difficult message for the people of Nineveh. The Lord was angry with Assyria for forcing the Jews to pay tribute or send presents to the king, so judgment was coming. But not for those who trusted in the Lord. He was a strong refuge for those who were close to Him. He still is.

Imagine you woke up to a home invasion and your children were at risk down the hall. Is there anything you wouldn't do to protect them? That's true no matter how upset you might have been with your children for some form of disobedience the night before. Nothing they could do would keep you from offering them a refuge in such a desperate moment, right? So it is with God.

You haven't lived a perfectly obedient life. In fact, you sin against the Lord and fellow humans every day. But you long for the day when this is no longer the case. Don't let your sin keep you from running to God during difficult times. He loves you and wants to offer His loving arm of protection.

Lord, I stand in awe of Your judgment and am humbled by
Your mercy. Thank You for providing a safe place
for me so I can escape the day of wrath.

FALL ON YOUR FACE

And the twenty-four elders who sit on their thrones before
God fell on their faces and worshiped God.

REVELATION 11:16 ESV

Just after the seventh angel blows his trumpet, loud voices from heaven will say, "The kingdom of the world has become the kingdom of our Lord and of his Christ, and he shall reign forever and ever" (Revelation 11:15 ESV). That leads the twenty-four elders, who are believed to represent the church, to fall on their faces to worship God.

How could they do anything but worship? And how can you do anything but worship here and now? You've been redeemed, justified, and are in the process of being sanctified. You are heaven bound if you have believed in Jesus and His atoning work on the cross for your sins. The proper response is worship.

What does your worship look like currently? Do you practice private worship during the week, maybe even falling to your knees or on your face? Do you regularly gather with other saints for corporate worship on the weekends, singing the praises of the Lord? If not, now is the time to start. By doing so, you'll get a small taste of eternity.

Lord, my heart often runs cold and leads me away from worship.
Forgive me. For I want to honor You for everything You've done for me.

GOD'S QUIET LOVE

"The Lord your God is in your midst, a mighty one who will save;
he will rejoice over you with gladness; he will quiet you
by his love; he will exult over you with loud singing."

ZEPHANIAH 3:17 ESV

Even though Israel was undergoing judgment at the time of Zephaniah, the prophet wanted them to know that "the day of the Lord is near" (Zephaniah 1:7 ESV). It would be a day in which He will have "prepared a sacrifice and consecrated his guests." He would save His people and rejoice over them with gladness.

Here, on Christmas Eve, the message remains the same. This world is under judgment, but the day of the Lord is near. It's even nearer since the birth of Jesus. Until He returns in all His glory, any who call on Him will be saved.

As you consider the incarnation today, consider the fact that the God of the universe loved you enough to leave heaven, take on flesh, speak words of life that you can still read and study, and then die a horrific death (and then rise again the third day) so you might be saved.

Consider God's own response to your salvation. He will rejoice over you, quiet you by His love, and exult over you with loud singing.

May you have a sense that He is doing all three for you today.

Lord, I'm in awe over the incarnation.
Quiet my heart today with Your love.

THE ETERNAL GOSPEL

Then I saw another angel flying directly overhead, with an eternal
gospel to proclaim to those who dwell on earth, to every
nation and tribe and language and people.

REVELATION 14:6 ESV

Bible commentators speculate that the angel in today's key verse may be one who will rapidly spread the eternal Gospel around the world, or maybe the angel will be a special messenger, or maybe it's symbolic for a group of believers who will carry the Gospel. There's no way to say for certain. But what is clear is that the birth of Jesus, and ultimately His death and resurrection, compels the believer to proclaim the Gospel to every nation, tribe, language, and people group.

On this Christmas Day, enter a time of worship for the baby who changed everything—including the trajectory of your life. You were once far from God, but Jesus brought you near. You were once someone who indulged the flesh, but now you walk in the Spirit. You were once someone who loved the darkness, but now you walk in the light.

With deepest thanks to Jesus Christ, especially on this holy day, happily and winsomely proclaim His good news to your family members and close friends.

Father, today is the day we celebrate the birth of Your Son, Jesus.
I'm humbled to be called Your child. Thank You for the privilege of
sharing Your life-giving message with those You've placed around me.

YOUR FAITH LEGACY

*"Do not be like your ancestors, to whom the earlier prophets
proclaimed: This is what the LORD Almighty says: 'Turn from your
evil ways and your evil practices.' But they would not listen
or pay attention to me, declares the LORD."*

ZECHARIAH 1:4 NIV

I srael strayed from the Lord almost every generation. They might honor and obey Him for a time, only to get lost and go back to their sinful, evil ways. In today's key verse, the prophet Zechariah delivered a familiar call from the Lord to leave behind the wicked ways of their ancestors and turn back to Him.

You may have noticed a similar pattern in your own family heritage. You've heard plenty of heartbreaking stories, maybe even over the past couple of days as you celebrated the Christmas season with family members. Thankfully, you don't have to be like your ancestors who lived far from the Lord.

Instead, heed the Lord's warning: "Where are your ancestors now? They and the prophets are long dead. But everything I said through my servants the prophets happened to your ancestors, just as I said" (Zechariah 1:5–6 NLT).

What sort of fail-safes can you put into place for your family now, as you contemplate heading into the new year, so that generations from now your immediate family will be remembered for the right reasons?

*Lord, may my immediate family shun the evil practices of
our ancestors so we can walk in ways that please You.*

HONOR YOUR NEIGHBOR

*And let none of you think or imagine or devise evil or injury
in your hearts against his neighbor, and love no false
oath, for all these things I hate, says the Lord.*

ZECHARIAH 8:17 AMPC

Joseph S. Exell, coeditor of The Pulpit Commentary series, makes these observations about Israel's pet sins during the days of Zechariah: "The prevalent sins at this time were not idolatry, but cheating and lying and injustice, vices learned in the land of exile, where they had turned their energies to traffic and commerce."

As is always the case, God's message for His people cuts to the heart of the matter, addressing the very sins they were struggling with at the time. But lying, backbiting, and harmful words continue to this day—even among God's people.

Consider how it would look for you, someone who is full of the Holy Spirit, to be honest in every circumstance of your life, and to always have people's best interests at heart. It would mean adhering to Jesus Christ's call to die to self. It would mean honoring the needs of others over your own. It would mean giving credit where credit is due. And it would mean owning your mistakes and failures rather than covering them with half truths.

This is the very life you are called to live.

*Lord, may I live out the intent of today's key verse
at work, at home, and anywhere else I go.*

COVER YOUR MOUTH

If you have been a fool by being proud or plotting evil,
cover your mouth in shame.

Proverbs 30:32 nlt

Body language experts say one sure sign that someone is lying to you is covering his mouth. It seems to be an automatic response to doing or saying something shameful. In today's verse, it's a device the believer is supposed to use to stop himself from foolishly propagating pride or plotting evil.

Of course, this can be a figurative action. The point it is, you are called to intentionally stop pride or plotting evil the second you recognize it in yourself. Is this something you are good at doing? Or do you often go too far, making things even worse? Proverbs 25:28 (ampc) says, "He who has no rule over his own spirit is like a city that is broken down and without walls."

The good news is, the Holy Spirit enables you to exhibit self-control in all areas of your life. You don't have to stay stuck in your old patterns. Titus 2:11–12 (esv) says, "For the grace of God has appeared, bringing salvation for all people, training us to renounce ungodliness and worldly passions, and to live self-controlled, upright, and godly lives in the present age."

Don't wait.

Lord, may Your grace train me to renounce all forms
of ungodliness and fill me with self-control.

KEEP YOUR HEART

Do not give your strength to women,
your ways to those who destroy kings.
PROVERBS 31:3 ESV

Proverbs 31 records the oracle that King Lemuel's mother taught him. Some believe Lemuel (which means "for God" or "devoted to God") is Solomon, while others do not. Either way, the king's mother wanted him to avoid the perils that come with adultery and fornication. It's not only sinful, but also a serious distraction that leads to destruction.

In what ways might you be giving your strength to women? Are you entertaining seemingly "innocent" flirtation? Does your mind toy with fantasies? Is it causing your attention to be divided? Understand that King Lemuel's warning isn't for kings only. Many men have fallen.

Stop playing games. Instead, heed the advice given in Proverbs 4:23–25 (ESV): "Keep your heart with all vigilance, for from it flow the springs of life. Put away from you crooked speech, and put devious talk far from you. Let your eyes look directly forward, and your gaze be straight before you."

Practically speaking, you can do such things by staying engaged spiritually by reading spiritually edifying material, by meeting with a small group of brothers to weed out impure thoughts, and by meeting with a larger group of believers regularly for worship.

Lord, I confess that I struggle to keep my mind pure. Help me find a
community of Christian men to spur me on in pursuit of righteousness.

THE FIVE CROWNS

And I saw the dead, great and small, standing before the throne,
and books were opened. Then another book was opened,
which is the book of life. And the dead were judged by what
was written in the books, according to what they had done.
REVELATION 20:12 ESV

Two sets of books will be opened at the judgment. One will contain every good or bad deed a person has committed. The other will list the name of every believer. Those who die in their sins will face judgment for every single sin.

Imagine the fear and trepidation of the lost as those books are opened and read. Conversely, those who die in Jesus Christ will face no condemnation (Romans 8:1). Even so, believers will (or will not) receive rewards (Matthew 5:12; Luke 6:23; 1 Corinthians 3:14, 9:18)

The Bible promises crowns (priceless rewards) for faithful believers based on their behavior: the crown of life (James 1:12, Revelation 2:10), an imperishable crown (1 Corinthians 9:24–27), the crown of righteousness (2 Timothy 4:6–8), the crown of glory (1 Peter 5:2–4), and the crown of rejoicing (1 Thessalonians 2:19).

Study these passages. Write down the characteristics you need to exhibit. Then begin to consciously and prayerfully live them out, for these are the marks of the transformed believer.

Lord, thank You for redeeming me and for being so clear
about how I can earn heavenly rewards and crowns.

THE NEW JERUSALEM

*Then I saw a new heaven and a new earth, for the first heaven
and the first earth had passed away, and the sea was no more.
And I saw the holy city, new Jerusalem, coming down out of heaven
from God, prepared as a bride adorned for her husband.*

REVELATION 21:1–2 ESV

J ohn presents the image of the new Jerusalem "as a bride adorned for her husband." The holy city will come down and everyone will look on it with awe. This will be God's permanent dwelling place. A loud voice from heaven will say, "The dwelling place of God is with man. He will dwell with them, and they will be his people, and God himself will be with them as their God" (Revelation 21:3 ESV). What a day that will be!

You are on the threshold of a new year. It won't be anywhere near as glorious as the new heaven and new earth, or the new Jerusalem, but it will be a fresh start. It's a chance to begin new habits while shunning old ones. You will fall short, no doubt, but you'll have the new Jerusalem to look forward to one day. Spend today imagining what it might look like.

*Lord, as this year ends, and the next one is about to begin,
it paints a picture of renewal and new opportunities.
It's just a glimpse of what's to come, but I can't wait!*

CONTRIBUTORS

Ed Cyzewski is the author of *A Christian Survival Guide: A Lifeline to Faith and Growth* and *Flee, Be Silent, Pray: Ancient Prayers for Anxious Christians* and is the coauthor of *Unfollowers: Unlikely Lessons on Faith from Those Who Doubted Jesus*. He writes about prayer and imperfectly following Jesus at www.edcyzewski.com. Ed's devotions are found in March and September.

Glenn A. Hascall is an accomplished writer with credits in more than a hundred books. He is a broadcast veteran and voice actor and is actively involved in writing and producing audio drama. Glenn's devotions are found in June and October.

David Sanford's speaking engagements have ranged everywhere from the Billy Graham Center at the Cove to UC Berkeley. His book and Bible projects have been published by Zondervan, Tyndale House, Thomas Nelson, Doubleday, and Amazon. His professional biography is summarized at www.linkedin.com/in/drsanford. His personal biography features his wife of thirty-seven years, Renée, their five children, and their fourteen grandchildren (including one in heaven). David's devotions are found in January and February.

Tracy M. Sumner is a freelance author, writer, and editor in Beaverton, Oregon. An avid outdoorsman, he enjoys fly-fishing on world-class Oregon waters. Tracy's devotions are found in May and November.

Marty Trammell, PhD, and his wife, Linda, enjoy leading relationship retreats. He is the coauthor of four books, the English Chair at Corban University, and the Worship and Family Pastor at Perrydale Church. Marty codirects redeemingrelationships.com and in addition to writing for Barbour, he has written for Moody, Tyndale, Thomas Nelson, Zondervan, Guideposts, and Bethany House. Marty's devotions are found in April and July.

Lee Warren is published in such varied venues as *Discipleship Journal*, *Sports Spectrum*, Yahoo! Sports, CBN.com, and ChristianityToday .com. He is also the author of the book *Finishing Well: Living with the End in Mind* (a devotional), as well as several Christmas novellas in the Mercy Inn Series. Lee makes his home in Omaha, Nebraska. Lee's devotions are found in August and December.

READ THRU THE BIBLE IN A YEAR PLAN

1-Jan	Gen. 1-2	Matt. 1	Ps. 1
2-Jan	Gen. 3-4	Matt. 2	Ps. 2
3-Jan	Gen. 5-7	Matt. 3	Ps. 3
4-Jan	Gen. 8-10	Matt. 4	Ps. 4
5-Jan	Gen. 11-13	Matt. 5:1-20	Ps. 5
6-Jan	Gen. 14-16	Matt. 5:21-48	Ps. 6
7-Jan	Gen. 17-18	Matt. 6:1-18	Ps. 7
8-Jan	Gen. 19-20	Matt. 6:19-34	Ps. 8
9-Jan	Gen. 21-23	Matt. 7:1-11	Ps. 9:1-8
10-Jan	Gen. 24	Matt. 7:12-29	Ps. 9:9-20
11-Jan	Gen. 25-26	Matt. 8:1-17	Ps. 10:1-11
12-Jan	Gen. 27:1-28:9	Matt. 8:18-34	Ps. 10:12-18
13-Jan	Gen. 28:10-29:35	Matt. 9	Ps. 11
14-Jan	Gen. 30:1-31:21	Matt. 10:1-15	Ps. 12
15-Jan	Gen. 31:22-32:21	Matt. 10:16-36	Ps. 13
16-Jan	Gen. 32:22-34:31	Matt. 10:37-11:6	Ps. 14
17-Jan	Gen. 35-36	Matt. 11:7-24	Ps. 15
18-Jan	Gen. 37-38	Matt. 11:25-30	Ps. 16
19-Jan	Gen. 39-40	Matt. 12:1-29	Ps. 17
20-Jan	Gen. 41	Matt. 12:30-50	Ps. 18:1-15
21-Jan	Gen. 42-43	Matt. 13:1-9	Ps. 18:16-29
22-Jan	Gen. 44-45	Matt. 13:10-23	Ps. 18:30-50
23-Jan	Gen. 46:1-47:26	Matt. 13:24-43	Ps. 19
24-Jan	Gen. 47:27-49:28	Matt. 13:44-58	Ps. 20
25-Jan	Gen. 49:29-Exod. 1:22	Matt. 14	Ps. 21
26-Jan	Exod. 2-3	Matt. 15:1-28	Ps. 22:1-21
27-Jan	Exod. 4:1-5:21	Matt. 15:29-16:12	Ps. 22:22-31
28-Jan	Exod. 5:22-7:24	Matt. 16:13-28	Ps. 23
29-Jan	Exod. 7:25-9:35	Matt. 17:1-9	Ps. 24
30-Jan	Exod. 10-11	Matt. 17:10-27	Ps. 25
31-Jan	Exod. 12	Matt. 18:1-20	Ps. 26
1-Feb	Exod. 13-14	Matt. 18:21-35	Ps. 27
2-Feb	Exod. 15-16	Matt. 19:1-15	Ps. 28
3-Feb	Exod. 17-19	Matt. 19:16-30	Ps. 29
4-Feb	Exod. 20-21	Matt. 20:1-19	Ps. 30
5-Feb	Exod. 22-23	Matt. 20:20-34	Ps. 31:1-8
6-Feb	Exod. 24-25	Matt. 21:1-27	Ps. 31:9-18
7-Feb	Exod 26-27	Matt. 21:28-46	Ps. 31:19-24
8-Feb	Exod. 28	Matt. 22	Ps. 32
9-Feb	Exod. 29	Matt. 23:1-36	Ps. 33:1-12
10-Feb	Exod. 30-31	Matt. 23:37-24:28	Ps. 33:13-22
11-Feb	Exod. 32-33	Matt. 24:29-51	Ps. 34:1-7
12-Feb	Exod. 34:1-35:29	Matt. 25:1-13	Ps. 34:8-22
13-Feb	Exod. 35:30-37:29	Matt. 25:14-30	Ps. 35:1-8
14-Feb	Exod. 38-39	Matt. 25:31-46	Ps. 35:9-17
15-Feb	Exod. 40	Matt. 26:1-35	Ps. 35:18-28
16-Feb	Lev. 1-3	Matt. 26:36-68	Ps. 36:1-6
17-Feb	Lev. 4:1-5:13	Matt. 26:69-27:26	Ps. 36:7-12
18-Feb	Lev. 5:14 -7:21	Matt. 27:27-50	Ps. 37:1-6
19-Feb	Lev. 7:22-8:36	Matt. 27:51-66	Ps. 37:7-26

20-Feb	Lev. 9-10	Matt. 28	Ps. 37:27-40
21-Feb	Lev. 11-12	Mark 1:1-28	Ps. 38
22-Feb	Lev. 13	Mark 1:29-39	Ps. 39
23-Feb	Lev. 14	Mark 1:40-2:12	Ps. 40:1-8
24-Feb	Lev. 15	Mark 2:13-3:35	Ps. 40:9-17
25-Feb	Lev. 16-17	Mark 4:1-20	Ps. 41:1-4
26-Feb	Lev. 18-19	Mark 4:21-41	Ps. 41:5-13
27-Feb	Lev. 20	Mark 5	Ps. 42-43
28-Feb	Lev. 21-22	Mark 6:1-13	Ps. 44
1-Mar	Lev. 23-24	Mark 6:14-29	Ps. 45:1-5
2-Mar	Lev. 25	Mark 6:30-56	Ps. 45:6-12
3-Mar	Lev. 26	Mark 7	Ps. 45:13-17
4-Mar	Lev. 27	Mark 8	Ps. 46
5-Mar	Num. 1-2	Mark 9:1-13	Ps. 47
6-Mar	Num. 3	Mark 9:14-50	Ps. 48:1-8
7-Mar	Num. 4	Mark 10:1-34	Ps. 48:9-14
8-Mar	Num. 5:1-6:21	Mark 10:35-52	Ps. 49:1-9
9-Mar	Num. 6:22-7:47	Mark 11	Ps. 49:10-20
10-Mar	Num. 7:48-8:4	Mark 12:1-27	Ps. 50:1-15
11-Mar	Num. 8:5-9:23	Mark 12:28-44	Ps. 50:16-23
12-Mar	Num. 10-11	Mark 13:1-8	Ps. 51:1-9
13-Mar	Num. 12-13	Mark 13:9-37	Ps. 51:10-19
14-Mar	Num. 14	Mark 14:1-31	Ps. 52
15-Mar	Num. 15	Mark 14:32-72	Ps. 53
16-Mar	Num. 16	Mark 15:1-32	Ps. 54
17-Mar	Num. 17-18	Mark 15:33-47	Ps. 55
18-Mar	Num. 19-20	Mark 16	Ps. 56:1-7
19-Mar	Num. 21:1-22:20	Luke 1:1-25	Ps. 56:8-13
20-Mar	Num. 22:21-23:30	Luke 1:26-56	Ps. 57
21-Mar	Num. 24-25	Luke 1:57-2:20	Ps. 58
22-Mar	Num. 26:1-27:11	Luke 2:21-38	Ps. 59:1-8
23-Mar	Num. 27:12-29:11	Luke 2:39-52	Ps. 59:9-17
24-Mar	Num. 29:12-30:16	Luke 3	Ps. 60:1-5
25-Mar	Num. 31	Luke 4	Ps. 60:6-12
26-Mar	Num. 32-33	Luke 5:1-16	Ps. 61
27-Mar	Num. 34-36	Luke 5:17-32	Ps. 62:1-6
28-Mar	Deut. 1:1-2:25	Luke 5:33-6:11	Ps. 62:7-12
29-Mar	Deut. 2:26-4:14	Luke 6:12-35	Ps. 63:1-5
30-Mar	Deut. 4:15-5:22	Luke 6:36-49	Ps. 63:6-11
31-Mar	Deut. 5:23-7:26	Luke 7:1-17	Ps. 64:1-5
1-Apr	Deut. 8-9	Luke 7:18-35	Ps. 64:6-10
2-Apr	Deut. 10-11	Luke 7:36-8:3	Ps. 65:1-8
3-Apr	Deut. 12-13	Luke 8:4-21	Ps. 65:9-13
4-Apr	Deut. 14:1-16:8	Luke 8:22-39	Ps. 66:1-7
5-Apr	Deut. 16:9-18:22	Luke 8:40-56	Ps. 66:8-15
6-Apr	Deut. 19:1-21:9	Luke 9:1-22	Ps. 66:16-20
7-Apr	Deut. 21:10-23:8	Luke 9:23-42	Ps. 67
8-Apr	Deut. 23:9-25:19	Luke 9:43-62	Ps. 68:1-6
9-Apr	Deut. 26:1-28:14	Luke 10:1-20	Ps. 68:7-14
10-Apr	Deut. 28:15-68	Luke 10:21-37	Ps. 68:15-19
11-Apr	Deut. 29-30	Luke 10:38-11:23	Ps. 68:20-27
12-Apr	Deut. 31:1-32:22	Luke 11:24-36	Ps. 68:28-35
13-Apr	Deut. 32:23-33:29	Luke 11:37-54	Ps. 69:1-9

14-Apr	Deut. 34-Josh. 2	Luke 12:1-15	Ps. 69:10-17
15-Apr	Josh. 3:1-5:12	Luke 12:16-40	Ps. 69:18-28
16-Apr	Josh. 5:13-7:26	Luke 12:41-48	Ps. 69:29-36
17-Apr	Josh. 8-9	Luke 12:49-59	Ps. 70
18-Apr	Josh. 10:1-11:15	Luke 13:1-21	Ps. 71:1-6
19-Apr	Josh. 11:16-13:33	Luke 13:22-35	Ps. 71:7-16
20-Apr	Josh. 14-16	Luke 14:1-15	Ps. 71:17-21
21-Apr	Josh. 17:1-19:16	Luke 14:16-35	Ps. 71:22-24
22-Apr	Josh. 19:17-21:42	Luke 15:1-10	Ps. 72:1-11
23-Apr	Josh. 21:43-22:34	Luke 15:11-32	Ps. 72:12-20
24-Apr	Josh. 23-24	Luke 16:1-18	Ps. 73:1-9
25-Apr	Judg. 1-2	Luke 16:19-17:10	Ps. 73:10-20
26-Apr	Judg. 3-4	Luke 17:11-37	Ps. 73:21-28
27-Apr	Judg. 5:1-6:24	Luke 18:1-17	Ps. 74:1-3
28-Apr	Judg. 6:25-7:25	Luke 18:18-43	Ps. 74:4-11
29-Apr	Judg. 8:1-9:23	Luke 19:1-28	Ps. 74:12-17
30-Apr	Judg. 9:24-10:18	Luke 19:29-48	Ps. 74:18-23
1-May	Judg. 11:1-12:7	Luke 20:1-26	Ps. 75:1-7
2-May	Judg. 12:8-14:20	Luke 20:27-47	Ps. 75:8-10
3-May	Judg. 15-16	Luke 21:1-19	Ps. 76:1-7
4-May	Judg. 17-18	Luke 21:20-22:6	Ps. 76:8-12
5-May	Judg. 19:1-20:23	Luke 22:7-30	Ps. 77:1-11
6-May	Judg. 20:24-21:25	Luke 22:31-54	Ps. 77:12-20
7-May	Ruth 1-2	Luke 22:55-23:25	Ps. 78:1-4
8-May	Ruth 3-4	Luke 23:26-24:12	Ps. 78:5-8
9-May	1 Sam. 1:1-2:21	Luke 24:13-53	Ps. 78:9-16
10-May	1 Sam. 2:22-4:22	John 1:1-28	Ps. 78:17-24
11-May	1 Sam. 5-7	John 1:29-51	Ps. 78:25-33
12-May	1 Sam. 8:1-9:26	John 2	Ps. 78:34-41
13-May	1 Sam. 9:27-11:15	John 3:1-22	Ps. 78:42-55
14-May	1 Sam. 12-13	John 3:23-4:10	Ps. 78:56-66
15-May	1 Sam. 14	John 4:11-38	Ps. 78:67-72
16-May	1 Sam. 15-16	John 4:39-54	Ps. 79:1-7
17-May	1 Sam. 17	John 5:1-24	Ps. 79:8-13
18-May	1 Sam. 18-19	John 5:25-47	Ps. 80:1-7
19-May	1 Sam. 20-21	John 6:1-21	Ps. 80:8-19
20-May	1 Sam. 22-23	John 6:22-42	Ps. 81:1-10
21-May	1 Sam. 24:1-25:31	John 6:43-71	Ps. 81:11-16
22-May	1 Sam. 25:32-27:12	John 7:1-24	Ps. 82
23-May	1 Sam. 28-29	John 7:25-8:11	Ps. 83
24-May	1 Sam. 30-31	John 8:12-47	Ps. 84:1-4
25-May	2 Sam. 1-2	John 8:48-9:12	Ps. 84:5-12
26-May	2 Sam. 3-4	John 9:13-34	Ps. 85:1-7
27-May	2 Sam. 5:1-7:17	John 9:35-10:10	Ps. 85:8-13
28-May	2 Sam. 7:18-10:19	John 10:11-30	Ps. 86:1-10
29-May	2 Sam. 11:1-12:25	John 10:31-11:16	Ps. 86:11-17
30-May	2 Sam. 12:26-13:39	John 11:17-54	Ps. 87
31-May	2 Sam. 14:1-15:12	John 11:55-12:19	Ps. 88:1-9
1-Jun	2 Sam. 15:13-16:23	John 12:20-43	Ps. 88:10-18
2-Jun	2 Sam. 17:1-18:18	John 12:44-13:20	Ps. 89:1-6
3-Jun	2 Sam. 18:19-19:39	John 13:21-38	Ps. 89:7-13
4-Jun	2 Sam. 19:40-21:22	John 14:1-17	Ps. 89:14-18
5-Jun	2 Sam. 22:1-23:7	John 14:18-15:27	Ps. 89:19-29

6-Jun	2 Sam. 23:8-24:25	John 16:1-22	Ps. 89:30-37
7-Jun	1 Kings 1	John 16:23-17:5	Ps. 89:38-52
8-Jun	1 Kings 2	John 17:6-26	Ps. 90:1-12
9-Jun	1 Kings 3-4	John 18:1-27	Ps. 90:13-17
10-Jun	1 Kings 5-6	John 18:28-19:5	Ps. 91:1-10
11-Jun	1 Kings 7	John 19:6-25a	Ps. 91:11-16
12-Jun	1 Kings 8:1-53	John 19:25b-42	Ps. 92:1-9
13-Jun	1 Kings 8:54-10:13	John 20:1-18	Ps. 92:10-15
14-Jun	1 Kings 10:14-11:43	John 20:19-31	Ps. 93
15-Jun	1 Kings 12:1-13:10	John 21	Ps. 94:1-11
16-Jun	1 Kings 13:11-14:31	Acts 1:1-11	Ps. 94:12-23
17-Jun	1 Kings 15:1-16:20	Acts 1:12-26	Ps. 95
18-Jun	1 Kings 16:21-18:19	Acts 2:1-21	Ps. 96:1-8
19-Jun	1 Kings 18:20-19:21	Acts2:22-41	Ps. 96:9-13
20-Jun	1 Kings 20	Acts 2:42-3:26	Ps. 97:1-6
21-Jun	1 Kings 21:1-22:28	Acts 4:1-22	Ps. 97:7-12
22-Jun	1 Kings 22:29- 2 Kings 1:18	Acts 4:23-5:11	Ps. 98
23-Jun	2 Kings 2-3	Acts 5:12-28	Ps. 99
24-Jun	2 Kings 4	Acts 5:29-6:15	Ps. 100
25-Jun	2 Kings 5:1-6:23	Acts 7:1-16	Ps. 101
26-Jun	2 Kings 6:24-8:15	Acts 7:17-36	Ps. 102:1-7
27-Jun	2 Kings 8:16-9:37	Acts 7:37-53	Ps. 102:8-17
28-Jun	2 Kings 10-11	Acts 7:54-8:8	Ps. 102:18-28
29-Jun	2 Kings 12-13	Acts 8:9-40	Ps. 103:1-9
30-Jun	2 Kings 14-15	Acts 9:1-16	Ps. 103:10-14
1-Jul	2 Kings 16-17	Acts 9:17-31	Ps. 103:15-22
2-Jul	2 Kings 18:1-19:7	Acts 9:32-10:16	Ps. 104:1-9
3-Jul	2 Kings 19:8-20:21	Acts 10:17-33	Ps. 104:10-23
4-Jul	2 Kings 21:1-22:20	Acts 10:34-11:18	Ps. 104: 24-30
5-Jul	2 Kings 23	Acts 11:19-12:17	Ps. 104:31-35
6-Jul	2 Kings 24-25	Acts 12:18-13:13	Ps. 105:1-7
7-Jul	1 Chron. 1-2	Acts 13:14-43	Ps. 105:8-15
8-Jul	1 Chron. 3:1-5:10	Acts 13:44-14:10	Ps. 105:16-28
9-Jul	1 Chron. 5:11-6:81	Acts 14:11-28	Ps. 105:29-36
10-Jul	1 Chron. 7:1-9:9	Acts 15:1-18	Ps. 105:37-45
11-Jul	1 Chron. 9:10-11:9	Acts 15:19-41	Ps. 106:1-12
12-Jul	1 Chron. 11:10-12:40	Acts 16:1-15	Ps. 106:13-27
13-Jul	1 Chron. 13-15	Acts 16:16-40	Ps. 106:28-33
14-Jul	1 Chron. 16-17	Acts 17:1-14	Ps. 106:34-43
15-Jul	1 Chron. 18-20	Acts 17:15-34	Ps. 106:44-48
16-Jul	1 Chron. 21-22	Acts 18:1-23	Ps. 107:1-9
17-Jul	1 Chron. 23-25	Acts 18:24-19:10	Ps. 107:10-16
18-Jul	1 Chron. 26-27	Acts 19:11-22	Ps. 107:17-32
19-Jul	1 Chron. 28-29	Acts 19:23-41	Ps. 107:33-38
20-Jul	2 Chron. 1-3	Acts 20:1-16	Ps. 107:39-43
21-Jul	2 Chron. 4:1-6:11	Acts 20:17-38	Ps. 108
22-Jul	2 Chron. 6:12-7:10	Acts 21:1-14	Ps. 109:1-20
23-Jul	2 Chron. 7:11-9:28	Acts 21:15-32	Ps. 109:21-31
24-Jul	2 Chron. 9:29-12:16	Acts 21:33-22:16	Ps. 110:1-3
25-Jul	2 Chron. 13-15	Acts 22:17-23:11	Ps. 110:4-7
26-Jul	2 Chron. 16-17	Acts 23:12-24:21	Ps. 111
27-Jul	2 Chron. 18-19	Acts 24:22-25:12	Ps. 112

28-Jul	2 Chron. 20-21	Acts 25:13-27	Ps. 113
29-Jul	2 Chron. 22-23	Acts 26	Ps. 114
30-Jul	2 Chron. 24:1-25:16	Acts 27:1-20	Ps. 115:1-10
31-Jul	2 Chron. 25:17-27:9	Acts 27:21-28:6	Ps. 115:11-18
1-Aug	2 Chron. 28:1-29:19	Acts 28:7-31	Ps. 116:1-5
2-Aug	2 Chron. 29:20-30:27	Rom. 1:1-17	Ps. 116:6-19
3-Aug	2 Chron. 31-32	Rom. 1:18-32	Ps. 117
4-Aug	2 Chron. 33:1-34:7	Rom. 2	Ps. 118:1-18
5-Aug	2 Chron. 34:8-35:19	Rom. 3:1-26	Ps. 118:19-23
6-Aug	2 Chron. 35:20-36:23	Rom. 3:27-4:25	Ps. 118:24-29
7-Aug	Ezra 1-3	Rom. 5	Ps. 119:1-8
8-Aug	Ezra 4-5	Rom. 6:1-7:6	Ps. 119:9-16
9-Aug	Ezra 6:1-7:26	Rom. 7:7-25	Ps. 119:17-32
10-Aug	Ezra 7:27-9:4	Rom. 8:1-27	Ps. 119:33-40
11-Aug	Ezra 9:5-10:44	Rom. 8:28-39	Ps. 119:41-64
12-Aug	Neh. 1:1-3:16	Rom. 9:1-18	Ps. 119:65-72
13-Aug	Neh. 3:17-5:13	Rom. 9:19-33	Ps. 119:73-80
14-Aug	Neh. 5:14-7:73	Rom. 10:1-13	Ps. 119:81-88
15-Aug	Neh. 8:1-9:5	Rom. 10:14-11:24	Ps. 119:89-104
16-Aug	Neh. 9:6-10:27	Rom. 11:25-12:8	Ps. 119:105-120
17-Aug	Neh. 10:28-12:26	Rom. 12:9-13:7	Ps. 119:121-128
18-Aug	Neh. 12:27-13:31	Rom. 13:8-14:12	Ps. 119:129-136
19-Aug	Esther 1:1-2:18	Rom. 14:13-15:13	Ps. 119:137-152
20-Aug	Esther 2:19-5:14	Rom. 15:14-21	Ps. 119:153-168
21-Aug	Esther. 6-8	Rom. 15:22-33	Ps. 119:169-176
22-Aug	Esther 9-10	Rom. 16	Ps. 120-122
23-Aug	Job 1-3	1 Cor. 1:1-25	Ps. 123
24-Aug	Job 4-6	1 Cor. 1:26-2:16	Ps. 124-125
25-Aug	Job 7-9	1 Cor. 3	Ps. 126-127
26-Aug	Job 10-13	1 Cor. 4:1-13	Ps. 128-129
27-Aug	Job 14-16	1 Cor. 4:14-5:13	Ps. 130
28-Aug	Job 17-20	1 Cor. 6	Ps. 131
29-Aug	Job 21-23	1 Cor. 7:1-16	Ps. 132
30-Aug	Job 24-27	1 Cor. 7:17-40	Ps. 133-134
31-Aug	Job 28-30	1 Cor. 8	Ps. 135
1-Sep	Job 31-33	1 Cor. 9:1-18	Ps. 136:1-9
2-Sep	Job 34-36	1 Cor. 9:19-10:13	Ps. 136:10-26
3-Sep	Job 37-39	1 Cor. 10:14-11:1	Ps. 137
4-Sep	Job 40-42	1 Cor. 11:2-34	Ps. 138
5-Sep	Eccles. 1:1-3:15	1 Cor. 12:1-26	Ps. 139:1-6
6-Sep	Eccles. 3:16-6:12	1 Cor. 12:27-13:13	Ps. 139:7-18
7-Sep	Eccles. 7:1-9:12	1 Cor. 14:1-22	Ps. 139:19-24
8-Sep	Eccles. 9:13-12:14	1 Cor. 14:23-15:11	Ps. 140:1-8
9-Sep	SS 1-4	1 Cor. 15:12-34	Ps. 140:9-13
10-Sep	SS 5-8	1 Cor. 15:35-58	Ps. 141
11-Sep	Isa. 1-2	1 Cor. 16	Ps. 142
12-Sep	Isa. 3-5	2 Cor. 1:1-11	Ps. 143:1-6
13-Sep	Isa. 6-8	2 Cor. 1:12-2:4	Ps. 143:7-12
14-Sep	Isa. 9-10	2 Cor. 2:5-17	Ps. 144
15-Sep	Isa. 11-13	2 Cor. 3	Ps. 145
16-Sep	Isa. 14-16	2 Cor. 4	Ps. 146
17-Sep	Isa. 17-19	2 Cor. 5	Ps. 147:1-11
18-Sep	Isa. 20-23	2 Cor. 6	Ps. 147:12-20

11-Nov	Ezek. 11-12	Heb. 4:4-5:10	Prov. 17:6-12
12-Nov	Ezek. 13-14	Heb. 5:11-6:20	Prov. 17:13-22
13-Nov	Ezek. 15:1-16:43	Heb. 7:1-28	Prov. 17:23-28
14-Nov	Ezek. 16:44-17:24	Heb. 8:1-9:10	Prov. 18:1-7
15-Nov	Ezek. 18-19	Heb. 9:11-28	Prov. 18:8-17
16-Nov	Ezek. 20	Heb. 10:1-25	Prov. 18:18-24
17-Nov	Ezek. 21-22	Heb. 10:26-39	Prov. 19:1-8
18-Nov	Ezek. 23	Heb. 11:1-31	Prov. 19:9-14
19-Nov	Ezek. 24-26	Heb. 11:32-40	Prov. 19:15-21
20-Nov	Ezek. 27-28	Heb. 12:1-13	Prov. 19:22-29
21-Nov	Ezek. 29-30	Heb. 12:14-29	Prov. 20:1-18
22-Nov	Ezek. 31-32	Heb. 13	Prov. 20:19-24
23-Nov	Ezek. 33:1-34:10	Jas. 1	Prov. 20:25-30
24-Nov	Ezek. 34:11-36:15	Jas. 2	Prov. 21:1-8
25-Nov	Ezek. 36:16-37:28	Jas. 3	Prov. 21:9-18
26-Nov	Ezek. 38-39	Jas. 4:1-5:6	Prov. 21:19-24
27-Nov	Ezek. 40	Jas. 5:7-20	Prov. 21:25-31
28-Nov	Ezek. 41:1-43:12	1 Pet. 1:1-12	Prov. 22:1-9
29-Nov	Ezek. 43:13-44:31	1 Pet. 1:13-2:3	Prov. 22:10-23
30-Nov	Ezek. 45-46	1 Pet. 2:4-17	Prov. 22:24-29
1-Dec	Ezek. 47-48	1 Pet. 2:18-3:7	Prov. 23:1-9
2-Dec	Dan. 1:1-2:23	1 Pet. 3:8-4:19	Prov. 23:10-16
3-Dec	Dan. 2:24-3:30	1 Pet. 5	Prov. 23:17-25
4-Dec	Dan. 4	2 Pet. 1	Prov. 23:26-35
5-Dec	Dan. 5	2 Pet. 2	Prov. 24:1-18
6-Dec	Dan. 6:1-7:14	2 Pet. 3	Prov. 24:19-27
7-Dec	Dan. 7:15-8:27	1 John 1:1-2:17	Prov. 24:28-34
8-Dec	Dan. 9-10	1 John 2:18-29	Prov. 25:1-12
9-Dec	Dan. 11-12	1 John 3:1-12	Prov. 25:13-17
10-Dec	Hos. 1-3	1 John 3:13-4:16	Prov. 25:18-28
11-Dec	Hos. 4-6	1 John 4:17-5:21	Prov. 26:1-16
12-Dec	Hos. 7-10	2 John	Prov. 26:17-21
13-Dec	Hos. 11-14	3 John	Prov. 26:22-27:9
14-Dec	Joel 1:1-2:17	Jude	Prov. 27:10-17
15-Dec	Joel 2:18-3:21	Rev. 1:1-2:11	Prov. 27:18-27
16-Dec	Amos 1:1-4:5	Rev. 2:12-29	Prov. 28:1-8
17-Dec	Amos 4:6-6:14	Rev. 3	Prov. 28:9-16
18-Dec	Amos 7-9	Rev. 4:1-5:5	Prov. 28:17-24
19-Dec	Obad-Jonah	Rev. 5:6-14	Prov. 28:25-28
20-Dec	Mic. 1:1-4:5	Rev. 6:1-7:8	Prov. 29:1-8
21-Dec	Mic. 4:6-7:20	Rev. 7:9-8:13	Prov. 29:9-14
22-Dec	Nah. 1-3	Rev. 9-10	Prov. 29:15-23
23-Dec	Hab. 1-3	Rev. 11	Prov. 29:24-27
24-Dec	Zeph. 1-3	Rev. 12	Prov. 30:1-6
25-Dec	Hag. 1-2	Rev. 13:1-14:13	Prov. 30:7-16
26-Dec	Zech. 1-4	Rev. 14:14-16:3	Prov. 30:17-20
27-Dec	Zech. 5-8	Rev. 16:4-21	Prov. 30:21-28
28-Dec	Zech. 9-11	Rev. 17:1-18:8	Prov. 30:29-33
29-Dec	Zech. 12-14	Rev. 18:9-24	Prov. 31:1-9
30-Dec	Mal. 1-2	Rev. 19-20	Prov. 31:10-17
31-Dec	Mal. 3-4	Rev. 21-22	Prov. 31:18-31

SCRIPTURE INDEX

31:3 – December 29

Ecclesiastes
3:11–12 – September 5
9:16–17 – September 8

Isaiah
1:14, 16–17 – September 11
9:2–3 – September 14
11:2–3 – September 15
25:8 – September 19
30:15 – February 1
40:28–29 – September 25
42:6–7 – September 26
45:22–23 – September 28
53:6 – October 1
53:9 – February 19
65:17 – October 6

Jeremiah
4:22 – October 8
9:23–24 – October 12
17:9 – October 15, December 19
31:13 – October 22
33:3 – October 24

Lamentations
3:26 – February 1

Ezekiel
3:27 – November 8
18:23 – November 15
22:30 – November 17
26:20 – August 2

Daniel
1:8 – December 2
1:17 – December 2
4:27 – December 4
9:4–5 – December 8

Hosea
6:1 – December 11
14:9 – December 13

Amos
3:3 – October 2
7:14–15 – December 18

Nahum
1:7 – December 22

Zephaniah
1:7 – December 24
3:17 – December 24

Zechariah
1:4 – December 26
1:5–6 – December 26
8:17 – December 27

New Testament
Matthew
5:2–3 – January 5
5:14 – January 29
5:16 – August 13
5:20 – January 19
5:44–45 – December 5
6:8–9 – January 7
6:21 – January 18
6:26 – November 22
7:12 – January 10
8:22 – June 16
9:10 – January 13
10:42 – January 16
12:14 – January 19
15:23 – January 26
16:16 – January 28
17:2 – January 29
18:5–6 – January 31
19:26 – February 3
22:23 – February 8
22:29 – February 8
23:3 – February 9
24:14 – February 10
25:15 – February 13
25:21 – May 1
26:75 – February 17
27:13–14 – February 18
27:57–58 – February 19
28:1 – February 20

Mark
1:21 – February 21
1:35–36 – February 22
1:40 – February 23
3:14, 19 – February 24
4:11–12 – February 25
4:13 - February 25
4:20 – February 25
5:22 – February 28
6:12 – February 29
6:34 – March 2
7:21 – December 19
8:18 – November 10
9:7–8 – March 5
9:24 – June 16
10:44–45 – March 8
12:16–17 – March 10
14:31 – March 14
15:37–39 – March 17

15:43 – February 19
16:7–8 – March 18

Luke
1:16–17 – March 19
2:27–29 – March 22
3:11–13 – March 24
4:6–8 – March 25
5:19–20 – March 27
6:31 – January 10
6:37 – March 30
8:2–3 – April 4
8:56 – April 3
9:41 – April 7
9:48 – April 8
10:23–24 – April 10
11:29 – April 12
11:34–36 – April 12
12:6–7 – April 14
12:29–31 – May 29
12:34 – April 15
13:24 – April 19
15:7 – April 22
16:13 – April 24
16:29 – April 25
16:31 – April 25
18:14 – April 27
21:2–4 – May 3
21:34 – May 4, August 26
22:45–46 – May 6
23:40–41 – May 8
23:42 – May 8
23:43 – May 8
23:50–51 – February 19

John
1:26–27 – May 10
3:14–15 – May 13
4:21–23 – May 15
6:5–6 – May 19
6:32–33 – May 20
6:67–69 – May 21
9:31 – May 26
10:27–28 – May 28
11:32 – May 30
12:13 – June 10
12:24–25 – June 1
13:12 – June 3
14:6 – June 4
14:27 – October 23
15:7 – May 11
16:12–13 – June 6
17:18 – June 8
19:3 – June 10
19:38 – February 19
19:38–39 – June 12

21:15 – June 15
21:17 – June 15

Acts
2:24 – June 19
3:6–8 – June 20
4:36–37 – June 22
8:7–8 – June 28
9:22 – July 1
10:4 – July 2
11:18 – July 4
11:24 – July 5
13:10–11 – July 6
14:15 – July 9
14:16–17 – July 9
17:11 – July 14
17:29 – July 15
19:11 – July 18
19:15 – July 18
19:32 – July 19
20:18–19 – July 21
21:13 – July 22
22:12 – July 24
23:2 – July 25
26:10 – July 29
27:3 – July 30

Romans
1:28–29 – August 3
2:4 – June 3
4:3 – August 6
4:20–21 – August 6
5:3–4 – August 7
8:26 – August 10
8:28 – June 23
9:3 – August 12
12:1 – August 16
12:10 – November 16
13:14 – August 18
15:1 – August 19
15:4 – February 12
15:7 – November 16
16:1–2 – August 22

1 Corinthians
1:10 – November 16
1:27 – April 29
2:12 – August 24
2:14 – October 17
4:12–13 – August 26
5:13 – April 7
7:4 – August 29
9:24–25 – September 2
10:13 – June 13
13:2 – September 6
15:32–33 – September 9

2 Corinthians
1:6–7 – September 12
5:16–17 – September 17
5:20 – October 19
6:2 – June 17
6:8, 10 – September 18
9:6–7 – September 21
10:8 – September 22
12:8–9 – September 24

Galatians
3:26–27 – September 29
4:6–7 – September 30
5:13 – November 16
5:16 – October 2
5:22–23 – August 8

Ephesians
1:13–14 – October 4
4:22–24 – October 7
4:29 – November 25
5:18 – November 21
6:4 – October 9

Philippians
1:27–28 – October 11
4:6–7 – October 14

Colossians
3:2–3 – October 17
4:5–6 – October 19

1 Thessalonians
3:9–10 – October 21
5:13 – October 23

2 Thessalonians
3:13 – October 25

1 Timothy
1:5–7 – October 26
4:7–8 – October 28
5:8 – May 29, October 29

2 Timothy
1:8 – October 31
2:23–24 – November 1
3:16–17 – November 2

Titus
1:9 – November 4
2:11–12 – December 28
2:13 – December 15
3:5 – November 6

Hebrews
3:12–13 – November 10
4:12 – November 11
5:13–14 – November 12
7:24–25 – November 13
8:13 – April 7
10:24–25 – November 16
11:7 – November 18
12:7–8 – November 20
13:5–6 – November 22

James
1:22 – November 23
2:14, 17 – November 24
3:10 – November 25
4:9–10 – November 26
5:16 – November 27

1 Peter
1:6–8 – November 28
1:13–17 – February 27
1:14–16 – November 29
2:9 – April 19
2:17 – November 30
2:19 – December 1
2:24 – February 17
3:12 – May 26
3:15 – December 14

2 Peter
3:3–4 – December 6

1 John
1:6 – December 7
1:8 – December 7
3:14 – December 10

2 John
1:7 – December 12

Jude
1:3 – December 14

Revelation
1:17–18 – December 15
3:5 – December 17
7:14 – December 21
11:15 – December 23
11:16 – December 23
14:6 – December 25
20:12 – December 30
21:1 –2 – December 31
21:3 – February 15, December 31